Breaking and Entering

Policewomen on Patrol

Susan Ehrlich Martin

UNIVERSITY OF CALIFORNIA PRESS

Berkeley • Los Angeles • London

University of California Press
Berkeley and Los Angeles, California
University of California Press, Ltd.
London, England
© 1980 by
The Regents of the University of California
First Paperback Printing 1982
ISBN 0-520-04644-7
Printed in the United States of America

1 2 3 4 5 6 7 8 9

Library of Congress Cataloging in Publication Data

Martin, Susan Ehrlich.
  Breaking and Entering: Policewomen on patrol

  Originally presented as the author's thesis, American University.
  1. Policewomen—United States.   I. Title.
HV8023.M37 1980   363.2'2   79-63555
ISBN 0-520-03908-4

Contents

Acknowledgments

This book was originally written as a Ph.D. dissertation in sociology for The American University. As is usual with such undertakings I owe thanks to many people, including Lieutenant Ed Simms of the Metropolitan Police Department, who first suggested that I do a study of the "policewomen on patrol" experiment being conducted in the District of Columbia and who made available his newspaper clipping file on policewomen; David Saari of The American University, who put me in touch with the policewoman who became my informant, critic, and good friend; and former District police chief Jerry Wilson, who made a suggestion that enabled me to gain admission to the Police Reserve Corps.

I want particularly to thank Muriel Cantor, the chairperson of my dissertation committee, and Karen Petersen of the department of sociology at The American University for their invaluable intellectual guidance, moral support, and critical reading of an enormous number of pages of the dissertation manuscript in several drafts.

My debt to Jessie Bernard is great. She served as a role model, sounding board for ideas, and friend who would always listen when I felt discouraged or when I had a new "inspiration."

The thoughtful reviews and many helpful suggestions made by Peter Manning and James Jacobs greatly facilitated the preparation of the manuscript for publication.

Special thanks must be reserved for the many men and women of the Metropolitan Police Department who must remain anonymous and to one particular policewoman whose assistance was essential for the project. Their toleration of my presence in scout cars and police stations and their cooperation in answering numerous questions made this book possible.

Finally, it is hard to describe adequately the emotional and intellectual support I received from my husband, Malcolm, throughout the years spent in graduate school, field work, and writing. His faith in me, willingness to be a "police husband" and babysitter for many months, and editorial assistance were invaluable.

Preface

The occupational world has long been sex segregated; there are "men's jobs" and "women's work." Occupations that confer high prestige, large incomes, or great authority as well as those that demand great strength or require courage in the face of danger have traditionally been reserved for men. Women have been left with the work that men do not want to do either because it offers low pay or is an extension of women's domestic tasks, which involve nurturing of or service to others. As a result, women entering occupations dominated by men and closely associated with masculinity face formidable obstacles and interactional dilemmas. They must cope with organizational policies and practices that put them at a disadvantage; isolation by and hostility from supervisors and coworkers who resent their presence; inappropriate behavior on the part of clients; an informal occupational social system that excludes them from networks of communication and sponsorship; and interaction rituals that press them into stereotypically feminine behavior which is inappropriate on the job. Highly visible and relatively powerless, these pioneering women must unlearn old patterns of behavior, and learn new skills in order to perform in their new role; they must ignore the subtle and not so subtle messages that women are expected to fail in their new jobs.

This study is an examination of one such group of women "breaking and entering" into police patrol, an occupation traditionally reserved "for men only." It explores the problems they face in learning their work role and entering the mainstream of police life, and examines the mechanisms they employ for coping with work-related problems, including male coworkers' tendency to treat them as interlopers in a male world.

We know very little about such women. Since work outside the home has been considered primarily the domain of men, most occupational studies focus on men's work. The majority of studies of women's work have focused either on women in traditionally female jobs, such as teaching, nursing, and clerical work, or on women entering nontraditional occupations at the professional level. Although there are a number of studies of female doctors, lawyers, and college professors, little is known as yet about the occupational lives of women who enter nontraditional blue-collar jobs requiring less planning and education. To date there are virtually no studies of women in the skilled crafts, insurance sales, or police work; this book is a step toward filling that void.

Women are not new to policing; the first sworn female officer in the United States was appointed in 1910. But women are new to patrol work. The first city to make extensive use of female patrol officers was Washington, D.C. In 1972 the department hired approximately one hundred female officers and assigned them to patrol duties. This "policewomen on patrol" program initially was regarded as an experiment, and an intensive evaluation of the women's performance in comparison with a group of rookie male officers was arranged and conducted by the Urban Institute, a Washington-based research organization. Bloch and Anderson (1974a and b), using primarily quantitative measures of the officers' performance, found that women were able to perform patrol duties satisfactorily. The study ignored, however, many of the qualitative aspects of the situation in which the women worked.

This book started from a different point. The issue of women's ability to perform patrol duties was largely put aside, and instead, I sought to understand the meaning and implications of the entry of female officers for their male coworkers, the department leadership, and for the women themselves. My goal was to explore the women's perspectives on their new work, the difficulties they faced in gaining a place in the police world due to clearly stated opposition by many male officers, the manner in which these factors affected job performance and morale, and the ways that the women coped with the resistance they faced. I was particularly interested in the conflicts female officers felt between cultural norms prescribing appropriate behavior for a woman and occupational norms regarding the behavior of police officers as they interact with citizens and coworkers.

To examine these issues I undertook an in-depth study of officers in one police district in the Metropolitan Police Department of Washington, D.C. This department was selected for both theoretical and practical reasons: when I began the research in 1975 there were more than three hundred female officers in the department of about forty-six hundred officers (comprising 7 percent of the total force), and there were approximately thirty women assigned to each police district. Thus it was possible to gather data in a single district and have a sufficiently large and heterogeneous sample for intensive examination. In addition, Washington, D.C., was selected because I was (and remain) a resident of the metropolitan area, was familiar with the city, and had a number of contacts which decreased (but did not eliminate) some of the difficulties of gaining access to the department to conduct the research.

The particular police district I studied will not be identified. It included part of the downtown business area, a middle-class residential area, and a segment of a lower-class black ghetto. It was selected because it had a fairly high crime rate, a socially heterogeneous population, and a mix of residential, religious, governmental, commercial, and recreational activities within its boundaries.

Following an initial planning phase, data collection began when I became a police reserve officer in October 1975 and continued full time until June 1976. From March through June 1976 my participant observation continued, with diminished frequency, as I conducted intensive interviews with a sample of male and female officers in the district in which I was a reserve officer as well as with seven policewomen involved in the "policewomen on patrol" program in the department. The final phase of the study consisted of analysis and writing with occasional participant observation to check on data obtained during the interviews and to fill information gaps. (For a fuller discussion of field research procedures, methodological problems, and ethical issues raised by this research, see the Appendix.)

As a police reserve officer I was able to gain intimate familiarity with a world with which I had previously had minimal contact. I got a taste of the excitement and boredom, the sense of independence and the feeling of constant surveillance, the fear in the pit of one's stomach and the cold sweat of relief after dealing with a dangerous situation, the occasional sense of accomplishment and the frequent frustration with the endless paperwork that make up a "policeman's lot." I was able to experience many of the feelings, view many of the dilemmas and pressures, and learn the meanings patrol officers attribute to various interactions as I worked with more than fifty officers during more than sixty tours of duty covering all shifts and all days of the week.

As a member of the Metropolitan Police reserves I was both participant and observer. I was never accepted nor treated as a "regular" officer and had limited duties. Reserve officers are unpaid citizens who wear uniforms hardly distinguishable from those of sworn officers, carry no firearms (but do have mace, handcuffs, and a nightstick), have no special police powers, and work alongside sworn officers. They are usually assigned to a scout car to work with an officer without a partner for the shift. The attitudes of officers toward reserves tended to be negative, although many were personally cordial.

My duties on patrol were few; I was not permitted to drive the scout car and only occasionally used the radio. For the most part I remained in the background, speaking only when citizens addressed me as an officer. In terms of dispatched assignments, the scout car in which a reserve is working is treated as a one-officer unit. I conducted occasional searches on female suspects, however, and assisted my partner with paperwork when I became familiar with departmental procedure.

Doing observation as a reserve had both advantages and disadvantages. The primary disadvantages were that I was not able to observe partners working together because I was assigned to work in one-officer units, and it was difficult to observe policewomen on patrol since few were assigned to patrol alone, while others had permanent station assignments. I did, however, have the opportunity to work with nine of the women, three on several occasions. An additional disadvantage was the fact that as a reserve (and female) I was not included in off-duty socializing.

Although my status in the police department was low, being a reserve had advantages. It permitted me to enter the police world, view its "backstage" activities, get to know a number of police officers, and experience some of their joy, pride, fear, and frustration on the beat. Without the responsibilities of an officer, I was freer to observe, and, in time, was treated as a "friend of the police." I was thereby able to gain the confidence and cooperation of officers who often are reluctant to be open with outsiders.

My perspective on police work as a participant observer was limited by the fact that I am female. As the report will make clear, women are treated as "different." Not "one of the boys," I was unable to gain access to the inner circles of the district organization. I did, however, experience some of the frustrations of the policewomen in their work and personal relationships with coworkers.

The interviews, including both open and closed questions, elicited information from officers about their background, work history, motivation for becoming a police officer, expectations and aspirations, and attitudes toward the department, citizens, fellow officers, and the work itself. They ranged in length from forty-five minutes to six hours with the majority lasting between one-and-a-half and two hours.

A total of 55 officers and 15 officials from the observation district were interviewed. I sought to include all of the women assigned to the district with one year of police experience, an equal number of male officers matched as closely as possible for length of service and race, and a variety of officials. I was able to interview 28 of the 33 women in the district as well as a corresponding group of 27 male officers. In addition a sample of 15 officials from the observation district and seven current or former policewomen connected with the police-women's program were interviewed. One of these women was my "informant" throughout the project.

Although one must exercise caution in generalizing from a case study based on data collected in a single district of one police department, it seems reasonable to assume that if the policewomen in a department committed to their integration face difficulties different from their male peers', female officers working in departments opposing their assignment to patrol will encounter (at the very least) many of the same problems and adopt similar coping strategies.

Two final limitations of the study merit comment. I have taken as "given" the existing police role and organizational structure and not raised important questions about the role of the police in the criminal justice system or in society. For a woman to be a "successful" officer in the context of this study means only that she successfully negotiated the existing system and conformed to the organizational and occupational norms as they currently exist for a patrol officer.

Finally, although I have attempted to be objective and neutral, the reader might do well to keep in mind the potential biases that arise from the fact that I perceived the police world through the eyes of an upper-middle-class white woman and feminist.

My feminist perspective may have affected the research in two somewhat contradictory ways. On the one hand it sensitized me to the many subtle ways in which language, interpersonal interaction, and institutions perpetuate and reinforce the social arrangements between the sexes. A feminist perspective permitted me to perceive and analyze much of the taken-for-granted behavior that shapes and reflects genderism as it operated in the police world. At the same time I began my research with a commitment to the idea of equality of opportunity for women and with the conviction that women can function effectively on police patrol. Because I was not neutral on the issue of policewomen—or women's rights in general—on a number of occasions I found myself inwardly annoyed (and probably outwardly defensive) when policemen glibly criticized or overgeneralized about policewomen's shortcomings. In several instances I might better (from a sociological perspective) have remained silent when policemen baited me about policewomen. To some of the men I appeared to be an advocate of policewomen and "women's lib," which may have inhibited their willingness to express negative feelings about the presence of patrolwomen and their impact on the police world and may have led them to alter their behavior in my presence in a variety of ways.

Part I

The Setting

Chapter I

Introduction

THREE OFFICERS

Jane, Tim, and Ann are officers in the Metropolitan Police Department of Washington, D.C., assigned to the same patrol district. Differences in their backgrounds, expectations, and, most importantly, in their experience as police officers have led them to quite divergent perspectives about their lives and work. A closer examination of these three officers will indicate some of the factors that make "breaking in" as a police officer a different experience for each.

Tim and Jane are both twenty-four years old. Both are from blue-collar families. Each graduated from high school in 1970, attended two years of college and joined the department in late 1974. Tim is a white man of average size (5'10", 170 pounds) with a muscular build. Jane is black, pretty, and petite (5'3", 118 pounds). During his high school years in a western city, Tim participated in "organized violence on the football field" which, he believes, helped prepare him for police teamwork. During her high school years Jane moved to Washington from the south and became a wife (she has since divorced) and mother.

Tim remembers his college experience as one big fraternity party and beer blast. He dropped out, took a "boring" clerical job for a year, and then worked in a factory for another year before becoming a police officer. He says of himself, about those years, "I was a bum." During that time, Tim had the opportunity to ride along with a police officer, found the work exciting, and decided to become a police officer himself. When it became clear that he would not be able to get a police job in his home town, he applied for a position with the Washington, D.C., Metropolitan Police Department.

Tim was attracted to policing because it offered him personal discipline plus adventure: "There's no more adventure left in America except in the police department. It's an active job where you're doing something most of the time rather than being cooped up behind a desk." He has not been disappointed in his choice. He feels he has found a lifetime career and, since joining the police, matured personally, noting, "people at home say I'm not as wild as I used to be. I assume more responsibility."

After Jane dropped out of college, she took a job as a secretary with a government agency. Denied a promotion she sought, Jane began looking for another job. She heard a radio advertisement describing job opportunities for women in the police department and was attracted by the prospect of doing investigative work, as well as by a substantial salary increase. She had never known nor was then acquainted with any police officers and received little encouragement from her family to pursue this work. Unlike Tim, Jane was unsure about her occupational choice, and anticipated sex discrimination.

After several years as a policewoman, Jane displays little enthusiasm for police work, but has not thought seriously of leaving the department because she does not want to resume secretarial work. She finds it difficult to predict what work she will be doing five years from now and is unable to describe any career goals. She is uncertain how long she will remain in the department, has no desire for promotion, and figures she is likely to end up in an "inside" (clerical or administrative) assignment. Although she would like to become a detective, that is unlikely to occur because she does not have a high rate of arrests and has done little to cultivate the necessary contacts and sponsorship.

Tim is more ambitious and more optimistic. He wants to be "at least" a sergeant in five years but will settle for an investigative assignment. He figures "someone eventually takes notice if you do a good job out there" and, in fact, has already been noticed. He received a commendation for his handling of a burglary that led to an arrest and conviction and in 1977 was given a permanent scout car assignment.

At the police academy Tim had little difficulty meeting the physical training requirements, but was annoyed at physical education instructors whom he felt "were easier on the girls" and at some of the women who made no attempt to meet the standards. He reported that one policewoman refused to practice self-defense exercises with him because she said he was too rough—although, he noted, citizens involved in street fights are not gentle.

Jane had difficulty with some of the physical training exercises at the academy but observed that the instructors were lenient on her, particularly when she appeared to make an effort. She felt inadequately prepared by her training to handle rowdy men. After a year of street patrol she still does not have a convincingly authoritative or imposing manner and is hesitant to act in situations where citizens threaten to disobey her directions.

Tim's optimism and Jane's apparent lack of commitment to the job also stem from their experiences in the police district to which they have been assigned. Although both were given permanent footbeats in residential neighborhoods, Tim is more frequently assigned to a scout car. Is it because of his race? his sex? his friendship with one of the sergeants? because he makes more arrests than Jane? because he is "one of the boys"? because he has clearly adopted and mastered many of the basic norms of policing including the expectation that officers assertively maintain respect for the police on the street? Jane is not sure why Tim rides and she walks (sometimes without a radio) but she is aware that a significant difference exists, and reflected about its effect on her attitude and behavior:

> I'm not gung ho. I just do what I have to. . . . I get disgusted when I get my assignment. . . . Others with less time in the section get to ride more often than I do and they also got better days off that went with their permanent assignments while I didn't. . . . So I'm not going to break my neck, especially if I don't have a radio. . . . I'm not that strong and . . . I'm not going to drag myself to a call box.

On patrol, Jane does not seek arrests, making only those that evolve from an assigned run when she is in a scout car. She takes little initiative, feels little need to be assertive and is uncertain about her ability to maintain respect. As a female officer, she feels she is at a disadvantage on the street:

> I have to try to act tough even though I'm not tough because situations come up where they don't understand when I talk nice to them. I have to portray being tough although it's just when I'm on duty.

Tim is a gung ho officer, who strives to make many arrests, which he believes are a direct reflection of his policing skills. He was careful to distinguish, however, between his style of policing and that of the "Wyatt Earp-type cop" who rigidly enforces the letter of the law and

"will lock someone up for disorderly conduct if they breathe funny."
With citizens he is "civil to all and polite to none" (a phrase he took
from a Joseph Wambaugh novel). His treatment of citizens depends
on their attitude toward him:

> If someone treats me right, with respect, I treat him the same way. If
> he's belligerent, he gets what's coming. . . . Then I have to react with
> force to show I'm not to be messed with.

Tim believes that policemen have fewer problems on patrol than
policewomen because of physical differences. He thinks a disorderly
citizen will hesitate to tangle with him whereas a woman is more
vulnerable to physical and verbal abuse. "Just because you're a man,"
he notes, "the violent will treat you with more respect." Jane agrees
with this judgment and generally avoids potentially violent interactions.

Tim feels that he is "definitely" accepted by the other male officers
in the district. After work he will frequently have a drink with a group
of policemen and, in general, centers his social life and friendships
around other officers. Tim plays on the section baseball team and is
clearly "one of the boys"; he is liked by the others, with whom he
"fits," and is viewed by his superiors as reliable and hard working.

Jane is less sure of her acceptance by other officers. Her social life
does not revolve around policing; none of her close friends are police
officers. Although she has occasionally been invited, Jane has never
joined fellow officers after work because she neither drinks nor feels
comfortable with a group of men. She was not permitted to play on
the men's basketball team but occasionally attends their games as a
spectator. She has dated only one policeman from the district and
avoids department officials, most of whom are white males. She
resentfully points out the dilemma she faces, noting that male officers
who are friendly with superiors often are rewarded with good
assignments. She is reluctant to talk with her superiors because she
does not know exactly what to say and is fearful of departmental
gossip and misunderstanding.

> If I'm friendly, being female, they'll approach me for a date, taking what
> I say the wrong way and then the sergeant will get mad (if I turn him
> down) and make me walk [a footbeat]. To avoid any problems I just
> don't act too friendly with them and take my chances about assign-
> ments.

Jane has weak social and personal ties with fellow officers, and her sense of belonging and being in the right job is tenuous at best. In addition, the nature of police work adversely affects her family life since changing work shifts and midweek days off prevent her daughter from living with her.

Tim is a rookie officer who has experienced a cycle of success. His initial enthusiasm coupled with his seeming "rightness" for the job as a white male resulted in his acceptance by the other male officers. His activism on the street has been repaid with good assignments. These in turn have fostered greater self-confidence. He has become integrated into both the formal and informal police world, has gained an increasingly positive image of himself as an officer, and has raised his career expectations correspondingly. His personal life is intimately related to his work; he experiences little if any conflict between his occupational role and other social roles.

Jane, black, female, shy and initially fearful, seems caught in a cycle of demotivation and failure. She has difficulties interacting with citizens on the street, is isolated from the world of locker-room camaraderie, receives little support or encouragement from fellow officers, and is fearful of developing close relationships with other officers or officials. Uncertain how to succeed, she believes that her lack of success is the result of sexual and racial discrimination. Such a perception further hinders any willingness to take risks or assert herself.

In assessing officers with whom he does not like to work it was easy for Tim to say that officers like Jane are "lazy and ignorant" and that they "sit there and giggle," doing little more than pulling down their pay check. Such a judgment, however, fails to take into account the factors that contribute to Jane's behavior. Nor are all policewomen like Jane nor policemen like Tim. A thumbnail sketch of another policewoman (Ann) will show that some female officers respond to the challenges of the police role by actively struggling to gain acceptance both as a person and as an officer.

Ann, a twenty-five-year-old black woman who grew up in Washington, D.C., is a married mother of three children and has been a member of the department since 1972. Turning down a college scholarship in order to help support her mother and a younger brother, she graduated from high school on a Friday and went to work the next Monday. She found her work as a telephone operator "stupid," mind deadening, and physically confining. Hearing her older brother, a police officer, talk about the satisfaction he got from his work, she applied to the department, and was accepted so quickly that she had little chance to reconsider. She got strong encouragement from her brother and support in her choice from her husband.

Initially, she expected to remain in policing for only a year but has been in the department for several. She does not want to talk about her expectations or aspirations five years from now; she simply cannot predict. On several occasions Ann considered quitting but reconsidered each time because she lacks the qualifications for work that she would prefer and because, although she is reluctant to state it, she finds the job challenging, involving, stimulating, and satisfying— despite her having some misgivings. Although confident that she could perform the duties, Ann has no desire to become a sergeant because she does not want to return to midweek days off and shift work, from her current administrative post. She is, however, seeking return to an investigative assignment.

An average-size woman (5'6", 120 pounds), Ann's personality and background contributed greatly to her success as a patrol officer. Neither athletic nor a team player like Tim, Ann sees herself as independent and adventurous. In addition she is outspoken, congenial and enormously self-confident. These qualities enabled her to deal with what she characterized as "racism, chauvinism, bigotry and everything else . . . both because I'm black and I'm a woman" in a manner quite different from Jane. She elaborated the dilemma of double discrimination:

> If you're a man and a police officer it's accepted that you can do the job. Nobody's watching to see if you can. . . . But if you're a woman everybody's watching to see how brave you are, how commanding you can be and how well you can take charge of a situation. You have to prove to the citizens that you're a police officer when you take over a scene and you have to do twice as much to prove to your partner and official that you can handle the job.
>
> As a black you have to be careful that others don't take your actions in a situation as leaning toward [favoring] a complainant if he happens to be black too.

Although she had no problems at the training academy, Ann indicated that as one of the first women assigned to patrol work she did not receive the usual post-academy training in the district to which she was assigned. Normally new officers go through a period known as certification before they are permitted to patrol alone. During this period they work in a scout car under the supervision of a training officer who teaches them patrol techniques, report writing skills, and district geography. In her case,

> I was certified when the sergeant came in, handed me a piece of paper and said, "sign this." I had been in the district about two months but had never ridden in a training car and did not know the streets. . . . The men who came into the district went into training cars . . . but I wasn't put into a training car or instructed—ever. Yet I was certified because they handed me a piece of paper and was put in a scout car alone that day. . . . I had to learn the hard way—through mistakes—but when I made a mistake they'd come down on me just as hard regardless of whether they'd trained me or not.

Ann survived the initial period of hazing and rejection through a combination of determination, reliance on her previous experience, and conformity to the informal rules of policing. She explained,

> I'm a survivor. . . . It was easier for me than some of the other policewomen because I'm from D.C. and had seen a lot as a kid. I'd seen people get drunk, raise hell and shoot guns. I'd seen stores robbed and the store owner get shot. The other women were terrified of many things that no longer frightened me. They were scared of lesbians, prostitutes and junkies. I'd seen them when I was growing up and knew they were just people.
>
> I had to do a great deal to prove myself but now nobody doubts my competence and nobody bothers me. They know there's no use picking on me so they harass someone else. . . . If you show that they can't get to you they'll leave you alone. My attitude is that I'm going to make it, regardless. . . . I don't make waves, I play by the rules. I come to work on time all the time. I wear a tie, iron my shirt, and shine my shoes. I played by the rules so straight that now if I don't play by the rules nobody seems to notice.

She proved herself in the way male officers prove themselves although the tests she faced were more frequent and she was more closely scrutinized than the men. She remained cool in several shooting incidents and participated in making a number of good arrests although they were not credited to her because "women weren't supposed to do well that first year. . . . If one did well, they didn't officially note it." She kept her mouth shut, accepted the assignments she was given, followed the rules, and maintained a low profile.

Following a transfer to a different police district, gaining acceptance among a new group of officers was less difficult. Ann explained that initially she was assigned to work with one "super gung ho" officer who had never worked with a female officer and indicated quite clearly he did not want to work with a woman.

> That first week together anything he got involved in, I got involved in,

one hundred percent. He went and told the sergeant, "This is a dynamite officer. I'd rather have her than most guys as a partner. She might not be as strong but I know she'll be right there with me. . . ." Getting his seal of approval was like getting the Pope's blessing and I stayed in a scout car with him.

Rather than feeling hesitant in dealing with unruly male citizens, Ann capitalizes on being female. She believes that citizens will frequently be cooperative because they expect a woman to be more understanding. Her policing style stresses her listening and interpersonal skills. In other instances she has a psychological advantage because "there still are some men out there who will respect you just because you're a woman" and because in a physical confrontation she recognizes and exploits the strong fear that some men have of a woman with a gun. To the man who asserts, "no broad can lock me up," she replies,

> "Yes I can, but this time if you cause any trouble you're going to get shot. . . . If a man was locking you up and you gave him trouble, he'd beat you up. I'm so confident that I couldn't beat you up that if you hit me . . . I'd probably go berserk and shoot you." . . . And they get locked up a whole lot easier for me than a man.

Despite her eventual acceptance as an officer and a partner, Ann is not "one of the boys"; her incorporation in the informal social networks of the department, which is vital to success, did not happen as readily as and remains more tenuous than Tim's. Unlike Tim, Ann could not join the men's sexual joking or banter because she was often the object of their remarks. In one instance she put down a particularly objectionable comment about her anatomy in scathing terms, humiliating the offending officer in front of the other men. This and similar incidents resulted in Ann's acquiring a reputation for being "stuck-up, snotty, and evil—even being a lesbian," but, she added, "I preferred it that way. They left me alone and I left them alone." Similarly, when a sergeant made unwanted sexual overtures she "nipped it in the bud" by making clear to him that if he did not stop she would file a complaint supported by evidence of his improper conduct.

Ann's social life does not revolve around police officers. She maintains a protective social and emotional distance between herself and other officers with the exception of two former male partners and two former policewomen with whom she has maintained close friendships. Outwardly friendly, she still prefers being a loner to social incorporation because it minimizes and masks her vulnerability to and dependence on others. When she occasionally socializes with other police officers, spouses and children are included.

Currently Ann has an administrative assignment. After several years on street patrol and then in an investigative assignment, she decided that, "when you don't have time to see your babies you know something is wrong!" She gave up the excitement of the street and the challenge of investigative work for a dull office job to "get out of the rat race of working ten and twelve hours a day," but after several months is restless and looking for another investigative assignment.

As I was sitting with Ann in her office, one of her male coworkers said to me,

> You know you're talking to one of the top ten policewomen in D.C. I'd say the top one but Monday morning she might not get through the door with a swelled head. . . . She's one of the better ones I've run across.

Thus, although she plays by their rules, carries her share of the workload, and is recognized as a highly competent police officer, Ann is not merely another officer but remains a "policewoman," an outsider who wants to maintain her distance from fellow police.

THEORETICAL PERSPECTIVES

These three officers have been described in detail to illustrate the main issues to be examined in this study. They have been selected because each exemplifies a different pattern of behavior in response to their occupational role demands. Their experiences indicate that while some problems in adapting to policing are common to all new officers, female officers face different expectations from clients and coworkers, and thus additional barriers and difficulties not encountered by the male recruit. All policewomen, however, do not cope with these problems the same way.

In examining the problems and role adaptations of female officers, the emphasis will be on organizational factors rather than individual or psychological differences. The structure and policies of the police department, and the district in which they work, affect the occupational behavior of policemen and policewomen. Thus the book's focus will be on the person, in a work role, within an organization. It will examine the impact of the work organization's formal and informal structures on the workers, as well as occupational role behavior they adopt in response to their situations.

The work draws upon studies of complex organizations and the ways that they function to shape the behavior of participants in them; analyses of police work as a unique occupation shaped both by the nature of the work and division of labor, and by the structure of the police organization within which the work is carried out; and interactional analyses of the ways in which verbal and nonverbal cues pattern male-female relations. The combination of these macro level (structural) and micro level (interactional) approaches permits a fuller understanding of how the organizational context influences participants and the ways in which individuals—in this case female officers— negotiate the system and establish patterns of interaction.[1]

The problems faced by policewomen "breaking and entering" into a nontraditional occupation derive from two primary and overlapping sources: organizational variables, particularly opportunity, power and numbers or proportional distribution of people of different kinds in an organization; these in turn are the result of culturally established sex role norms and behavior patterns, which for policewomen conflict with their occupational role norms as police officers.

Organizational Variables

In her recent study of men and women in a large corporation, Kanter (1977b) noted that our understanding of work-related behavior frequently has been hindered by the application of an individual model which locates the source of problems in the actions and attitudes of individual men and women, rather than a system model which examines how the large organization, as a system of organized roles and opportunities, presses the individual toward subsequent success or failure by shaping work-related contingencies. She suggests that there are three primary variables for understanding occupational role performance in organizations—power, opportunity, and numbers—which constrain and shape possibilities for action and press people to adapt to their situation, although they do so in a number of different ways depending on the circumstances, the individual, and the

1. There are a number of other studies of organizations that adopt what Silverman (1971) termed an "action frame of reference" to examine the ways actors interpret others' meanings and behaviors and negotiate the organizational rules. See, for example, Roy (1953 and 1954), Dalton (1964), Crozier (1964), and Kanter (1977b).

means available to achieve a sense of dignity and meaning in the occupational role.[2]

Opportunity and Power. Kanter (1977b) suggests that men and women behave differently in corporations because men have greater opportunities for mobility and more real power in such organizations than women. These differences are generally attributed to sex differences and have come to be seen as "natural." Yet, she observed, people of either sex, when placed in powerless and low mobility situations, respond similarly: they lower their aspirations and develop different patterns of occupational behavior from those with wider opportunities and more power. By limiting motivation for improving their situation the former set in motion a downward cycle of deprivation and discouragement. Individuals with power and/or opportunities for upward mobility, on the other hand, are able to use these resources to gain allies and supporters who provide further opportunities for success, triggering a different kind of cycle. Thus opportunity and power rather than sex per se make the difference. The structure of the work situation produces organizational behavior and creates feedback loops and cycles of success and failure so that "you can't" and "I don't want to" follow one another in circular fashion. In this way opportunity shapes values which in turn affect further opportunities. Those individuals who perceive opportunities (although they may be quite limited in reality) will work for them; those who feel blocked (although opportunities may actually exist) seek alternative sources of satisfaction.

In examining the opportunities for mobility and the distribution of power within an organization it is necessary to look at the nature of the work and the division of labor within an occupation and between occupational groups. One must also note both formal career ladders, hierarchies of positions, and mechanisms for the distribution of power and opportunity, and the informal networks and patterns of influence and sponsorship, which lead some members toward success and consign others to failure.

While a police department is similar to an industrial organization in many respects, its unique work and paramilitary structure, in which

2. By "occupational role" is meant "the patterned behavior associated with an occupational group. It includes the privileges attached to a social position in the workplace" as well as the job responsibilities (Stewart and Cantor, 1974:8). For many it is not merely a set of tasks that provide income but a socially organized set of activities and social roles which give meaning and direction to their lives.

most officers spend their careers as undifferentiated generalists (patrol officers) at the lowest rank, shape the organizational environment and channel opportunities and power. Police work involves the officer in a wide variety of tasks, but the primary responsibilities involve the maintenance of public order and enforcement of the law.[3] The potential for violence and the need and right to use coercive means to enforce his/her definition of the situation are unifying factors in police work (Bittner, 1970). The threat of danger to and vesting of discretionary authority in the police officer produce the officer's "working personality" (Skolnick, 1966), isolate the officer from the community (Banton, 1964; Westley, 1970) and have resulted in a highly developed and closed occupational subculture. Acceptance of the subculture's principal norms and acceptance into the subculture's informal social network are the keys to opportunity for mobility within the organization.

The paramilitary organizational structure of the police department both shapes the distribution of power and opportunities, and contributes to the officers' informal subculture, which in turn subverts the formal controls. To limit the street officer's discretion and potential to abuse his authority, police departments since their inception have been organized on a military model employing ranks, uniforms, a detailed set of internal rules and regulations, and close punitive supervision. Yet the actuality of police work precludes guidelines for every imaginable situation and necessitates the discretion of patrol officers. The isolation of the officer on the beat and atomized police operations frequently lead to unresponsiveness to top command; supervisors have difficulty controlling the work behavior of subordinates, and their attempts at control are perceived as arbitrary and unpredictable. Thus the reality of police work thwarts efforts by the department to militarily control or manipulate police officers; instead it has led to the development of "the code of the system" (Wilson, 1963) which powerfully affects work behavior. The fiction of a military organization, when in fact officers are guided by an alternative set of "practical" norms, and the reality of unmilitary, informal power and opportunity arrangements work doubly against women. The fiction of military discipline leads to the belief that women are

3. There are a number of excellent discussions of police work and the effect of the work and organizational structure on police officers and their behavior. See Rubinstein (1974) for a detailed ethnography of police work. Also see Skolnick (1966), Wilson (1968), Bittner (1970), Westley (1970), Cain (1973), Muir (1977), and Manning (1977).

inappropriate for the job, and results in males, particularly veterans, being given preference on job registers and promotional ratings. At the same time, the reality of an informal power structure based on personal ties and political maneuvering makes it very difficult for a female "outsider" to gain membership, acceptance, or sponsorship in the "in" group.

Opportunities for advancement in a police organization are limited and, although nominally open to all through promotional examination, in fact depend on the ratings of supervisors, which reflect informal patterns of acceptance and sponsorship based on the individual's apparent "rightness" for the work and place in the existing social system. Only those who can be trusted to play by the (informal) rules can be considered for promotion. While both formal and informal hierarchies of power and influence, and various routes of upward mobility exist within all large organizations, the nature of police work and structure of the police department create a particularly wide gulf between the formal distribution of power and opportunity, and the informal reality—the inability of the organization to control much of the officers' behavior. This, in turn, magnifies the importance of the informal understandings: mobility options rest on an officer's fitting into the informal peer group, adhering to the informal norms, and gaining sponsors through the "buddy system."

Relative Numbers: The Problem of "Tokens." Hughes (1944) observed that there tends to grow up about a status, in addition to its specific characteristics (e.g., a doctor must be trained and licensed) a complex of expected auxiliary characteristics. Within an occupational group expectations concerning members' appropriate auxiliary statuses become interwoven with the group's values and procedures, serve as a basis of its informal code of behavior, and guide the selection of informal leaders. The arrival of an individual with different characteristics results in discomfort and anxiety for the members of the dominant group; they focus on the "wrong" status in their interactions with the newcomer. Although the deviant auxiliary status may be irrelevant to the task at hand, it nevertheless becomes the salient status (Epstein, 1970). Members of the majority group tend to respond toward the minority or "token" individual with an unexpected auxiliary status on the basis of their informal assumptions about someone with such different characteristics: women and blacks who enter occupations in which the majority of workers are male or white, for example, face dilemmas as token members of the group which make their occupational role problematic and interfere with their ability to function effectively.[4]

Kanter (1977a and 1977b) observed three perceptual phenomena associated with the presence of such minority individuals or tokens, each of which has consequences for their position in the group: they are highly visible, and so capture a disproportionate share of others' awareness; they polarize the differences that exist between tokens and dominants; and their attributes become distorted by dominants to fit the latter's generalizations about tokens' social types. These perceptual phenomena, in turn, lead to: increased performance pressures on tokens who threaten dominants' shared understandings; heightened dominants' group boundaries against "outsiders"; and entrapment into familiar stereotypic roles "appropriate for someone of the token's type," limiting self-expression and role flexibility. As tokens, police-women face experiences which require them to adopt a variety of mechanisms to ease the stresses of their occupational situation.

Tokens may respond by attempting to assimilate with the dominants by stressing fulfillment of the occupational role through additional striving, maintaining a low profile, and disavowing identity with their "type" by being "the exception." Alternatively, they may emphasize their "differentness," accept token status, and rely on some of the "benefits" that status confers in terms of lowered expectations of their occupational performance.

Cultural Patterns and Male-Female Interaction

Overarching organizational structures and the division of labor in an organization are culturally prescribed sex role norms which shape the interactions of males and females on the job and elsewhere. For policewomen these sex role norms lead to dilemmas and conflicts that are not an artifact of power, numbers, and opportunity alone. Cultural mandates defining "appropriate" behavior for men and women are enacted through interpersonal interaction which affects occupational role performance.

All societies impose on the biological differences between men and women a set of cultural definitions of what it means to be male and

4. Hughes (1944) illustrated the dilemma with the case of the woman engineer who, after designing a new airplane wing, was expected to go on its maiden flight and give a (stag) dinner for coworkers. She was urged by fellow workers not to go (i.e., to act like a lady rather than as an engineer). She chose to take the flight and give the party like an engineer. After the food and one round of drinks, she left the party, like a lady.

female, and establish differing norms of behavior for members of each group. For policewomen sex role norms of appropriate "female" behavior conflict with occupational role definitions of behavior appropriate for a police officer, affecting day-to-day occupational interactions of policewomen and evoking a variety of interactional dilemmas.[5]

The term "sex role" is empirically fuzzy but appears to involve four elements: a label, behavior, expectations, and a social location (Angrist, 1969; see also Lipman-Blumen and Tickamyer, 1975). Accompanying the label "male" or "female" is a constellation of traits and behavior patterns considered characteristic of and appropriate to members of each sex. Sex role norms in our society call for and reward certain qualities in women including "personal warmth and empathy, sensitivity and emotionalism, grace, compliance, dependence, and deference" (Epstein, 1970:20). Men, on the other hand, are generally expected to be independent, objective, logical, active, competitive, and adventurous. They are taught to be specialists in the world of power, authority, and the manipulation of things. Generally, men have higher social rank than women, so that in male-female interactions, certain asymmetrical patterns of deference and demeanor prevail (Goffman, 1956 and 1976; Spradley and Mann, 1975).

These culturally defined sex roles are learned from infancy, becoming a basic part of an individual's self-concept. Often taken for granted, they condition interactions in which all individuals participate, but because they are ubiquitous, are often ignored or taken as "given" by sociologists analyzing the social interaction of male and female actors in other role performances.

Many occupations, particularly those offering the greatest income, prestige, and power, call for qualities that are antithetical to the female role and "femininity." Most women resolve the potential normative conflict between "appropriate" occupational role and sex role behaviors by engaging in jobs in which the tasks involve service to or nurturance of others and in which they are the subordinates of men. Women rarely work as peers of men and when women become

5. The notions of "dilemmas and contradictions of status" (Hughes, 1944) and "conflicting status obligations" (Merton, 1957:382) are part of the larger body of concepts grouped together as role theory. For a discussion of role theory and associated concepts see Merton (1957); Sarbin (1954); Biddle and Thomas (1966); Sarbin and Allen (1968); and Levinson (1959). For discussions of role stresses and conflicts see Gross et al. (1957); Goode (1960); Goffman (1961); and Kahn et al. (1964). For an application of Merton's schema to the study of professional women see Epstein (1970).

supervisors their subordinates ordinarily are other women or children.

Problems arise when women "step out of place" into work that calls for "masculine" characteristics or when they enter a work situation as a peer of men. When they do so, their behavioral options are constrained by the potency of sex role norms. As Spradley and Mann (1975:6) observed:

> Women not only assume their roles, the traditional and the new, they also learn to play them in ways that others can recognize as feminine. It is often easier for a society to allow women to occupy new roles than to allow them some new style of performance within these roles. A woman can become a college professor, a surgeon, a managing editor, a bank president or a tennis player but "she should still act like a woman."

Since male-female interaction is governed by asymmetrical norms, while police officers relate to each other as peers and equals and have status superiority over most citizens, confusion is likely to develop in policewomen when deciding what rules apply with both colleagues and clients. When and how does a policewoman act "like a cop" and still act "like a woman"? If she acts "like a woman" how does that affect her occupational role performance on the street? her relations with male colleagues? her options for occupational mobility? What are the consequences of not acting "like a woman" on the job? This study will examine how the cultural constraints characteristic of the male-female relationship affect the micro-level dynamics of interaction between men and women in the specifically structured context of the police department.

Chapter 2

The Changing Role
of Women in Policing

Since its inception in the early nineteenth century, policing has been and remains a male-dominated occupation, closely associated with masculinity. Yet policewomen are not a new phenomenon. Women have served as sworn officers for more than half a century (although their assignment to patrol is a recent development). Why is policing a male-dominated occupation? Why has the number of women officers been so limited and their work role so circumscribed? What has led to the recent changes in the work assignments of female officers in many departments? The answers to these questions will contribute to a fuller understanding of policewomen's current dilemmas by putting them in an historical perspective.

HISTORY OF WOMEN IN POLICING

The Origins of Policing and of the Policewomen's Movement

The history, organization, nature, and conditions of policing all have contributed to its past—and continuing—definition as "men's work," as well as the initial exclusion of women, and the grudging admission of a limited number of female officers.

The assignment of the policing role exclusively to men was a logical extension of the existing division of labor in society. Traditionally men have acted as warriors and soldiers, and borne the responsibility for the physical protection of the herd, home, family and community. Women and children were regarded as socially and physically subordinate groups in need of the men's protection. When medieval towns in England hired watchmen, the predecessors of modern police officers, the employment of men was regarded as natural and appropriate to the task.

The modern police were initiated in England, and shortly thereafter in the United States in the first half of the nineteenth century in the midst of growing urban mob violence, crime and social disorder. The 1829 act establishing the London police created the first police force in the world organized to prevent crime by providing constant patrol. Created at a time of political crisis over parliamentary representation for the middle classes, the fundamentally political role of the police met with great public suspicion and resistance. To win broad public support the commanders of the new force created a police removed from partisan politics. They sought to create a public image of policemen as a moral and symbolic force, impartial representatives of the law to which they were subordinated. To gain citizen respect and cooperation necessary for its success, the department was organized on a military model with strict discipline and limited officer discretion. The men selected had to be superior physically, intellectually and temperamentally. Officers were required to be above average in height and in strength; in addition, to emphasize the appearance of physical superiority and strict discipline, they wore uniforms with tall hats (Miller, 1973).

In the United States policemen were more political, and armed with lethal weapons. In both societies despite organizational differences, the essential elements of policing—the exercise of authority and the ability to use force—were responsibilities long assigned to men and denied to women. Women, disenfranchised and part of the protected "weaker" class, could hardly have represented the moral authority of the state, nor did they have the physical characteristics considered symbolically and practically important for the job. Therefore, the employment of men selected for physical brawn as police officers was merely an extension of the existing division of labor between the sexes. Although social conditions, the definition of the police role, and the sexual division of labor have changed somewhat in the last fifty years, and although the authority and legitimacy of the police have long been established, the core of policing remains the use of authority in potentially violent situations in which males, by virtue of their physical stature, socialization, and society's assumptions about them, are at an advantage.

The initial entrance of women into policing early in this century was the result of the convergence of several social reform movements, including the women's rights movement and an attempt to reform a variety of police practices. Prior to this, however, the groundwork was laid during the "pre-policewomen" phase of what was termed "the policewomen's movement." During this phase, which extended from before the Civil War until the early twentieth century, reformers sought to ensure that women and young girls held in custody in public institutions were supervised by women. From 1845, when New York City hired the first woman prison matron, until the end of the century an increasing number of municipalities and states employed women in this capacity.

The next step involved the use of female officers as protectors of women and children prior to incarceration. As women entered the labor force, public concern about the social and moral conditions of women and girls led first to a public outcry and then to a movement extending special protection and guidance.

The Specialist Phase: 1910-1930

In 1910 Alice S. Wells became the first sworn policewoman with the powers of arrest. Convinced that she could be more effective in preventive and protective work with women and children if she had police powers, Ms. Wells petitioned and gained appointment from the police department and city council of Los Angeles. She soon was deluged with requests for help in introducing women into police agencies throughout the United States and the Western world. By 1915 at least twenty-five cities had appointed policewomen (Horne, 1974:18-19) and by 1918, 220 towns and cities were using policewomen and matrons (Task Force Report: The Police, 1967:229).

To promote the policewomen's movement, Ms. Wells took the lead in organizing the International Association of Policewomen in 1915 during the annual Conference of Charities and Corrections. The goals of this organization were to provide information about the work of policewomen, raise work standards, and promote the concept of preventive and protective services by police departments.

The earliest policewomen's literature makes clear their sense of being part of a social movement with a special mission, their advocacy of a distinct role for policewomen, and their reformist zeal and idealism. As women attempted to reshape their place in society and alter society's major social institutions, they sought employment in police agencies as a part of a social crusade tied to larger reforms. The struggle to "save" wayward youth and helpless women from the evils of industrialism, alcohol, and other abuses led to the doorstep of the stationhouse, and the women marched in. They joined departments as specialists, carving out for themselves a unique role.[1]

The early policewomen faced many barriers, including higher entrance requirements, admission quotas, and separate promotion lists. Policemen frequently fought against what they felt was "an unwarranted invasion of the uniformed man's field of work" (Hutzel, 1933:2-3), fearing that women would seek to take over men's functions. Others felt that "preventive policing was an unjustified excursion into social work" (Owing, 1968:203). They questioned the physical ability of women, their emotional stability, and their ability to work under paramilitary discipline.

As their numbers slowly increased, questions of where and how to incorporate women into the police organization arose. About one-third of the jurisdictions employing women, including most of the larger urban departments, eventually established separate women's bureaus which permitted the policewomen to develop their own leadership, programs, and a sense of unity and mission as "a socializing agency to the whole police force" (Van Winkle in Owing, 1968:x). The women's bureaus frequently were independent police departments in miniature, composed of women who were "kept at arm's length from the main organization and, perhaps, a little despised by the remainder of the force" (Hutzel, 1933:3). Protected by ideology and organization, policewomen in women's bureaus were isolated and nearly powerless; those women not in women's bureaus were unorganized and probably lacked the sustaining ideology prevalent among organized policewomen.

Women were able to stake a claim in policing as a result of several factors including: the societal demand for better protection of women and children in urban settings; the increasing participation of women in a variety of occupations; the acceptance of a limited and special role within policing, which was an extension of women's traditional sex

---

1. An example of the women's idealistic and reformist activities was the establishment in New York City of a special women's precinct. Housed in a refurbished house in the Hell's Kitchen section under the leadership of Mary Hamilton, it was to be a place where women could come for information, advice, and aid. The experiment was aborted shortly after it began. See Hamilton (1924) for further details.

role; and public pressures echoed by a few progressive police reformers for changes in police practices.

In the early twentieth century, as a result of widespread criticism, a movement to reform the police grew from within police circles. Reformers sought to adopt more advanced strategies of crime prevention to supplement traditional techniques of control. The early policewomen's movement grew in conjunction with this police reform movement, echoing its sentiments and goals; its fortunes have waxed and waned with reform's popularity. Periods of police reform such as the 1920's and late 1960's, challenging the "traditional" goals, tasks, organizational structures, and personnel policies of police departments, created conditions which permitted women—whose goals paralleled those of the reformers and who were thus useful to the latter—to gain some of their objectives by riding in on the reformers' coattails.

The leading advocates of police reform in the first two decades of this century sought to emphasize the community service and crime preventative functions of the police. Fosdick, in his classic book, *American Police Systems*, noted (1920:371):

> Police work cannot be isolated from other welfare agencies of the community concerned with social problems. It cannot be divorced from all the organizing influence . . . working for better conditions in city life. . . . The new policing demands a type of officer interested and trained in social service.

The policewomen's movement not only strongly shared these sentiments and advocated a similar goal (although its particular emphasis was on provision of protection and services to women and children), it offered women as uniquely qualified for these new functions. In an era when social work was a newly emerging profession almost exclusively dominated by women, policewomen represented a cadre of officers with the requisite interest and, in many cases, the training that very few men, and far fewer male police recruits, had acquired. The policewomen's movement took the very feminine attributes that had been used to disqualify females from policing and turned them into occupational assets, enunciating their police mission as an extension of women's roles as mothers, guardians of children and protectors of the public morals. In addition, the women were willing to undertake some of the jobs that policemen disdained, including the clerical tasks. They developed a specialized role which was complementary to—rather than in competition with—the traditional enforcement tasks of the male officers. Although they were a small and not very powerful group, for more than half a century policewomen represented a model of the highly educated, socially oriented officer seeking a "more socialized police practice" (Owing, 1968:217).

In contrast to female officers' present-day efforts, the police-women's movement of the early twentieth century did not seek equality for women in policing. Accepting a division of labor based on sex, this movement attempted to place women in areas of policing believed to be less dangerous and less demanding of physical strength, in which they could utilize their "feminine" skills. Thus they became specialists within police departments before specialization became the general trend, adapting a police role congruent with the conventional view of women.

Latency: 1930-1970

The depression halted the growth of the policewomen's movement as well as most police reform efforts. For the next forty years women on urban police forces worked with juveniles, prisoners, and type-writers, without significant changes in their status or duties. The missionary zeal and rhetoric faded as the first generation of reformers and pioneers retired, while the organizations supporting women's inclusion in other aspects of police work turned to new issues or faded into oblivion.

During the depression, hiring of policewomen slowed to a trickle and women's bureaus were criticized as "expensive frills" departments could eliminate (Williams, 1946). The 1930 U.S. census reported a total of 1,534 policewomen and detectives "gainfully employed" in both public and private agencies; the 1940 census reported that this number had increased to only 1,775 (both figures from U.S. Bureau of the Census, 1958). Although the number of female police officers increased during World War II, many were laid off after the war. The 1950 census (U.S. Bureau of the Census, 1956) reported 2,610 publicly employed policewomen, comprising slightly more than 1 percent of all police and detectives; this increased to 5,617 policewomen and 2.3 percent of all publicly employed officers in the 1960 census. Thus the silent fifties marked the quiet growth in number and percentage of female officers, but saw little change in their police role. By the 1970 census the number of policewomen had again doubled, but they still comprised about 2 percent of the total sworn police personnel (Crites, 1973).[2]

Between 1930 and 1970 the duties of a few policewomen broadened to include investigative work but the vast majority of female officers continued to be specialists employed in secretarial or juvenile work.[3] The limitations and constraints on recruitment, training, salary, work role, and promotion remained. Many departments continued to refuse to hire any female officers; others maintained a limited number of "policewoman" positions and would only hire a new female officer to replace another woman, regardless of the former's qualifications. In no department was there a single list for both male and female recruitment candidates.

During the 1960's crime became a national concern, as urban riots and civil disorders swept across the U.S. A blue-ribbon panel, The President's Commission on Law Enforcement and the Administration of Justice, was established to examine the failure of the criminal justice system—particularly the police—to cope effectively with these problems and make suggestions for sweeping changes in the system. Among the Commission's many recommendations was the following:

> Policewomen can be an invaluable asset to modern law enforcement and their present role should be broadened. Qualified women should be utilized in such important staff service units as planning and research, training, intelligence, inspection, public information, community relations, and as legal advisors. Women could also serve such units as computer programming and laboratory analysis and communications. Their value should not be considered as limited to staff functions or police work with juveniles; women should also serve regularly in patrol, vice, and investigative divisions. Finally, as more and more well

2. For further statistical information about policewomen during this period see Williams (1946) and Women's Bureau, *Outlook for Women in Police Work* (1949).

3. For a bibiliography of material on policewomen between 1945 and 1972 see Sherman and Sherman (1973). For illustrations and discussions of the special preventive-protective role of policewomen and their work see Boyd (1953); Buwalda (1945); Fagerstrom (1958, 1960, 1964); Gibbons (1956); Higgins (1947, 1950, 1951, 1956, 1958a, 1958b, 1958c, 1960, 1961, 1962a, 1962b, 1962c); Leevy (1949); Melchionne (1960a, 1960b, 1961); O'Connor (1955); Olson (1957); Owens (1958); Purcell (1960); Rinck (1954); Rink (1963); Salzbrenner (1963); Snow (1956); Sweeny (1959); Tenney (1953); Torres (1953). For an overview of the history of women in policing and the areas to which they were assigned see Breece and Garrett (1974); Crites (1973); Higgins (1947, 1951, 1958, 1960); Horne (1972); and Milton (1972).

qualified women enter the service, they could assume administrative
responsibilities. (The President's Commission on Law Enforcement and
the Administration of Justice, 1967:125)

Although Milton (1972) noted that little change had occurred
during the ensuing five-year period, the role of women in policing has
been noticeably altered since 1972. For the first time women have been
employed and assigned on an equal basis with men, and perform the
same patrol functions rather than specialized tasks.

The Contemporary Period

Because there are approximately 40,000 separate police jurisdictions in the United States, using a variety of titles and ranks, it is
difficult to compile accurate information about recent changes in the
role of female officers, although a growing body of data on policewomen and their work has become available.[4] The statistics that
follow are based on all available data for the nation's thirty-two cities
with a population of more than 400,000 according to the 1970 census
(tables 1 and 2).

No statistics on total sworn police personnel are available for 1924.
Although the number of policewomen increased between 1924 and
1946 in most cities, it is not possible to determine whether this also
represented an increase in the percentage of women engaged in police
work.

Between 1946 and 1971 no noticeable change occurred in representation of policewomen in the departments for which data are
available. The 1946 mean percentage of women in the total police
forces of the twenty-two cities for which data were obtained was 1.6
(see table 2). Twenty-five years later in 1971 the mean percentage of
sworn female police department personnel in the thirty-two largest
American cities was 1.3. By 1974 policewomen comprised 2.4 percent
of the total personnel in these cities and in 1975 they made up 2.9
percent of the police forces (excluding New York, for which data were
unavailable). The layoff of about 400 newly hired policewomen by
New York City, as a result of its financial crisis, led to a decrease in
1976, when policewomen comprised 2.6 percent of the sworn officers

4. See Eisenberg et al. (1973); Bloch et al. (1973a, 1973b); Washington (1974); Bloch
and Anderson (1974a and 1974b); Edmundson (1975); and the FBI's annual Uniform
Crime Reports, which since 1971 list "sworn police personnel" separately by sex.

of these cities (excluding Nashville, for which statistics are unavailable). Thus the representation of sworn women in the country's largest police departments, while still very small, has grown slightly.

In 1971, policewomen comprised less than 1 percent of all sworn officers in sixteen of the thirty-two major cities; by 1974 the number of departments with less than 1 percent female officers was only six. In 1975, despite the setback in New York, women made marked gains in several other cities. That year female officers comprised at least 2 percent of the sworn personnel in nineteen of the thirty-two departments, and in five departments more than 5 percent of the sworn personnel was female.

A detailed explanation of the reasons why in some cities, such as San Antonio and Minneapolis, less than 1 percent of the sworn force consists of female officers while in others, such as Indianapolis, Atlanta, and Washington, D.C., women comprise more than 7 percent would require another full scale study of the demographics and political history of each city. (A study of the history and current status of policewomen in major U.S. cities is being conducted by the Police Foundation.) In some instances explanations are available and idiosyncratic. Long hailed as a leader in the use of policewomen (who in 1946 comprised more than 10 percent of its force), Indianapolis had the high proportion of female officers because, until 1970, civilian positions in the police department were political appointments. In order to ensure loyal long-term secretarial assistance to police officials, the department hired female officers: in 1971 well over half of its 74 policewomen, including most sergeants, were used as secretaries.

In many instances changes in the number and proportion of policewomen in a department arose in response to legal pressures brought to bear on the department. In 1973 and 1974, hoping to avoid a lawsuit, New York voluntarily doubled the number of policewomen. Large increases in the number of policewomen in Philadelphia and Chicago, on the other hand, were the direct result of court orders mandating the hiring of a specified number of policewomen.

It appears that in those cities with large black populations (e.g., Washington, Atlanta and Detroit) the sexual and racial integration of the police department have proceeded furthest. In strongly ethnic group-dominated cities (e.g., Buffalo, Boston, Philadelphia and Minneapolis) the forces of traditionalism and resistance to change, including the sexual and racial integration of policing, have retarded the hiring of policewomen.

TABLE 1
Policewomen Employed in Cities over 400,000

City	1924a	1946b	1966c	Dec. 31, 1971d	Oct. 31, 1972e	Oct. 31, 1973f	Oct. 31, 1974g	Oct. 31, 1975h	Oct. 31, 1976i
New York	61	174	305	322	311	622	715	j	294
Chicago	30	60	56	119	125	310	190	207	207
Los Angeles	8	–	113	165	161	150	151	156	154
Philadelphia	–	10	60	67	63	65	74	73	179
Detroit	31	60	88	100	93	124	140	282	353
Houston	1	5	–	48	50	55	77	137	141
Baltimore	5	6	–	53	53	53	52	60	62
Dallas	0	–	–	20	38	67	71	80	103
Washington, D.C.	21	35	36	108k	168	157	250	340	319
Cleveland	5	22	36	43	41	53	51	48	45
Indianapolis	19	56	–	76	72	76	82	74	93
Milwaukee	0	2	–	16	25	25	25	27	26
San Francisco	3	19	–	9	j	13	13	44	59
San Diego	–	1	–	12	22	26	59	54	49
San Antonio	–	–	–	4	4	3	6	9	9
Boston	5	15	5	4	14	23	22	28	26
Memphis	5	–	–	21	37	37	49	51	55
St. Louis	18	18	16	19	19	18	29	34	40
New Orleans	1	–	–	10	11	14	17	68	28
Phoenix	–	3	–	9	17	27	28	34	49

TABLE 1 *(Continued)*
Policewomen Employed in Cities over 400,000

City	1924[a]	1946[b]	1966[c]	Dec. 31, 1971[d]	Oct. 31, 1972[e]	Oct. 31, 1973[f]	Oct. 31, 1974[g]	Oct. 31, 1975[h]	Oct. 31, 1976[i]
Columbus	2	3	–	19	20	20	20	30	29
Seattle	–	–	–	20	20	19	17	24	26
Jacksonville	0	11	–	6	14	13	18	27	18
Pittsburgh	5	12	14	14	14	13	11	9	29
Denver	3	1	–	18	21	20	32	41	47
Kansas City, Mo.	–	–	–	5	9	11	13	15	25
Atlanta	2	6	–	3	16	50	129	131	121
Buffalo	5	4	–	16	15	19	18	16	17
Cincinnati	–	–	–	9	10	12	12	13	12
Nashville	2	–	–	13	11	14	21	22	n
San Jose	–	–	–	13	24	19l	18	21	24
Minneapolis	3	6	–	8	6	8	5	9	7
TOTAL	235	529	729	1261	1504	1956	2415	(2139)m	2644o

[a]Source: Owing, Chloe, *Women Police* (Montclair, N.J.: Patterson, Smith, 1968, pp.283-90).
[b]Source: Williams, Carol M., *The Organization and Practices of Policewomen's Divisions in the United States* (Detroit: National Training School of Public Service, 1946).
[c]Watson, Nelson A. and Robert Walker, eds., *A Symposium on Women and Policing* (Washington, D.C.: IACP, 1966).
[d]*Uniform Crime Reports for the United States—1971* (Washington, D.C.: U.S. Department of Justice, Federal Bureau of Investigation).

TABLE 1 *(Continued)*

eUniform Crime Reports for the United States–1972 (Washington, D.C.: U.S. Department of Justice, Federal Bureau of Investigation).

fUniform Crime Reports for the United States–1973 (Washington, D.C.: U.S. Department of Justice, Federal Bureau of Investigation).

gUniform Crime Reports for the United States–1974 (Washington, D.C.: U.S. Department of Justice, Federal Bureau of Investigation).

hUniform Crime Reports for the United States–1975 (Washington, D.C.: U.S. Department of Justice, Federal Bureau of Investigation).

iUniform Crime Reports for the United States–1976 (Washington, D.C.: U.S. Department of Justice, Federal Bureau of Investigation).

jNo breakdown of employees by sex available to Uniform Crime Reports.

kFigure for January 1972 supplied by Metropolitan Police Department of Washington, D.C., in private communication.

lData missing in Uniform Crime Report. Figure taken from Washington, *Deployment of Female Policewomen in the United States* (Gaithersburg, Md.: IACP, 1974), p. 24.

mNot a meaningful total because of the absence of New York City figures.

nData missing from Uniform Crime Reports.

oData on Nashville missing from total.

TABLE 2
Percentage of Women in the Police Force
in Cities over 400,000

City	1946[a]	1971[b]	1974[c]	1975[d]	1976[e]
New York	1.1	1.0	2.3[g]	[f]	1.1[j]
Chicago	0.7	0.9	1.4	1.5	1.6
Los Angeles	0.8	2.3	2.0	2.0	2.1
Philadelphia	0.2	0.8	0.9	0.9	2.2[g]
Detroit	1.7	1.8	2.6	5.1[h]	7.0[g]
Houston	1.5	2.4	3.3	5.2[h]	5.2
Baltimore	0.3	0.8	1.5	1.7	1.8
Dallas	[f]	1.1	3.7	4.0	5.1[g]
Washington, D.C.	2.0	2.1	5.4	7.9	7.4
Cleveland	1.4	1.8	2.2	2.1	2.2
Indianapolis	10.4[k]	6.9[i]	7.5	6.8	8.6[g]
Milwaukee	0.8	0.7	1.2	1.2	1.2
San Francisco	1.5	0.4[j]	0.7	2.4	5.5[h]
San Diego	0.3	1.2	5.3[h]	4.6	4.6
San Antonio	[f]	0.4	0.5	0.7	0.8
Boston	0.7	0.1	0.9	1.1	1.1
Memphis	[f]	1.9	3.8[g]	3.8	4.2
St. Louis	0.9	0.8	1.3	1.5	1.9
New Orleans	[f]	0.7	1.2	4.1[h]	1.9[i]
Phoenix	2.6	0.8	2.1[g]	2.2	3.1
Columbus	0.9	1.8	1.7	2.6	2.7
Seattle	[f]	1.6	1.6	2.2	2.5
Jacksonville	4.8	0.8[i]	2.0[g]	1.8	1.8
Pittsburgh	1.1	0.8	0.8	0.6	2.1[g]
Denver	0.2	1.4	2.3	2.9	3.5
Kansas City, Mo.	[f]	0.4	1.0	1.2	2.0
Atlanta	1.5	0.2[j]	8.1[h]	9.2[g]	9.7
Buffalo	0.3	1.1	1.4	1.2	1.4
Cincinnati	[f]	0.9	1.0	1.1	1.1
Nashville	[f]	1.9	2.4	2.5	[f]
San Jose	[f]	2.3	2.6	2.9	3.1
Minneapolis	1.2	0.9	0.6	1.0	0.8
TOTAL PERCENTAGE	1.6[l]	1.3	2.35	2.9	2.6

TABLE 2 *(Continued)*

[a]Williams, Carol M., *The Organization and Practices of Police-women's Divisions in the United States* (Detroit: National Training School of Public Service, 1946).

[b]*Uniform Crime Reports for the United States—1971* (Washington, D.C.: U.S. Department of Justice, Federal Bureau of Investigation).

[c]*Uniform Crime Reports for the United States—1974* (Washington, D.C.: U.S. Department of Justice, Federal Bureau of Investigation).

[d]*Uniform Crime Reports for the United States—1975* (Washington, D.C.: U.S. Department of Justice, Federal Bureau of Investigation).

[e]*Uniform Crime Reports for the United States—1976* (Washington, D.C.: U.S. Department of Justice, Federal Bureau of Investigation).

[f]No data available.

[g]Represents a growth of more than 1 percent in the representation of women in the police department for the period.

[h]Represents a growth of more than 2 percent in the representation of women in the police department for the period.

[i]Represents a decrease of more than 2 percent of women on a particular police department for the period.

[j]Represents a decrease of more than 1 percent (but less than 2 percent) of policewomen on a particular police department for the period.

[k]Italics show cities in which more than 5 percent of the total sworn officers are female.

[l]The data are standardized across the cities by indicating for the various dates the percentage of the total police force women comprise in that city. The mean of these percentages was then calculated, producing a mean unweighted by the size of the city.

Changes in the large cities are paralleled by those in other jurisdictions. Table 3 shows that similar growth has occurred in smaller cities, suburban departments, sheriff's departments, and in university campus security forces. By 1976 policewomen made up 2.4 percent of all city sworn police personnel, an increase of .7 percent from 1973. More impressive is the increase of women in suburban agencies, where they now comprise more than 4 percent of the sworn personnel, and in sheriff's departments, where they comprise over 8 percent. Similarly, as campus security increased (from 3,525 to 4,590 officers, up 30 percent, from 1973 to 1975), the relatively high proportion of women rose from 13 to 17 percent of the total.[5]

5. These officers have limited police powers and lower incomes than regular police.

TABLE 3
Percent Distribution of Female Sworn Police Officers by Agency Type: 1971-1975

Population Group	1971[a]	1973[b]	1975[c]	1976[d]
Group I				
Total (over 250,000)	1.3	1.7	1.7	2.6
Over 1,000,000	1.3	1.7	1.7	2.1
500,000 to 1,000,000	1.2	1.9	3.1[e]	3.1
250,000 to 500,000	1.3	1.5	2.4	3.0
Group II				
100,000 to 250,000	1.4	1.7	2.3	2.6
Group III				
50,000 to 100,000	0.9	1.2	1.7	1.9
Group IV				
25,000 to 50,000	1.2	1.1	1.6	1.7
Group V				
10,000 to 25,000	1.8	1.8	2.0	2.2
Group VI				
Under 10,000	2.9	2.8	2.1	2.6
Suburban agencies	2.7	3.6	4.1	4.2
Sheriff	5.7	7.0[e]	8.1[e]	7.7
University security forces	11.0	13.0[e]	17.0[e]	17.2
TOTAL CITIES	1.4	1.7	2.2	2.4

[a]*Uniform Crime Reports for the United States—1971* (Washington, D.C.: U.S. Department of Justice, Federal Bureau of Investigation).

TABLE 3 *(Continued)*

[b]*Uniform Crime Reports for the United States–1973* (Washington, D.C.: U.S. Department of Justice, Federal Bureau of Investigation).
[c]*Uniform Crime Reports for the United States–1975* (Washington, D.C.: U.S. Department of Justice, Federal Bureau of Investigation).
[d]*Uniform Crime Reports for the United States–1976* (Washington, D.C.: U.S. Department of Justice, Federal Bureau of Investigation).
[e]Increase of more than 1 percent during the period.

Increasing numbers and altered policies toward policewomen are found in federal and state agencies as well. Women have been admitted on an equal basis with men in the Executive Protective Service since its inception in 1970, the Secret Service since 1971, and the FBI since 1972 (Horne, 1974). As of February 1976 there were forty-three female FBI agents (Unger, 1976:29), and 12 percent of all army military police were female (Kinzer, personal communication). A number of states now employ female troopers, including Pennsylvania (since 1972) and Maryland (since 1974).

More significant than the increasing number of female officers (still quite small) is the change in their assignments. In many departments they are placed in criminal investigation units; and women are on patrol in at least nineteen of the nation's thirty-two largest cities (data were unavailable for seven of these) (Washington, 1974). The long period in which a limited number of women served as specialists has ended, with the emergence of policewomen in patrol assignments acting as generalists.[6]

6. The use of women officers abroad varies widely. Great Britain has been a pioneer in their use. The Women's Police Service, a volunteer organization, was set up at the outbreak of World War I to keep the activities of women and children under surveillance. During the course of the war nearly 1,000 women were trained and employed on or near military bases and munitions factories. Like the American policewomen, these largely middle-class women had been activists in pre-war social reform movements. In November 1918 the London Metropolitan Police hired women and organized them in the Division of Women Police Patrols, which by 1919 had expanded to 110 female officers (Allen, 1925). Their main function was to deal with sex offenses, prostitution, white slave traffic, female prisoners, wayward girls, and all juvenile cases. The growth of their movement came to a halt when the policemen's federation mounted an effort to eliminate them. In 1922 the government-sponsored Geddes Report called for the abolition of women police. The Division survived

FACTORS RELATED TO THE
CHANGING ROLE OF POLICEWOMEN

The new phase in the history of women in police work is the result of social changes in the 1960's and early 1970's. Although changes in the law have been the most important factor in causing police departments to hire and assign officers without regard to sex, social and economic trends fostered these legal changes, while various problems and pressures faced by police departments contributed to the changing role for policewomen.

In the late 1960's police departments faced a number of severe challenges: a growing shortage of qualified personnel; strong public pressure to reduce the rising crime rate; and widespread demand for a radical alteration in their relationship with the community. When federal money and new technology failed to solve these problems, other solutions had to be considered. A few departments abandoned "business as usual" approaches and included female officers in a wider variety of assignments, including patrol.

At the same time, changes in the general legal, economic, and social roles of women led to a renewal of demands for equality and organized challenges to laws and habits which were formerly seen as "natural." The convergence of society-wide trends and departmental problems thus contributed to changing the role of policewomen.

Changing Pressures Facing the Police

Crime and Social Disorder. Crime, rarely mentioned during the 1960 presidential campaign, had become a national political issue in 1964, and by 1968 had reached the top of the Gallup Poll list of domestic issues troubling Americans (Saunders, 1970:1). In 1965 the President's Commission on Law Enforcement and the Administration of Justice (called the Crime Commission) was established. Its findings,

---

although the number of policewomen was cut to 20 and hiring outside London was stopped.

For the next four decades the role of women remained limited as their numbers grew slowly. In 1966 there were 4,000 women out of 95,000 officers (Berkeley, 1967:67). In 1973 promotion lists were merged and in 1974 women's salaries were made the same as men's (Horne, 1974).

Other countries that now use policewomen include the major Western European nations, Japan, Guyana, Israel, Australia, and New Zealand. For further historical and statistical data on policewomen abroad see Allen (1925); Wyles (1952); Condor (1960); Higgins (1964); Berkeley (1967); Milton (1972); Horne (1974).

published in 1967, "documented the devastating impact of crime on
the national consciousness" (Saunders, 1970:2). It recommended more
than two hundred proposals for action, including changes in police
departments' monolithic personnel structure, higher standards of
selection and training, more effective community relations, better
management, and better coordination of services and functions
among the 40,000 police forces in the United States.

Beyond the rising crime rate, the Crime Commission pointed to the
huge gulf that separated the police from the communities they were
employed to serve. In the 1960's police became the vortex of the social
storm sweeping the country. The civil rights movement, through
national media coverage, called attention to widespread police practices that were illegal and brutal. "Bull" Connors became a national
symbol, an indication that the police contributed to the nation's social
problems. Relations between the black community and the police
grew worse following a series of urban riots which made clear that the
police were generally viewed by blacks as oppressive "occupying
army" rather than public servants or protectors.

The police response to the student and peace movements, including
officers' behavior in several incidents labeled "police riots," indicated
that the alienation of the police was not only a racial matter, and that
profound changes in police organization, function, and personnel
policies were necessary. "Law and order" was not enough; the police
would have to become responsive and responsible to the community,
and operate under the law to regain public confidence.

"Manpower" and Recruiting. The Crime Commission's *Task Force
Report: The Police* urged departments to subordinate strength and
aggressiveness, previously highly regarded selection criteria, to emotional stability, intelligence, and sensitivity to minority problems. It
recommended changing recruitment standards, including height,
weight, age and vision requirements, that frequently eliminated many
otherwise highly qualified potential officers, including women; and it
urged the employment of more minority, college-educated, and female
officers. The recommendation that police departments reflect the
spectrum of their community and employ officers on the basis of their
interpersonal skills facilitated the consideration of women for police
work.

Despite these recommendations "manpower" problems continued
through the 1960's as an unusually high number of retirements

occurred and police salaries trailed wage increases in the private sector.[7] Also contributing to the recruitment problem was the negative police image. The political upheavals during the decade led to a new stereotype of the police as "pigs" among the very groups—blacks and college students—from which they were seeking to recruit.

Despite massive recruitment campaigns, the police failed to attract enough officers from these groups. The problem was less a lack of applicants than an insufficient number of "qualified" applicants. Some departments accepted male recruits with lower IQ scores and less education rather than alter their height requirements or the limitation on the number of positions legally or informally allocated to female officers which had been in effect for many years.[8] Thus women were ignored by the recruiting drives of the late 1960's.

In 1971 the Police Foundation, as part of a larger police manpower examination, began studying the feasibility of using more women in police work. Its report (Milton, 1972) once again documented numerous barriers to their employment as well as the underutilization of existing female personnel.[9] It suggested the benefits that the expanded use of female officers would bring to the police and community, including a reduction in violence between officer and citizen, an increase in crime-fighting capabilities, a better public image, improved service to citizens, greater community representation, a general re-

7. Generally, turnover ranges between 5 and 10 percent of total personnel annually. As officers recruited following World War II became eligible for retirement, turnover rates climbed sharply. For example, in 1967, 41 percent of the Los Angeles police department was eligible for retirement (*Task Force Report: The Police*, 1967). In addition, the relative pay for police declined in the 1950's; and by 1960 the median salary of craftsmen and foremen was $5,699 while that of police officers was $5,321 (*Task Force Report: The Police*, 1967:135). In 1966 the median starting salary for an officer in a city over 500,000 was $5,834. In 1968 *Fortune* reported that patrolmen's pay in major cities, about $7,500, was one-third less than that needed to sustain a family of four in moderate circumstances (Reichley, 1968).

8. In New York City the IQ scores of male recruits dropped from an average of 107 in 1962 to 93 in 1969. Although the IQs of the women were notably higher (the policewomen admitted to the department in 1966 had an average IQ of 110) the New York department stopped hiring women when the allotted positions for "policewomen" were filled although many qualified women were still available (Milton, 1972:73).

9. The barriers discussed include: hiring quotas; entrance examinations, training practices, and promotion procedures which differed from those for men; unequal pay; segregation into women's bureaus; the silence of the law on policewomen's rights; and male officers' negative view toward changing the role of policewomen.

thinking of personnel policies, and accelerated racial integration of the police.[10]

Changing Crime Patterns. A sharp increase in female and juvenile criminality and a rise in reported rapes have led to a greater need for women officers. Although the causes of these increases are not clear,[11] arrests of females and juveniles (of both sexes) in the 1960's rose at a far greater pace than the overall crime rate.[12] Since searches of female prisoners are performed exclusively by policewomen, the increase in female crime alone is likely to have required more female officers or a change in some women's assignments.

The national concern with the increase in reported rapes, and the inadequacy of police handling of rape victims, also appears to have contributed to the change in policewomen's role. The focus on rape and the victim, while largely a product of the women's liberation movement, resulted in part from the almost doubled rate of reported rapes during the 1960's.[13]

Police departments responded to the national concern with rape and other serious sex crimes by adopting many innovative procedures, including an increase in the number of women assigned to sex crimes units and an increase in the size of these units in general. A national study of police handling of rape concluded that, "The emerging professional role of women within the criminal justice system is being assisted and advanced by their increased involvement in the investigation and prosecution of forcible rape" (Chappell, 1976:134). It found that 66 percent of all police agencies and 91 percent of agencies serving

10. This is due to the fact that the proportion of black policewomen to white policewomen has consistently been higher than that of black to white male officers. According to the 1960 census less than 5 percent of all public policemen and detectives were nonwhite; 10 percent of the female officers and detectives were nonwhite. By the 1970 census the figures were 8 percent and 14 percent respectively.

11. For a discussion see Rita James Simon (1975).

12. In 1960 female offenders accounted for 10.9 percent of all arrests; in 1972 they accounted for 15 percent—an increase of 85.6 percent. Male arrests over the same period increased 28.2 percent. For serious (index) crimes (excluding rape) women arrested increased from 10.3 percent to 18 percent (FBI Uniform Crime Report, 1972). From 1968 to 1973, for serious crimes arrests of males were up 8 percent; arrests of females increased by 52 percent. Also striking was the increase in arrests of female juveniles, who have long been the responsibility of policewomen. Between 1968 and 1973 arrests of females under 18 rose 35 percent, while arrests of males under 18 rose 10 percent (FBI Uniform Crime Report, 1973).

13. Chappell (1976, footnote 7) noted that the number of rapes, per 100,000 females between 5 and 75, rose from 21.9 in 1960 to 41.3 in 1970.

cities of more than 500,000 had special rape investigation units. Twenty-two percent of the investigators in these special units, and 35.5 percent of the investigators in these larger cities were female (U.S. Department of Justice, 1977). Because the percentage of women investigators is so high, although women have traditionally been barred from investigative units, it is likely that many departments have responded to political pressure to change their policies by hiring more policewomen for, or reassigning female officers to rape investigation units.[14]

From the existing available data it is impossible to determine whether the recent increase in the number of female officers was due to pressures related to the rape issue or the result of other factors; and whether the larger number of women assigned to investigative units was the result of increased hiring or merely due to the reassignment of existing female personnel. Even if some departments did hire more policewomen in response to the rape issue, the numbers are not likely to have been significant. Nevertheless, the issue may have had importance in altering attitudes and practices within departments where women were restricted to low-status clerical work, or juvenile and community services units, by opening prestigious investigative assignments to some women officers.

From the point of view of the police administrator, the above pressures pointed to the feasibility of hiring more female officers for a wider variety of assignments. It was suggested that women could "gentle-ize" the department, improve the tarnished public image of the police, and provide a pool of heretofore untapped personnel who were both well educated and sensitive to individuals, as well as dedicated to community service. These factors, which led a few progressive chiefs to change department policies before legal pressures were brought to bear, have also helped legitimize in the eyes of some officers and the public the changing use of policewomen.

Societal Factors Affecting the Role of Policewomen

Viewed from a societal perspective, the entry of women into patrol work reflects many of the social changes that have occurred in the past

14. Data from several cities indicates this to be the case. In 1973 the police department of Cincinnati employed 10 policewomen, all of whom were assigned to the Youth Division. Rape was initially investigated by the homicide squad and if found to be of a "non-serious nature" (*sic*) was referred to Youth Aid Bureau. In September 1975, the department reported that it had hired 4 new women.

several decades. While the legal changes have had a direct, immediate, and demonstrable effect on department policies with respect to policewomen, these in turn are rooted in broader alterations of the place of women in society, particularly changes in sex role definitions and women's participation in the labor force which have recently come into focus as a result of the women's liberation movement.

The Women's Liberation Movement. Legal changes in the position of policewomen have grown out of wider efforts by the women's liberation movement to alter the social, economic, and legal position of women throughout the society. This movement, which blossomed in the early 1970's, in turn resulted from the less noticeable increase in working women that began in the 1950's. While a discussion of the historical sources and goals of the movement will not be attempted here, it is important to view changes in the policewomen's role in the wider context of a national movement that grew from and fostered changes in women's work patterns, sex role definitions, and social position.[15] Once set in motion, the movement has created a dynamic pattern whereby legal changes alter social attitudes that lead to further demands for legal changes, and in turn reshape attitudes—an interactive process of cause and effect.

One of the most striking shifts in labor force patterns, the increase in the number of working mothers including those with pre-school children, is of particular importance for police work.[16] Due to upper age limits for police recruits, which tend to eliminate women who return to the labor force after their children are grown, the principal source of female police recruits is young women. The entry of mothers of young children into the labor market has thus increased the pool of potentially qualified women from which the departments can recruit.

Also contributing to the expansion of the recruitment pool of female officers are the financial attractiveness of police work for women, particularly those with only a high school education, and changes in sex role definitions and public images of women. While

15. For a discussion of the development of the women's liberation movement and its goals see Hole and Levine (1971) and Freeman (1975).
16. Since 1948 the proportion of working mothers with children between six and seventeen years of age has risen from 31 percent to nearly 55 percent in 1974. The labor force participation of women with children under six years has risen from 13 percent of all such women in 1948 to 37 percent in 1974. In 1967, 38 percent of all mothers with children under eighteen were in the labor force; by 1974 that number had risen to 46 percent (1975 Handbook on Women Workers:25).

policemen's median income is quite similar to the median income of men in lower clerical and skilled blue-collar jobs, the median salary for women in these categories is much lower than the median salary for policewomen. As indicated by table 4, policing compares quite favorably in terms of income with all but professional and technical occupations for women. In light of changing sex role norms, and with the elimination of minimum height and college degree requirements for women in many departments, policing is likely to appeal to a growing number of women, increasing further the pool of qualified applicants from which departments may choose.

TABLE 4

Median Income[a] of Full-Time Year-Round Workers
by Sex and Non-Farm Occupation Group, 1973[b]

Major Occupation Group	Median Wage or Salary Income[c]	
	Women	Men
Professional, technical workers	$9,093 ($8,074)[d]	$14,306
Managers, administrators (except farm)	6,667	14,519
Sales workers	4,650	12,296
Clerical workers	6,469	10,627 ($11,269)[e]
Craft and kindred workers	6,144	11,245
Operatives (including transport)	5,358	9,503
Service workers (except private households)	4,588	7,937
Private household workers	2,069	f
Nonfarm laborers	4,956	8,158

[a]Excludes those with no wage or salary income.

[b]Persons 14 years of age and over.

[c]U.S. Bureau of the Census: Current Population Reports, P-60, No. 93 (advance report). Reprinted in 1975 *Handbook on Women Workers*, p. 135.

[d]Median income of policewomen in 1973 according to the EEOC (1973:44).

[e]Median income of policemen in 1973 according to the EEOC (1973:49).

[f]Fewer than 75,000 men.

Shifts in sex role attitudes resulting from the women's liberation movement have, in turn, affected women in policing. The alteration of traditional concepts of masculinity and femininity throughout society are reflected in changed definitions of what is appropriate work for policewomen, including a rejection of the traditional specialist role.

Recently the mass media have legitimized the new roles and norms of behavior adopted by women in law enforcement, as witnessed by frequent newspaper articles and books.[17] Several television shows feature female officers as heroines.[18] The image of the policewoman as an unattractive "bull-dyke" has given way to a new image. Pepper Anderson, Jamie Sommers, and Charlie's Angels are women who are strong, determined, ambitious, brave and competent but still sexy and clearly female. They demonstrate that brains and guile often succeed where brawn proves useless. Although these media heroines have followed real changes for women in policing and other occupations, they have encouraged women to seek similar roles, have provided role models where none previously existed, and have helped the public accept female detectives and patrol officers.

While an active women's movement does not necessarily assure equal opportunities for female officers, the movement has helped produce a new social climate that has affected police departments both by challenging the legal status quo and by influencing social mores. In addition, the women's liberation movement has played a direct and important role in changing the law as it relates to women. Feminists have brought a number of important cases that the courts have decided in favor of women, and have been sponsors of and

17. See, for example, Abrecht (1967) and Fleming (1975).

18. For a more thorough analysis of the image of women in the public media see Weibel (1977). She points out that in general women are outnumbered by men in drama and adventure/drama programs and that those women appearing in TV programs are portrayed in traditional and outdated images.

In the adventure/drama programs that have replaced the Western in the 1970's, male supercops are shown as professional, analytic crime fighters radiating college education, good breeding, and staunch personal loyalty to fellow officers in their work group. Only a few women have appeared as members of these familylike groups. Even in the post-liberationist era of the mid-1970's on television working women are assigned subordinate positions. Until 1974 females in adventure series programs were "anemic"; the teen-cop Julie in "Mod Squad" who served primarily as a decoy in the enemy midst, was a passive heroine who used neither gun nor judo. Similarly, in "The Rookies" and "McMillan and Wife" wives and female relatives were used as assistants/confidantes for male crime fighters.

In the mid-1970's two programs featuring female police officers appeared as did several other shows in which the main character is female. Although in "Get Christie Love" the star was a comic heroine not taken seriously by either work associates or criminals, Pepper Anderson in "Policewoman" presents a more promising image of women. Like Love, Anderson occasionally must assume roles overtly suggestive of prostitution, but when she does, the fact that it is a role is not in doubt. With her partner and with colleagues Anderson is cool and competent. She is a "crack shot" and can outshoot her partner, who appreciates her skill which on a number of occasions has saved his life.

lobbyists for the passage of legislation affecting women, including the 1972 amendments to the Civil Rights Act which applied that law to state and local government employees and thus directly affected policewomen.

Legal Changes. The law has both limited the employment of women in police work and been a major remedy to occupational discrimination. For many years policing was one of the few occupations in which women were ineligible for promotion—a result of being barred by laws or ordinances from patrol duties. Since 1972, changes in the laws have made it illegal to deny a woman equal opportunity in a law enforcement career. Although enforcement of nondiscriminatory employment policies by police departments has been inconsistent and certain legal issues remain to be clarified, the burden of proof has shifted to the employer. The major breakthroughs were the passage of the 1972 Amendments to Title VII of the Civil Rights Act of 1964 and the adoption of the Crime Control Act of 1973.

Title VII of the Civil Rights act prohibits discrimination on the basis of race, creed, color, sex or national origin with regard to compensation, terms, conditions or privileges of employment. It specifically forbids an employer to "omit, segregate or classify his employees in any way which would deprive or tend to deprive any individual of employment opportunities . . . because of such individual's sex."[19] The 1972 amendments extended coverage of the act to public employees including police officers. The act also established the Equal Employment Opportunity Commission (EEOC) to enforce the new law by promulgating regulations, investigating complaints, conciliating, and (since 1972) suing on behalf of a complainant. In the case of a public agency, the U.S. Justice Department brings suit. In addition to suits brought by the EEOC or Justice Department, private individual and class actions may be brought under the act. A body of law has developed under Title VII including several important principles that apply to policewomen.

Since 1972 police departments must adhere to EEOC guidelines which prohibit discrimination in employment except where sex is a Bona Fide Occupational Qualification (BFOQ)[20] "reasonably neces-

19. Sec. 703a 42 USC 2000a 2(a) (1972).

20. Sex is considered a BFOQ only if the employer can demonstrate that the sex of the employee is necessary to the normal operation of that business or enterprise for reasons of authenticity, morality, and entertainment where sex appeal is essential. Sex

sary to the normal operation of that particular business or enterprise."[21] In the case of *Rosenfeld* v. *Southern Pacific Company*, which drastically limited the use of the BFOQ defense, the court ruled against an employer who argued that women as a class were physically unsuited for a job requiring long hours and heavy physical effort. The court rejected the employer's attempt to raise a commonly accepted characterization of women as the "weaker sex" to the level of a BFOQ. It concluded that the purpose of Congress in enacting Title VII was to forbid subjective assumptions and traditional stereotyped conceptions regarding women's physical ability to perform a particular job, and thus construed the BFOQ exception to cover only sexual characteristics crucial for the successful performance of the job (such as a wet nurse) or for reasons of authenticity or genuineness (such as in the case of an actor or actress).[22]

In the case of *Griggs* v. *Duke Power Company* the Supreme Court established the principle that the plaintiff in a job discrimination case does not need to prove discriminatory intent. If it is shown that job qualifications which appear neutral disproportionately exclude a group or class, the burden falls on the employer to show that the given requirement is a BFOQ directly related to the work and that other selection devices could not reasonably be substituted for the contested standard.

This principle was recently applied to strike down the minimum height requirements and a pre-training physical agility test which had made it virtually impossible for women to qualify as police officers in San Francisco.[23] The court ruled that departmental studies failed to

---

discrimination is not considered a BFOQ on the following grounds: some or many of the members of one sex cannot or do not want to perform the work; customers or coworkers would prefer workers of a certain sex; the job has traditionally been the preserve of one sex; the job involves heavy labor, manual dexterity, late hours, overtime, or work in a dangerous area; the job requires travel with a coworker of the other sex; physical facilities for the other sex are unavailable; the job requires personal characteristics not exclusive to either sex such as tact, charm, or aggressiveness.

21. Sec. 703a, 42 USC 2000a 2 (1972).

22. In the *Rosenfeld* case, the court concluded, "In the case before us there is no contention that the sexual characteristics of the employees are crucial to the successful performance on the job. . . . Rather, on the basis of a general assumption regarding the physical capabilities of female employees, the company attempts to raise a commonly accepted characterization of women as the 'weaker sex' to the level of a BFOQ." *Rosenfeld* v. *Southern Pacific Company* 444 F. 2nd 1219 (9th Circuit, 1971).

23. *The Officers for Justice et al.* v. *The Civil Service Commission of the City and*

show any correlation between the height requirement and an officer's ability to perform police duties. It also discounted the government's attempt to validate the physical agility test, noting that other major police departments give no pre-selection test but rely on the police academy training to develop the necessary abilities.[24]

When a court finds an employer illegally engaged in discriminatory hiring practices, it can order a hiring quota. Such affirmative relief has been used to force the police departments in Philadelphia, San Francisco, and Detroit, among others, to hire women.[25]

Another legal change benefitting policewomen was the passage of the Crime Control Act of 1973. This act amends the Omnibus Crime Control and Safe Streets Act of 1968, by prohibiting discrimination against women in the employment practices of any agencies that receive Law Enforcement Assistance Administration (LEAA) funds. Prior to passage of the Crime Control Act of 1973, and following the Supreme Court decision in *Reed* v. *Reed* which extended the equal protection guarantees to women as a class, LEAA issued guidelines banning sex discrimination on the basis of the equal protection clause of the Fourteenth Amendment. Pursuant to the 1973 act the LEAA established a new set of Equal Employment Opportunity guidelines that required major recipient agencies to assess their recruiting and hiring practices, analyze promotion and training procedures, formulate an equal employment opportunity program, and file it with the

County of San Francisco Civil n. c-73-0657RFP (N.D. Calif.) Memorandum and Order dated May 2, 1975.

24. Recently in *Mieth* v. *Dothard* (418 F. Supp.1169) a district court ruled the height and weight requirements for Alabama state troopers violate the equal protection clause of the Fourteenth Amendment as well as Title VII. Later, in *Dothard* v. *Rawlinson* (433 U.S. 321) the Supreme Court rejected the imposition of height and weight requirements, this time for the job of "correctional counselor" (prison guard). In this case the court held that height and weight standards were demonstrated to have a discriminatory impact and that these criteria alone could not be taken as indicative of the strength that the state maintained is essential for efficient job performance.

25. The police department of Philadelphia was ordered to hire 50 percent women for one academy class so that the performance of the men and women could be compared (*Brace* v. *O'Neill et al.*, Civil n. 74-399 [E.D. Pa.]; and *United States* v. *City of Philadelphia* Civil n. 74-400 [E.D. Pa.] order of the court dated January 29, 1975). In San Francisco the police department was required to hire fifteen women for every class of forty until sixty women had been hired and their performance could be studied. (*The Officers for Justice et al.* v. *The Civil Service Commission of the City and County of San Francisco* Civil no. C-73-0657RFP [N.D. Cal.], memorandum and order dated May 2, 1975). In 1974 a Detroit court ordered a 50 percent hiring quota to redress past discrimination (*Schaefer* v. *Tannian,* 394 F. Supp. 1128 [6th Cir. 1974]).

state planning agency through which most of its monies are disbursed. An additional set of guidelines prohibited minimum height requirements, which have been shown to discriminate against women in police recruiting but lack correlation with success on the job.[26]

These regulations clearly prohibit much of the discrimination against women in law enforcement, and require the LEAA to withhold payments to grantees who do not comply with its regulations after a hearing. Loss of these funds could seriously threaten many departments.

Enforcement, however, has been problematic. The LEAA's Office of Civil Rights Compliance has a very small staff which has devoted so much of its time to dealing with individual complaints that few compliance reviews have been undertaken.[27] Top LEAA administrators have shown little determination to eliminate sex discrimination in law enforcement agencies.[28] Eighty percent of LEAA's funds are distributed to local jurisdictions through state planning agencies whose efforts to enforce compliance with departmental equal employment opportunity plans have not been monitored by LEAA. Only recently has LEAA held up payment of funds to a department because of failure to hire female officers, despite the fact that twenty-six of the fifty largest police departments receiving LEAA funds were parties to lawsuits alleging discriminatory practices (U.S. Commission on Civil Rights, 1974). The withholding of both LEAA funds and monies under the General Revenue Sharing Act from the City of Chicago and the Chicago Police Department in late 1974 indicated a tougher federal enforcement policy which appears to have had a "ripple effect" around the country (Gates, 1976). Nevertheless, the large number of

26. The traditional height requirement of 5'7" for officers excluded approximately 95 percent of all American women from police jobs (Crites, 1973).

27. According to the U.S. Commission on Civil Rights (1974:371) as of 1974, the Office of Civil Rights Compliance of LEAA had performed only seventeen complete compliance reviews. Ten of these required criminal justice agencies to take immediate steps to increase employment opportunities for women and upgrade their status in those departments. However, this is a very small number of reviews: there are approximately 40,000 police departments in the U.S., and a high percentage of those investigated were found to be in violation of the law. Furthermore, the closure rate on complaints is slow. Of the forty-three sex discrimination complaints received in fiscal year 1972, twenty were still open in June 1973 and six of these remained unsettled by February 1975.

28. The U.S. Commission on Civil Rights found that the LEAA was not enforcing equal employment opportunity for women because "it believes sex may be a valid criterion for selecting persons for police work" (U.S. Commission on Civil Rights, 1974:366). It based this conclusion on a letter written by the agency's director to the Civil Rights Commission.

departments makes eliminating sex discrimination a very laborious task, even if LEAA administrators were strongly determined to do so.

REMAINING ISSUES AND BARRIERS

Despite legal changes there remain a host of discriminatory practices, reluctance on the part of many departments to enforce the law with respect to policewomen, and uncertainty about a number of unresolved legal issues. Although women can no longer be excluded from police departments simply because of their gender, selection procedures keep their numbers low; most departments hire a much smaller percentage of female applicants than male applicants (Eisenberg et al., 1973:11).

Differences in educational requirements for men and women have been eliminated by most departments (Eisenberg et al., 1973) but many continue to illegally maintain separate eligibility lists for male and female candidates. Questions remain about the content and validity of written entrance examinations, since certain questions place women at a disadvantage. For example, women tend to do poorly when tested on spatial relations and mechanics. While examinations must now be validated, and the job relatedness of the questions must be demonstrated, many departments continue to use unrevised entrance examinations unless threatened with a lawsuit.

Many departments maintain physical strength and agility tests which require a candidate to perform exercises in which women are generally untrained or which are difficult for women because of differences between male and female musculature. Although the law requires that all selection criteria for employment be related to the tasks the employee will actually perform, many departments continue using unvalidated physical agility tests despite the San Francisco case.

Another remaining barrier is the preference given by many departments to veterans. Eisenberg et al. (1974:48) found that about 65 percent of all agencies surveyed give preference to veterans and 57 percent of the municipal agencies granted absolute preferences.[29] Since less than 2 percent of all veterans are female, it is clear that such preference gives male applicants an advantage, despite the fact that men with military service experience were not rated higher as police officers than those who had not served in the military (Bloch and

29. An absolute preference places the veteran at the top of the list of eligibles regardless of his examination score.

Anderson, 1974b). Challenges to the constitutionality of veterans preference have thus far been unsuccessful.[30]

In training, although most departments now have unisex police academy programs, questions about the content of and standards for physical education remain. Whether women should do the same exercises as men and pass identical tests, for example, is an unresolved question.

Promotion and assignments, too, are problematic. Before 1968 no women were assigned to the backbone of policing, patrol duty. In the past several years police departments have begun placing women on patrol, but despite Title VII, many agencies continue to resist giving women patrol assignments. Washington (1974) found that only 95 of 258 city, county, and state agencies surveyed had women on patrol. While more departments now employ women, many still are reluctant to give them street assignments.

For many years policewomen were handicapped by the maintenance of separate promotion lists and different promotion examinations (Williams, 1946; Shpritzer, 1959). Eisenberg et al. (1973) found that only 19 percent of the agencies surveyed had women in supervisory or command ranks, although 54 percent of the agencies reported having the same promotion procedures for male and female officers.[31] Currently only a few departments have female officials and/or detectives. In some, women lack the seniority required to be eligible for promotion so that it will be several years before the number of female officials can significantly increase even if there were no further discrimination. A low promotion rate for women is likely to continue, however, since in most departments, promotion is based on both written examinations and ratings by one's supervisors; the criteria on which the officers are evaluated are often unclear; and sponsorship by a (male) supervisor is, in fact, a necessity—few female officers are likely to gain such support. As more women become eligible and find that they are not promoted, however, lawsuits challenging these promotion systems can be expected.

Also unresolved are questions regarding maternity leave. While the EEOC guidelines mandate that pregnancy shall be treated as any

30. Challenges in both Pennsylvania (*Feinerman* v. *Jones*) and Minnesota (*Koelfgen* v. *Jackson*) have lost. Recently in *Massachusetts* v. *Feeney* the Supreme Court vacated a lower court ruling that absolute preference for veterans deprives women of their Fourteenth Amendment equal protection rights.

31. In all the reporting agencies there was a total of only 304 women above the entry level rank, including 118 detectives and 139 sergeants (Eisenberg et al., 1973:34).

other temporary disability, still to be decided are issues related to termination and subsequent rehiring, selective granting of maternity leave, insurance benefit issues, denial of seniority credits during maternity leave, denial of maternity benefits to unmarried women and denial of sick, disability, and vacation benefits during maternity leave.

Despite the legal and social changes that have led to an increasing number of policewomen who are performing a wider variety of policing duties including patrol during the past five years, opposition to policewomen remains strong. Underlying the continued resistance to compliance with the law is the view of most policemen of all ranks that women are inherently unfit for police work. The remainder of this study will examine the changing role of women in one large urban police department, the problems these women face and difficulties they pose for male coworkers, and the strategies the women adopt for gaining acceptance and fulfilling the demands of their occupational role.

Chapter 3

The Setting:
Community, Department, and Officers

To adequately understand the problems facing female officers entering patrol duties from which policewomen had previously been excluded, it is necessary to examine the setting into which they are "breaking in" and the background of the officers themselves. Settings, including both the community and the department (which is intimately linked with the community), may be quite diverse (see Wilson, 1973). Communities differ in political structure which affects the problems to which the police must respond and in the characteristics of their resident population. Not only do suburban and urban communities differ from each other in character but large cities differ with respect to the socioeconomic status, racial, ethnic, and age characteristics of the residents, their civic traditions, and the character and mix of the work done in the community. These, in turn, shape the problems to which the police must respond and the organizational context in which police personnel work as well as the background personal characteristics and likely aspirations of those individuals who become police officers.

In a number of ways Washington, D.C., the site of my study, is unique and its Metropolitan Police Department different from other urban police departments. Similarly, recruitment to the metropolitan police is conducted on a nationwide basis so that in certain respects the characteristics and expectations of its officers and leadership differ from those in other urban departments.

THE COMMUNITY

Covering an area of sixty-eight and one-quarter square miles, Washington, D.C., has grown in the past fifty years from a small, provincial, southern town to a major social, cultural, economic, and political center. In 1920 its resident population was 438,000; today its 734,000 residents live in the ninth largest city and seventh largest metropolitan area (SMSA) in the United States, with a population of nearly three million inhabitants.

Washington is unique in a number of ways. A city with a black resident majority—blacks today comprise 71 percent of the city's inhabitants and control the local government—Washington's workers are found predominantly in white-collar jobs: 29 percent are classified as professional, technical or kindred workers and another 25 percent are in clerical or kindred positions (*People of the District of Columbia*, 1973:51-52). Despite its generally high median income level and low rate of unemployment, a substantial minority of the population lives in poverty.[1]

Law and government in Washington, too, are unique. As a federal city until December 1973, when Congress approved "home rule," the local government was controlled by Congress and actual power rested in the hands of a few congressional committee chairmen. Since January 1975, the city has been ruled by an elected mayor and a thirteen member city council. Congress retains veto power over certain city ordinances and controls the annual federal payment which makes up 25 percent of the fiscal city budget.

Years of congressional control of the local government have freed the Metropolitan Police Department from much of the local political factionalism, party politics, and corruption that is frequently associated with other city police departments. Officers note with pride the department's good reputation and lack of scandal, adding that this can be attributed to the relatively low level of organized crime in the city and the fact that Washington is not an international drug importation center.

The federal presence is felt in other ways as well. While most urban police departments recruit locally and their officers have longstanding ties to the community, in Washington a national recruitment campaign in the late 1960's and early 1970's and a nationally admin-

1. Using the Census Bureau's definition of poverty, 12.6 percent of all families and 17 percent of all residents of the city were living in poverty in 1970 (*People of the District of Columbia*, 1973:18 and 22).

istered civil service entry examination have brought officers from all parts of the country.

There is also a burgeoning law enforcement community in the Washington metropolitan area. In addition to the police departments in the five surrounding jurisdictions, there are a number of federal police and law enforcement agencies in Washington.[2] This offers the metropolitan police officers the opportunity to meet and compare notes with colleagues employed by other departments and agencies, to be part of a grapevine of job opportunities, and to switch agencies if they are dissatisfied with the local police department and still remain in the area. There appears to be a ranking of the area agencies, and a number of metropolitan police officers aspire to "move up" to federal agencies where they will have permanent civil service status, deal with a "higher class of clientele," and have the opportunity to travel.

Another aspect of the federal presence is illustrated by the effect of the Nixon administration's emphasis on "law and order" and its determination to make Washington a national showcase rather than the "crime capital" it was reputed to be. With White House pressure the Metropolitan Police Department increased from a force of 2,958 officers at the end of 1968 to a high of 5,070 sworn officers late in 1972. During fiscal years 1970 and 1971 the department hired 1,398 and 1,260 new officers respectively. (The number of officers has since declined to approximately 4,600.) This rapid growth reflected both the expansion of the department desired by the President and an intensive effort to recruit more black officers. Due to a high rate of resignations and retirements during these two years (499 and 777 officers separated from the force in 1970 and 1971 respectively), the large number of officers promoted in rank, and the increase in the number of detectives and other nonpatrol personnel, there was virtually a complete turnover of patrol officers between 1969 and 1972. A "new breed" which was blacker, younger, and more service oriented arrived on the scene. During this time the department underwent radical reorganization as well.

This period of rapid expansion was probably a very important factor in the recruitment and acceptance of women as patrol officers. Faced with enormous difficulties in finding qualified recruits, some

2. These agencies include the Executive Protection Service (including the Secret Service); Federal Protective Service; U.S. Park Police; Capitol Police; Alcohol, Tobacco and Firearms Agency; Drug Enforcement Agency; U.S. Marshall's Office; FBI; and a host of special police forces and federal cabinet and departmental investigative units.

top administrators were more willing to accept female patrol officers than they might have been under different, more "normal" circumstances. Similarly, given high mobility opportunities, many other changes in the department, and the poor quality of many of the recruits in the early 1970's, lower ranking officers were less personally threatened in their career paths and more tolerant of the entry of patrolwomen into the department than they might have been had the department remained stable or reduced its size and mobility opportunities.

DEPARTMENT AND DISTRICT

The Metropolitan Police Department, like most other departments around the country, has a paramilitary structure with power flowing from the top of the organizational pyramid downward. The department is divided into four bureaus: field operations; administrative services; technical services; and inspectional services. Field operations is the largest bureau and the focus of line activities. It includes all officers in the patrol, criminal investigation, traffic, youth, and special operations divisions. The Patrol Division, in turn, consists of the seven police districts into which the city is divided. The distribution of officers within the department and an approximation of the number and percentage of policewomen assigned to each unit as of June 1975 is presented in table 5.

District Organization

Over three-fifths of the department's sworn personnel work out of one of its seven districts, each of which is like a miniature department. The commander of the district is the inspector, who has control of the organization, operation, and deployment of "manpower" in his district. Each district is divided into three patrol sections, and has an administrative, community service (including youth services), and investigative (detective) unit. In addition there are units such as casual clothes, scooter, auto intercept, vice, gambling and liquor, and canine and evidence technicians squads.

To assure that there are officers on the street twenty-four hours a day, three eight-hour shifts of officers patrol daily. Each patrol officer is assigned to one of the three patrol sections (labeled A, B or C) and rotates shifts every two weeks so that all officers spend an equal amount of time on the day, evening, or midnight shift. In some districts

TABLE 5
Police Personnel by Unit and Sex as of June 30, 1975

	Total	Number of females	Percent females in unit
District 1	490	27	5.5
District 2	449	30	6.7
District 3	460	28	6.0
District 4	412	28	6.8
District 5	439	28	6.3
District 6	343	21	6.1
District 7	382	25	6.5
Field Operations Headquarters	9	0	0
Criminal Investigation Division	205	a	a
Traffic Division	90	1	1.1
Youth Division	68	3	4.4
Special Operations	281	11	3.9
Administrative Services	560	85[b]	15.2
Technical Services	286	17	5.9
Inspectional Services	208	2	0.9
Office of the Chief	4	1	25.0
General Council's Office	16	1	6.0
TOTAL SWORN PERSONNEL	4,702	308[c]	6.5

Source: Fiscal Year 1975 Annual Report, Metropolitan Police Department of Washington, D.C.

[a]Department statistics do not indicate whether a police officer assigned to the Criminal Investigation Division with the rank of detective is a male or female. The exact number of policewomen in C.I.D. June 30, 1975, is not available; in October 1976 there were 12 females in the division, most of whom were assigned to sex squad.

[b]Among the females assigned to Administrative Services are those who were students at the training academy as well as more experienced officers permanently assigned to that bureau. It is impossible to separate these two groups.

[c]This figure underrepresents the number of female officers in the department since it lists separately as "policewomen" only those female officers with that title. The women in the department who are ranking officials and detectives or plainclothes officers are not distinguished by sex. At that time (June 1975) there were approximately eight women officials and ten female plainclothes officers.

sections are further divided into platoons or sectors. Each section, regardless of other subdivisions, consists of eight to twelve squads (of five to eight officers) each commanded by a sergeant. The section and squad are the important units to the patrol officer. Each section has its permanent station crew as well as several officers assigned to the station on a day-to-day basis. Dispatching for the whole department is done from headquarters.

Training and the Rookie Officer

New officers spend approximately four months at the training academy and the remainder of their probationary year assigned to a patrol section in one police district. During the rookie year socialization to the work and the department begins, and the new officer tends to adapt and become accepted by fellow officers or remain isolated.

At the police academy the rookie officer receives formal instruction on departmental regulations and procedures, the communications system, community relations, court and judicial procedures, operation of the scout car and general patrol techniques, first aid, the D.C. Code, the law of arrest, the use of weapons including firearms training, and self-defense. In addition, rookies participate in a general physical training program. Learning is individualized through a module system; when the rookie passes all the tests, he or she leaves the academy. There is no street experience or on-the-job training included in the academy curriculum.

Following academy training the rookie is assigned to a patrol section in one of the seven police districts. Here he or she goes through an initial period known as certification before being permitted to patrol alone. Certification procedures vary among districts and sections but the period generally lasts between eight and fourteen weeks. Some rookies work almost exclusively with one training officer; others float among different cars and experienced officers.

During certification the rookie learns the geography of the district and how to handle situations on the street. Initially he or she watches the experienced officer, is encouraged to ask questions, is expected to write all reports, and may be "given" arrests involving minor infractions to gain familiarity with the courts and the problems associated with handling property. Gradually the rookie is permitted to take charge of situations and develops her or his own style. During this initial period, the rookie also begins adjusting to the rigors of shift work, irregular hours and mid-week days off as well as the job-related tensions which frequently cause strains on family life. In addition, the rookie learns the norms and values of policing, as well as the rules of the game for surviving in the occupation, department, and district. He or she develops relationships with fellow officers and officials and acquires a reputation that will follow her or him through the policing career.

Assignments and Mobility

Assignments are made daily by the operations sergeant in each section and announced at roll call. Most senior patrol officers have permanent assignments to scout cars, footbeats or the station house. The newer officers may work in scout cars for officers who are on leave, in court, or on their day off or may be given footbeats, special details or station duties as needed.

Although most police remain at the lowest rank in the department (officer) throughout their careers, there is a great deal of horizontal mobility and different assignments are available within the district as well as in other units of the department. In the district about half of the officers are on foot or scout car patrol. Others ride scooters, serve warrants, act as evidence technicians, work in casual clothes as crime prevention officers, function as community service workers, or handle the paperwork for the district (see table 6).

To get a scout car or other permanent assignment an officer must apply when a vacancy is announced. After the probationary year in the district, an officer may apply for any vacancy in the department. Because departmental policy mandates that scout cars must be racially integrated, scout car openings are informally racially earmarked. While seniority is respected, particularly in assignment to scout cars, it is sometimes balanced with other factors by officials who make such decisions. In addition, many vacancies are not widely advertised, so that an officer desiring a new position must be tied into an informal communications network, and must have a sponsor (the higher the rank the better) as well as an adequate, but not necessarily outstanding, record. Many officers noted that who you know rather than what you have done is most important in getting choice assignments—the "rules" are followed when it is convenient; they are changed or ignored when it is not. Rules serve as a means for the officials to justify their actions, particularly when seniority and racial integration guidelines conflict.[3]

3. One such situation was when a white junior officer and black officer with more education and police experience, both female, sought a position in a special unit in the

TABLE 6
Assignments in a Police District

Assignments	Number	Percent
Supervisors (sergeants and other officials)	70	16.5
Investigators (detectives, vice, gambling, and liquor squads)	40	
Casual clothes and auto theft squad	25	
Print and K-9 officers	20	
Warrants squad	5	34.1
Scooter/Crime Prevention	20	
Community services and youth officers	20	
Administration (including desk sergeants)	15	
Officers actually on street patrol (in scout cars or on footbeats)	210	49.4
TOTAL	425	100.0

Note: Within each district many officers listed as being in the Patrol Division perform functions other than street patrol.

After three years in the department an officer becomes eligible for promotion, based on two factors: an efficiency rating score assigned by supervisors and a score on a promotional examination. Because there are currently very few openings for new sergeants the competition is very stiff and the officer who does not receive a top efficiency rating (the criteria for which are unclear and subjective) is not promoted. The result is that despite universalistic rules and supposed equal and widespread opportunity for advancement, the department supervisors in fact determine who is actually eligible for promotion.

Recent Changes

Several important internal changes have occurred during this decade which have altered the work environment into which police-women have entered. These changes include attempts to "profession-

---

district. The latter officer was both personally contentious and physically unattractive. The former got the job, the latter was told, in order to maintain racial balance in the unit. Others suspected that the officials did not want to give the job to an unattractive and "troublemaking" black woman and used the racial balance issue to justify the action that would have been taken in any case.

alize" the police, the sexual and racial integration of the department, the recruitment of a number of officers who brought a new set of values into policing, and the creation of procedural safeguards for officers through police unions and EEO regulations. They have resulted in a generation gap among officers, challenges to the prevailing norms, weaker solidarity among officers, alteration in the position of the individual officer in the department, and the growth of new factions struggling to control the department.

While the movement to "professionalize" the department brought closer supervision and a "command controlled police" (Bordua and Reiss, 1966), it has also produced more universalistic application of the rules and thus undermined prevailing informal practices.

The recruitment of a large number of officers who do not "fit" has contributed to the weakening of officers' solidarity and led to strong pressures for increased officers' rights. Demands for change come not only from the many black officers who are struggling for individual protection against arbitrary supervision as well as for control of the police department, but from a number of young white officers as well. The mavericks in the department now openly question the authority of officials to control officers' personal lives and challenge a number of long-accepted practices, such as traditional racial etiquette, racial and sexual discrimination, and a system of favoritism for "drinking buddies" and "snitches" of the officials. They demand justification for punishments that are meted out and an explanation of the awarding of a coveted assignment to an officer when it is contrary to the stated rules. Some have questioned the "rule of silence" and the norm of backing up a partner, right or wrong.

What has permitted the open challenge to the system in the past few years is the opening of a number of formal channels of complaint and redress. Officers now can turn to Equal Employment Opportunity regulations if they believe they are the victims of discrimination. They are represented by a union that aggressively investigates complaints and formally files grievances on behalf of the officers. Black officers have created a militant "Afro-American Police Association" and policewomen early in 1977 established Policewomen in Action, an organization to identify problem areas unique to female officers and inform the women about established channels of complaint.

The older generation of officers and officials still dominate the department but their power has been challenged and limited.[4] It is

4. A clear illustration of changes in the police department, the generation gap, and

likely that similar changes have occurred in other police departments around the country. They appear to have advanced further and are more pronounced in Washington, D.C., however, due to the rapidity and extent of changes in the department's size, organization and personnel in the early 1970's.

OFFICERS IN THE STUDY

The twenty-seven policemen and twenty-eight policewomen who were interviewed for this study were not selected randomly, and are not representative of the officers in the district or department. In comparison with the rest of the department these officers are less experienced, younger, and a higher proportion of them are black. The men and women in the interview sample, however, have similar socio-economic characteristics, although the black officers tend to be younger and have less police experience than the whites.[5] Approximately one-half of the males and one-third of the females have had at least one semester of college with part of the difference attributable to race (see table 7).

Male and female officers differ with respect to marital and parental statuses, which may bear on their aspirations and commitment to the department. Less than one-half of the officers of both sexes are currently married (eleven of twenty-seven men and eight of twenty-eight women) and are parents (fourteen of twenty-seven men and twelve of twenty-eight women). Ten of the twelve policewomen who are mothers, however, are single parents, while only one of the fathers is.

---

racial politics is provided by the "hair issue." To a black, wearing an Afro may be a political or personal statement. For white men, wearing long hair, sideburns, a beard or mustache is fashionable while a military cut sets them apart from others of their generation. The officials have the power to order an officer to get a haircut or trim when his hair becomes longer than specified in police regulations. Many officials, upset by the "sloppy" and "girlish" appearances of some men, maintain that the officers' appearance is a matter of public concern. Many officers insist that the style of their hair in no way affects the manner in which they police and feel it should be a matter of personal choice. The newly organized officers brought a lawsuit over this matter, saying it symbolized individual rights of the officer and the department's power to control him, an issue on which black and white officers were united. Although the officers lost their suit they made clear their willingness to unite and challenge departmental policy.

5. The average age for female officers was 27.2 years for white, and 23.9 for black women. White men averaged 26.8 years, compared with 23.8 for black officers. The average length of service at time of interview was just over 30 months for black officers, and approximately 39 months for white officers.

TABLE 7
Education of Officers by Race and Sex

Education	Female			Male		
	White	Black	Total	White	Black	Total
High school or equivalency	3	15	18	4	9	13
Some college	4	6	10	7	7	14
TOTAL	7	21	28	11	16	27

Socioeconomic Origins and Prior Work History

The socioeconomic origins of the male and female officers in the sample are similar—most officers come from working-class backgrounds.[6] Only seven of the policemen's fathers and eight of the policewomen's fathers are in white-collar or higher status occupations. Fifteen of the men's fathers and thirteen of the women's fathers, on the other hand, are in blue-collar occupations. (This probably distorts the picture, since ten of twenty-seven women and eleven of twenty-six men for whom data were available did not grow up to the age of eighteen living with both parents. Those without economic support of a father are likely to have more economically deprived origins.) Similarly, although eight men and seven women had mothers whose occupations they stated as "housewife," this term includes both non-employed wives of working men and "welfare mothers." Several officers of each sex indicated that they had come from very deprived circumstances as children. Thus variation in social origins of officers appears to be greater within each sex group than between male and female officers (see table 8).

The prior work histories of male and female officers were also similar with respect to the level of job held.[7] Officers of each sex,

6. Other examinations of the social origins of policemen (McNamara, 1967; Neiderhoffer, 1969; Westley, 1970; and Hahn, 1974) noted that policemen come from primarily working-class and lower middle-class origins. Little is known about the socioeconomic origins of policewomen in general. A recent study of black officers in Washington, D.C. (Beard et al., 1976) found that black officers, both male and female, come from working-class families; 60 percent of the officers' fathers were unskilled or skilled blue-collar workers.

7. For some of the officers prior work experience was very limited or non-existent. Seven males had been employed only as police cadets before becoming sworn officers,

TABLE 8
Occupations of Officers' Parents by Sex of Officer

| | Policemen | | Policewomen | |
Occupation	Father	Mother	Father	Mother
Professional, semi-professional and technical	1	6	5	2
Proprietor, manager and official	5	1	3	1
Clerical, sales, and kin	1	5	0	5
Protective service and military	5	0	4	0
Skilled crafts and foremen	5	0	2	0
Unskilled, semi-skilled (including laborers, operatives and service workers)	5	4	7	8
Farmer	2	0	0	0
Housewife	–	8	–	7
Deceased in early childhood or no known occupation	1	1	5	2
Missing data	2	2	2	3
TOTAL	27	27	28	28

however, held jobs traditionally assigned to members of their sex. Seventeen of the twenty-two policewomen with prior work experience held lower level white-collar (clerical or sales) jobs. Among the male officers with prior work histories, seven of nineteen worked as laborers or factory operatives immediately before joining the police department and eight came from clerical and sales positions, although some had previously done manual labor (see table 9).

There is little in the work history of the policewomen that would indicate they would choose a nontraditional occupation. Only three had previously held jobs that might be considered nontraditional, such as driving a bus. What may distinguish many policewomen from other women in the population is the large proportion who describe themselves as having been independent, athletic, or "tomboys" when

---

while one entered police work from the military and another after college graduation. Similarly, four of the women worked only as cadets, one was a housewife with no prior work experience outside the home and one had been a full-time student.

A police cadet is a full-time paid employee of the police department between the ages of 18 and (currently) 21 who performs a variety of functions but is neither armed nor given arrest powers. At 21 a cadet may become a sworn officer.

TABLE 9

Occupation Immediately Prior to Policing by Sex

Occupation	Policemen	Policewomen
Professional, semi-professional and technical	1	3
Proprietor, manager and official	1	0
Clerical, sales, and kin	7	17
Military	1	0
Skilled crafts and foreman	1	0
Unskilled and semi-skilled (including laborers, operatives and service workers)	8	2
Police cadet	7	4
Student	1	1
Housewife	–	1
TOTAL	27	28

they were girls.[8] One woman replied, "Tomboy? I didn't want to be a girl when I grew up"; another left home immediately after high school to travel the country "to see if I could make it on my own." Only five women said they had not been independent, tomboyish or athletic, and three of these were among the female officers judged by their peers as least competent.

While almost all the policewomen had worked in "women's jobs" before joining the police department this may be for lack of non-traditional opportunities open to them. Several stated that they had seriously considered careers in the military, and another said she had wanted a nontraditional career, considered herself management material, but after high school had found nothing available but "women's work." In addition, five of the women said they had aspired to be police officers before actually entering the job market, and another four had applied or inquired about police department positions before the educational or height requirements were changed. While the women in the sample came from school, home, and "women's work" backgrounds, a substantial number of them had considered policing

8. One study (Tangri, 1972) found female college students who planned to enter nontraditional occupations to be autonomous individuals. A striking proportion of the women in the present sample viewed themselves similarly: eleven said they had been tomboys, and two others rejected the pejorative connotation of the term while they clearly described childhood behavior that was independent and adventurous. Four others described themselves as athletic (one was on the school tumbling team).

or other nontraditional jobs; when the opportunity for police work came, they took advantage of it.

Job Choice

In choosing an occupation, an individual feels negative responses to some occupations and positive "pulls" from others. The pulls may be intrinsic (i.e., related to the nature of the work) or extrinsic (i.e., factors such as salary, fringe benefits, and the work environment). Research on male officers indicates that they are usually attracted to police work by the extrinsic factors of job security and income, while they gain little personal satisfaction from the social service aspects of their work (McNamara, 1967; Neiderhoffer, 1969; Westley, 1970; Hahn, 1974). Not much is known about pre-patrol policewomen's motivation. A recent study of black officers in Washington, D.C., found some difference between the men's and women's motivation for joining the department.[9]

Alex (1976) noted several characteristic patterns in police officers' career choice. Some officers were motivated by extrinsic factors; other intrinsically motivated officers adopted what he called a social orientation to the work, expressing their motivation in terms of prestige, tradition, self-realization, and autonomy. This group included both those he termed "police career oriented" (i.e., seeking police work as a central life interest) and others labeled "action oriented" (i.e., seeking adventure, excitement, and manliness in their work). A final group consisted of "indifferently oriented" officers who drifted into police work with neither strong commitment to nor any particular preference for policing over other occupations.

Interviews with the fifty-five officers in this study indicated that the women initially were less attracted by retirement and security factors; that the men and women were equally concerned with personal gratification; and that the women were slightly less inclined to be altruistically motivated to helping people or the community than the

9. While both men and women were attracted primarily by pay (54.9 percent of the men and 47.6 percent of the women) and by "the opportunity to help others" (50.7 percent of the men and 52.4 percent of the women) the men indicated greater concern with job security (51.8 versus 31.7 percent of the women), fringe benefits (28 percent to 18.3 percent), and with assisting in crime reduction (27 percent to 19.5 percent). The women were more frequently attracted by variety in the work (mentioned by 40.8 percent of the men and 47.6 percent of the women; Beard et al., 1976). Part of the difference may be related to differences in age and marital status, since the men in the sample were older and more were married than the women.

men. Adopting three categories based on Alex's distinctions—the intrinsic or social, the extrinsic, and the indifferent—an equal number of male and female officers in the present study expected social (intrinsic) rewards from police work (see table 10). A difference by race, similar to that noted by Alex, is observable; twenty-one out of the thirty-seven blacks and fourteen out of the eighteen whites initially sought intrinsic rewards. A sex difference is also apparent: six men and three women desired economic security in joining the police; seven women and four men were indifferent. All seven indifferent females, however, are black. While the same percentage of males and females were attracted to policing by intrinsic factors, a greater proportion of whites—both male and female—than blacks reported that they sought personal or social rewards in their work.

TABLE 10
Motivation for Job Choice by Sex and Race

Motivation	Male			Female		
	White	Black	Total	White	Black	Total
Intrinsic or social	8	9	17	6	12	18
Extrinsic or economic	2	4	6	1	2	3
Indifferent	1	3	4	0	7	7
TOTAL	11	16	27	7	21	28

Several indifferents and extrinsics of both sexes noted that since joining the department they have changed their perspective, and find "new values" in their work. Such a change made it easier to acknowledge an initial motivation that did not jibe with the image the department seeks to project.

Perhaps because the men frequently state that women enter police work only for the money, eight women (and only two men) noted specifically that money had not been a primary factor in choosing police work, explaining that they were principally dissatisfied with their previous jobs or, in two cases, had been frustrated by blocked opportunity for advancement. In contrast, the men who denied being motivated by income said that they were in satisfying but insecure jobs and sought economic security.

Security seems to have been a far more important factor for the men, particularly the blacks, than the women. The policewomen more frequently speak of jobs rather than careers, income or money rather than security. While several men stated that they were attracted by the fringe benefits and prospects of retirement after twenty years, only one woman mentioned retirement and none spoke of medical or other benefits.

Several women appear to have become police officers by chance rather than by choice. Unemployed or uncertain about what to do, they discovered that the police department was recruiting and applied without a great deal of thought or commitment to the role:

> Why did I join? I have never been able to answer that. It's just a job. Something I do for eight hours. At school I took many tests . . . to have something to do. . . . I have to work. . . . There's nothing extra about the job that thrills me. I have to work so it's the same as another job. . . . It's nice being outdoors.

> There was no special reason I joined. I heard people on radio talk shows saying how hard the tests [for admission] were. I wanted to see if the test was really that hard. It wasn't. I passed but then didn't think about it. I was going to be laid off later and a job was a job at that time.

> I needed a job at the time. I couldn't be choosy. I didn't think of it. I went to the employment office, saw a sign, and took the test. It was my last alternative. It didn't cross my mind before that.

Fewer men drifted into police work by this route. Despite the lack of other options, two of the indifferents actually struggled against becoming officers before they accepted the job at the strong urging of a friend who was an officer in the department.

The women were attracted to policing for personal, rather than the altruistic motives frequently attributed to women. They sought personal gratification and were lured by the sense of excitement or challenge. In contrast to the routine of the typist or telephone operator, policing offered variety in daily activities, a chance to be outdoors, interaction with a variety of people, and a test of one's abilities to handle delicate situations. They said, for example:

> I was attracted by the excitement of different types of people and situations.

> In college I hated the police. . . . Then I decided I wanted to see how the other side made it. I thought it would be exciting and challenging.

Several women noted they had relished the prospect of being a rare woman in a male world. The women expressed little orientation to "helping people"; although five women said they joined the department to meet or work with people, their statements were not couched in service-oriented terms. Only five clearly articulated the desire to help others as a reason for choosing police work, stating, for example:

I was going to be Miss Social Worker and save the world.

I thought I could give something of myself to the community and feel gratified.

I saw a chance to change some things. I was sure I'd do things differently than other officers did.

Several of these women who initially envisioned themselves as social workers in the police department have changed their view of policing since joining the department and now define their occupational role in crime-fighting terms.

The women's uncertainties about the job were more personal than political. None expressed concern about community rejection or becoming a "brutal police officer," nor did most of them anticipate the problems they might face because of race or sex, which, as one noted, was "pretty naive." Their doubts about the job seemed to have centered on performance rather than the effect of police work on them personally.

In contrast to the women, policemen were more future oriented and motivated to become officers by extrinsic factors (including job security and early retirement) and the promise of individual rewards, including excitement and community service. Several alluded to the desire for authority and status. As one man put it, "I didn't want to be a common laborer. . . . As an officer you're on the inside; it puts you on a pedestal and helps as far as morale goes." Others referred to fulfilling responsibilities to their families; one man noted, "One day I started thinking, what am I going to do with myself? How am I providing for my family?" He concluded that police work was a financially secure occupation as well as "something I could get involved in."

The white men tended to be more enthusiastic about the job initially and to have expected greater intrinsic work satisfaction. None reported having had qualms about the effect the job might have on them personally. They had not experienced animosity to the police in their adolescence—one officer noted that he had been given a number of "breaks" by local police officers and sought to be like them. For white men becoming an officer did not involve the psychological discomfort of going over to "the other side" or "joining the oppressor." Nor had they anticipated isolation from their peer group in selecting police work.

In joining the police department, the black men were more interested in security, less attracted by excitement, and more concerned with their ability to "help the community" (rather than act merely as a repressive force) than the white men.

What distinguished the black males from both the black females and white men was a clear ambivalence about the police. For the young black male the decision to become a police officer seems to have led to introspection, doubts, and the resolution to be "different." The words of the men make their internal conflict and its resolution clear.

> Police work was always in the back of my mind but I tried to find something else . . . because I felt police officers were brutal. . . . I felt I couldn't treat people *not* in the right way so I thought I wouldn't fit in. . . . My cousin on the department told me police don't have to act like "baddies" and that the department was looking for new talent.

> The police department had a pretty good package to sell and I bought it, but also I had an inward thing. I'm someone who wants to be on the inside looking out. If I didn't like the police, I'd find out about it, put myself on the other end of the line, and do something about it.

In all, ten of the sixteen black males expressed ambivalence about the police and a determination, in becoming a policeman, to be "different," community-oriented officers while satisfying their personal needs for a job, income, and security.

Why did the black women not feel a conflict between their race and occupational role so pointedly felt by the black men? The men's conflict stemmed from the nature of the work, rather than doubts about their ability to physically handle the job. The black women's reservations about police work stemmed from concerns about their ability to cope with the demands of the work. Focusing more on their sex than racial issues, they perceived themselves as women and did not fear being "brutal."

The differences in life experiences of the men and women also contributed to their varied concerns about joining the police. Black working class juveniles spend a great deal of their time "in the street." They are frequent targets of police surveillance and intervention; prime suspects in crimes and disturbances, they are frequently stopped and questioned. Their experiences with the police often lead to bitter feelings and hostility. Adolescent females are given a great deal less freedom. The rarely "hang out," drink in groups, or get rowdy in public. Statistically they are far less likely to be involved in street crime, and thus they arouse far less suspicion on the part of the police. Since a male officer may not search or frisk a female, he is far less likely to stop her. While the black woman may share the perception (widely held in the black community) of the police as outsiders who "occupy" the neighborhood, she is less likely to have any unpleasant personal contact with the police. On the other hand, many inner city women turn to the police as protectors when faced with domestic violence. Their view of the police is not wholly negative. One policewoman noted that as a small child she had frequently called the police for her mother; to her the police had been frightening but protective heroes.

Officers attributed two other motivating factors to members of the other sex (and occasionally to those officers of their own sex whom they wished to censure). The men, in addition to saying the women were in policing "only for the money" (implying that the male officers were not), alleged that women join the department to find a husband, pointing to the high proportion of women dating or married to policemen as evidence.

The women, on the other hand, say that a number of the men are insecure and entered policing to prove their masculinity. Ann (see chapter 1) observed:

> Entering police work is perfectly logical for women. We're tired of demeaning work, tired of low pay, tired of doing the work men won't lower themselves to do. . . . Women come and stay in the police department to avoid dull jobs and get good pay. . . . Policing beats sitting in an office all day anytime. . . . But the men come on for strange reasons. They're a bunch of egomaniacs; they're insecure and want to bolster themselves and prove their manhood. They try to be big shots and feel like men by bossing people around. . . . The men say the women aren't aggressive enough. . . . But that's 'cause women aren't searching for manhood; we don't need to bully people.

Undoubtedly some men did choose police work to feel more like "real men" and some women entered it seeking an opportunity to meet "available" men—which points to the need for caution in examining interview data. It is impossible to determine with certainty whether interviewees stated their "real" motives or presented an image they believed would please the interviewer; or, in many cases, whether the officers were even fully conscious of the many factors that affected their job choice. Nevertheless, on balance their statements indicate that the factors shaping the job choice for male and female officers were similar. At the same time, the men emphasized long-term rewards whereas the women adopted a more short-term perspective. With more limited occupational options, the possibility of quitting work to become a housewife in the future, and less pressure or encouragement to think in terms of a "career," many more women entered policing in a tentative way, to "give it a try," and several happened into policing without much sense of active choice.

Having chosen to enter police work, most officers remain in the department for the same reasons they joined, others find new value in their work, and some discover that they are unsuited for the job. There appears to be little difference between male and female officers' stated reasons for remaining in police work. Eight of the women (seven of whom are black) remain for exclusively extrinsic reasons:

> I stay for the money.

> I stay for the same reason I joined: I needed a job. It's alright; it's a job. I don't have high expectations.

> It's a lonely job. . . . I don't quit because I have no other skills to get me the money to keep my apartment and pay my bills. . . . My typing is rusty so I'm stuck unless I find an unknown rich relative or hit the lottery.

A recurrent theme in these statements is the sense of being trapped. Having found a job that was much better paying than what they had previously had or expected, these women get scant satisfaction from their work, but see no alternatives that would permit them to continue living in the style to which they have become accustomed.

In contrast, the intrinsics find personal rewards in policing:

> I stay because I like the work I'm doing. I can't think of another place I'd rather be. . . . I'm not seen as a "typical woman" and I get a different approach from people. I like to be taken as someone with a career.

> I really love this job. It's exciting. For my 21 years I've learned so much and seen so much—things that make me think. I feel I've responsibility for making important decisions.

Most men, too, remain police officers because they find the work personally satisfying as well as economically rewarding, although more black than white men remain for only extrinsic reasons. Part of this racial difference results from differences in previous work experience; part stems from the different frames of reference adopted by black and white men.

In assessing their work situation the black men tend to look toward the black community and compare themselves with friends and former classmates, many of whom are unemployed. For most, the price they paid in "going over to the other side" seems worth the personal benefits of job security and the opportunity to achieve personal goals. "I like the work and I like the job security," one noted. "When I see others laid off and jobless I feel I made the right choice."

In contrast, the white men measure their satisfaction in terms of prior work experiences. Nine of the eleven white policemen in the sample had joined the department after a series of unsatisfying jobs with which police work compares favorably in terms of income and personal fulfillment. Thus they remain not only because of the job security but because, as one man noted, "after a while, police work gets in your blood."

Aspirations and Expectations

The work aspirations of male and female officers overlap to a large extent, but differ in certain respects. Nearly all officers hope to leave patrol eventually and "move upward," although to different assignments. While many officers now enjoy patrol work, they noted that after five years the routine, the shifts, close supervision, and higher status of other assignments all lead to a desire for reassignment. An equal proportion of the officers of each sex desire promotion (about half) or an investigative assignment. Similarly, approximately the same number of men and women desire to leave policing for another occupation (including full-time homemaking on the part of two policewomen).

The principal difference between the aspirations of the men and women is the desire expressed by several female officers for promotion or investigative work (including casual clothes), "inside" assignments to youth services and administrative posts. Eight of the twenty-eight women, and only one out of the twenty-seven males, aspire to such positions.

The aspirations of black and white officers differ as well. Six of the seven white policewomen, but only seven of twenty-one black policewomen desire promotion. A larger proportion of black than white

TABLE 11
Five-Year Aspirations of Officers by Sex and Race

| | Female | | Male | |
Goal	White (N=7)	Black (N=21)	White (N=11)	Black (N=16)
Promotion	6	7	6	8
Detective	2	9	4	3
Casual clothes	0	1	0	2
Mobile crime/K-9 or other uniform unit	2	1	1	1
Youth or community relations	0	3	0	1
Administrative or inside job	1	4	0	0
Patrol	0	0	2	0
Do not know	0	4	0	2
Resign from department	1	5	1	5

Note: Officers expressed several goals or aspirations, so that the total number of stated aspirations is greater than the number of officers.

female officers expressed interest in areas of policing traditionally reserved for women. Uncertainty about their goals or a desire to leave the police department is also more characteristic of black than white policewomen. A higher proportion of the former group view marriage and childrearing as career alternatives that affect their aspirations or cause greater uncertainty about their future in the police department. Five of the black policewomen hope to leave the department within five years, and four more stated no career aspiration or goal. One-third of the black policewomen desire assignments in the traditional places in the department for women which will be more "comfortable."

There is a less extreme but similar pattern for the white and black men. While a similar proportion aspire to rise in rank (about one-half) or enter non-uniformed units (about one-third), the black men expressed greater uncertainty about their goals and greater dissatisfaction with police work. Five black and only one white male hope to leave the department during the next five years.

While the aspirations of the male and female officers in the sample for upward mobility are quite similar, their expectations for five years hence differ. The men are far more optimistic about their chances of promotion, foresee career contingencies (i.e., factors that affect the development or outcome of their careers) which are job related, and are more willing to predict what their work futures hold than the women.

Ten of the sixteen men who aspire to promotion said they expect it, although four added qualifiers indicating that they recognize that promotion is unlikely. Most of the optimists are the newer men who had not yet taken the promotional exam and whose optimism may be short-lived.

The men's career contingencies are career determined; none expects family or personal circumstances to affect their careers, although several said they expect to marry. They prefer to remain on street patrol rather than to assume an inside assignment if they fail to attain a promotion or investigator status. While ten of the women could not make a prediction about their future, only five men expressed similar uncertainty.

In addition to uncertainty, the women, particularly the blacks, are less optimistic than the men about attaining their goals. Of the six white policewomen who desire promotion only two are sanguine about their chances and two others expect to attain alternative goals; only one could not predict what she would be doing in five years. Only one of the black women desiring promotion cautiously predicted that she would attain this goal or would have an inside assignment. Two of the nine aspiring detectives foresee success in attaining those assignments. More than half (twelve of twenty-one) of the black policewomen could not make predictions, although three of these expect to remain in the department (see table 12).[10]

10. The value of individuals' predictions of their future assignments is illustrated by table 12, which indicates the assignments of the officers in the study a year and a half after the completion of the last interview. None of the officers anticipated being sick or injured, yet one was forced to retire on disability and two were recovering from injuries (another was on maternity leave).

None of the officers in the study had expected to be promoted from the old promotional list and a new examination was not given until March 1978 so that, not surprisingly, no interviewees were promoted. Only two of the officers who had expected to resign have done so; two other men who resigned left for unforeseen personal reasons. (Both returned to their former hometowns for family reasons.) All the women are still in the department, two after having had babies.

Five officers transferred out of the district: the male officer as a result of a serious conflict with a sergeant; the women to become dispatchers (only one of the four had expected to do so). Within the district, one man attained an investigative assignment,

TABLE 12
Assignments of Interviewees by Sex
on December 12, 1977

Assignment	Male	Female
Remain in previous assignment	15	14
Reassigned within the district	5	6
Temporarily detailed	0	1
Transferred to another district of division	1	4
Sick leave	1	2
Retired on injury	1	0
Resigned from department	4	0
TOTAL	27	28

The women's views of their futures in the department are more pessimistic (and more realistic) than those of the men. Their lack of optimism and their uncertainty are related both to their personal lives and their perception of departmental opportunities open to them.

Personal contingencies, including age, marital and parental statuses, appear to affect the expectations of even the most satisfied and enthusiastic policewomen. At the time of their interview all of the women in the sample were thirty years old or younger, fifteen of the twenty-one black and five of the seven white women were not married, and twelve blacks and four whites had no children. Seven black and one white woman noted they anticipate and desire marriage and/or childbearing which might interfere with their work. One woman who stated that she is "enchanted" with her job added, "If I marry a man who opposes my being a police officer I'll find an inside job." Another mused, "Maybe my husband won't let me continue when I have a child." A third woman, after saying her current boyfriends accept her work, added, "The only way I won't stay for twenty years is if I should get snowed and the man asks me to quit . . . although that would be a turnabout." Such a reversal, however, remains a "thinkable" and perhaps a desirable possibility for the women, while none of the men

---

and one man and one female officer went to casual clothes assignments they desired. One women who desired (but had not expected) to be assigned to community services attained her goal. The rest remain in their previous assignments, have been assigned to scooter squad, or have been reassigned to patrol from other duties.

foresee marriage or parenthood affecting their work. Like many other young women, some policewomen are hesitant to commit themselves to their work expecting, and for some, hoping that marriage and motherhood will remove them from the occupational or the police world. One policewoman expressed the conflicts and ambivalence several others appear to feel:

> I stay because I like the job. I considered quitting when I worked with Officer L—— but there is no way for a black woman with a high school education to make what money I make. . . . I like the good parts [of my job]. They make me feel really good. . . . I am considering going back to patrol now . . . but the hours kill me. . . . I prefer to be in uniform because in uniform you have positive relations with people. I don't want to work but . . . if I have to work that's where I want to work. . . . I can't be a nurse or the president. . . . There's nothing else I could do. . . . I'd like to be here twenty years but I'm not planning that. If I get married which won't be for four or five years, then I'll probably have a baby since a man wants one of his own . . . and maybe I'll stay home. It depends on whether the job continues to make me happy.

The nature of her assignment affects a woman's ability to plan; work conditions of assignments vary considerably. Patrol work poses the greatest uncertainty in one's work schedule. While all patrol officers face certain conflicts between their work and family life, women, particularly those with young children, may encounter enormous strains as a patrol officer or sergeant, and thus tailor their occupational goals to mesh with nonwork related expectations. With no twenty-four-hour-a-day child care centers available for the woman whose shift changes every two weeks, and no opportunity to work as a part-time police officer, one way to reduce the strain is to seek an assignment more compatible with family life. Particularly appealing are assignments that involve straight day work with weekends off, including most administrative and "downtown" assignments. These factors, rather than any particular attraction to clerical work, appear to explain some women's stated goals and uncertain expectations. One woman stated simply, "I'd quit before I'd go back on patrol but if I can stay where I am now I'll stay to retirement."

The differences in the aspirations and expectations of male and female officers are also related to their perception of the opportunities within the department. As the remaining chapters will make clear, in addition to personal life circumstances the policies of the department, informal relationships and patterns of behavior, and the openly expressed attitudes of the men as reflected in their behavior strongly affect the women's views of the work, as well as their place within the police world and themselves. "Inside" assignments not only mesh well with personal life, they are the jobs in which policewomen are most "acceptable." Several women deemed inadequate as street patrol officers have been pushed or urged by male peers to find other (inside) assignments which they have readily accepted. By seeking and attaining such an assignment a woman can reduce some of the stresses and pressures patrolwomen face interacting with both the male officers and citizens.

Uncertainty and limited expectation of the future also serve as ego-protecting devices. If the likelihood of failure to attain a goal is high, indifference and/or ambiguous expectations help ward off a sense of failure and frustration. This helps explain the great uncertainty and limited expectations of the black women, who face double discrimination (on the basis of both race and sex). Many have adopted an "it's just a job" attitude that often leads to a self-fulfilling prophecy. While the department has made strides, increasing the hiring of blacks and women and eliminating racial and sex discrimination, the black women tend to see themselves as newcomers in a system that highly values seniority—outsiders both as blacks and women, and additionally disadvantaged by their youth and lack of other work experience. They recognize that the department is still dominated by white men and that three-fourths of their supervisors are whites who are unlikely to choose them for sponsorship or as protégés. Feeling these multiple disadvantages, they have shaped their aspirations accordingly. The white policewomen, too, are aware that as women they face discrimination and a myriad of subtle disadvantages which restrict opportunities in the department, and lead many to lower their aspirations and expectations.

Part II

Breaking and Entering

Chapter 4

Police Work and the
Policemen's Views of Policewomen

The incursion of women into traditionally "male" occupations has been opposed, resisted, and undermined wherever it has occurred. In few other occupations, however, has their entry been more vigorously fought—on legal, organizational, informal, and interpersonal levels— than in policing. Why is this so? What threats or challenges to the status quo, real or imagined, do women pose to the occupation, to the informal work group, and to the men as individuals?

The men's reactions to women on patrol are often based on fears of what sexual integration implies for the occupational role, the basic norms of police work, and the division of labor itself; the informal work group's cohesion which is based, in large part, on the men's shared definition of their masculinity; the social prestige of policing as an occupation; and thus, ultimately, their own personal identities. In short, the occupation of police officer affords many men a means of asserting their masculinity, an important fringe benefit. The integration of women into police patrol work as coworkers threatens to compromise the work, the way of life, the social status, and the self-image of the men in one of the most stereotypically masculine occupations in our society.

While most of the men oppose the assignment of women to street patrol (and several oppose their presence in the department altogether), a few men regard the change favorably and a third group accepts it with a certain amount of ambivalence.

POLICE WORK AND THE POLICE DEPARTMENT

More than a series of tasks and a source of income, one's work is intimately associated with all aspects of life. One's occupation is a social role. The incumbents of a particular role learn and exercise certain skills, meet with certain types of people, cope with organizational constraints, and often face a unique set of problems, all of which shape their behavior and their views of themselves. From their common experiences and common problems people in an occupation become part of a cohesive social group which establishes a set of norms that guide occupational behavior on the job, offers a particular perspective on the world, and, in many instances, serves as the basis for members' social lives outside the workplace. One's work is the primary determinant of one's socioeconomic status and social prestige and, finally, "a man's work is one of the most important parts of his social identity, of his self" (Hughes, 1958:43). To understand the implications of and opposition to the sexual integration of police work, it is necessary to examine the nature and organization of the work. These, in turn, shape the manner in which policemen carry out the job, the informal norms that guide the work group, and the impact of policewomen on male officers.

Police work today involves a demanding, often conflicting assortment of tasks and responsibilities. Officers are expected to prevent crime, protect life and property, enforce the laws, maintain peace and public order, and provide a wide range of services to citizens twenty-four hours a day. They attend fires; investigate all deaths that occur without a physician in attendance; direct traffic; disperse dangerous assemblies, while protecting the rights of those who have peacefully assembled; report violations of building and health codes; apprehend criminals of many types; and respond to calls for police assistance from citizens. They have paramilitary responsibilities, quasi-judicial functions, and serve as "the social agency of last resort for the impoverished, the sick, the old, and the lower socioeconomic classes" (Garmine, 1972:4). Informally they adjudicate conflicts of ethnic and class moralities, enforcing social customs in the various segments of the population, all the while protecting the property of the upper classes. They function variously as marriage counselors, medical assistants, legal advisors, psychologists, building inspectors, and providers of information and services.

This wide array of sometimes conflicting duties have frequently been classified into three primary areas of activities: law enforcement; order maintenance; and the provision of services.[1] The common central features of police work involve social control responsibilities. Bittner (1970:38-39) observed:

> Many puzzling aspects of police work fall into place when one ceases to look at it as primarily concerned with law enforcement and crime control, and only incidentally and often incongruously concerned with an infinite variety of other matters. It makes much more sense to say that the police are nothing else than a mechanism for the distribution of situationally justified force in society.

Thus what ties the police officer's work together, whether pursuing a robber, attempting to restore peace to a scene of domestic disturbance or issuing a traffic ticket, is the potential for violence and the need and right to use coercive means to enforce the officer's definition of the situation. The understanding that the police act as the representatives of the coercive potential of the state, and the legitimate users of force in everyday life, enables one to make sense of the gaps between the reality of police work and the public image of the police, and to explain a number of attitudes and behaviors characteristic of the police.[2]

One myth about police work is that it primarily involves the officer in crime fighting; both the mass media and police organizations and officers have sought to convince the public that the work centers around the apprehension of criminals. The facts, however, indicate that the police could not eradicte crime even if it were their only responsibility, and that most of the patrol officers' time is not devoted to law enforcement. Several studies have shown that most citizens'

1. Cumming, Cumming and Edell (1965) discuss the service functions. Regarding order maintenance as distinct from law enforcement, Banton (1964) notes the difference between "law officers" and "peace officers"; Bittner (1967) distinguished between "law enforcement" and "keeping the peace" in his analysis of patrolmen's handling derelicts on Skid Row; Wilson (1973) concentrates on the maintenance of order as differing from enforcement of the law. Other discussions of the police patrol functions and the conflicts among the various facets of the role include Skolnick (1967); Neiderhoffer (1969); Bayley and Mendelsohn (1968); Chevigny (1969); Bittner (1970); and Rubinstein (1974).

2. Muir (1977) examines "the paradoxes of coercive power" that shape police behavior. While his book focuses on the moral dilemmas faced by officers and the different ways in which officers respond, he, too, defines coercive authority as central to the police role.

requests are for service, or involve order maintenance functions.[3] The crime-fighting focus remains salient, however, because it is the aspect of the work with dramatic and symbolic value for the department and community. Crime fighting is visible, publicly valued and rewarded, and felt to be the most satisfying part of the work by the officers. The middle-class public can agree that it wants its property and physical safety protected, and rewards the police for successfully apprehending those whose behavior most clearly threatens the community.[4] The department rewards its crime fighters with plaques, award ceremonies, and assignments to the detective bureau that offer more pay, prestige and personal autonomy on the job. The informal work group esteems the "good pinch" (arrest) and the officers who make them. Finally, for the officer, the apprehension of criminals is associated with danger, bravery and heroism, marking police work as a "man's job" and enhancing both his professional and personal self-image.

The reality of police work, often carefully hidden from the public and denigrated by the officers themselves, is far less glamorous. It involves them in the "peace officer" role, thrusts them into situations in which emotions and tensions are often high and citizens may be hostile, and calls for the exercise of discretion in interpreting citizen behavior and in applying the law and interpersonal skills to the specifics of the situation. It requires skills in understanding and manipulating people rather than bravado and heroics.

The police claim the law is the basis of their authority to "maintain order" in the face of potential violence, noncompliance, and conflict. In many situations, however, the law only abstractly defines the range of events requiring police intervention and thus cannot serve as an adequate guide to police action. Laws legitimize the use of coercive force, function as one resource among many used by the police for

3. Wilson (1973:18) in a survey of citizens' complaints radioed to patrol vehicles in Syracuse during a one week period in June 1966, found that 37.5 percent of the calls were for service, 30.1 percent involved order maintenance functions, 22 percent required information gathering largely of a clerical nature, and only 10.3 percent of the calls were for law enforcement activities. For similar findings see Neiderhoffer (1969:75 footnote 26); Cumming, Cumming, and Edell (1965); Parnas (1967); and Reiss (1971).

4. An example of the public acclaim for police crime-fighting activities is the Washington Metropolitan Police Department's "Sting" operation. With FBI financial backing, the department set up a phony fencing operation that led to the arrest of many criminals and the recovery of a substantial amount of stolen property. The style and flair of the detectives in carrying out the operation was the center of press attention, favorable public comment, and departmental self-congratulations for several weeks.

dealing with disorder, and permit officers to rationalize their actions (Wilson, 1968; Bittner, 1970; Manning, 1977).

Discretion is built into the officer's job.[5] Particularly in "order maintenance" situations, the law may not have been violated but citizens pressure the officer to act as a controller or social mediator. While most criminal laws define acts that are illegal, laws regarding disorderly conduct implicitly assert that there is a condition, "public order," that can be increased or decreased by various actions. Yet, what constitutes "public order" is a matter of opinion, a delicate "judgment call" the officer is frequently required to make. Even in situations where the law has been clearly violated, the officer is expected to exercise discretion rather than automatically enforcing the law to the fullest.[6] Yet in making these situation-based judgments the officer, in essence, takes sides in a dispute. Being "for" one party means acting "against" the other, and the resentment or hostility of one party then become redirected at the officer. Similarly, in selectively enforcing certain laws, the police officer evokes public resentment and resistance to his authority: citizens may protest, "Why did he give me the speeding ticket when others are speeding, too?" or pointedly tell an officer that he or she should do "real" police work (i.e., catch criminals) instead of "wasting time" enforcing traffic regulations.

An additional dilemma officers face in applying the law to ambiguous situations arises from the procedural constraints that protect individual rights from police abuse. (See Skolnick [1967] for a discussion of the conflict between law enforcement and procedural restraints.)

Pressured by the public to apprehend criminals and reduce crime, and rewarded by the department for making arrests, officers are simultaneously limited by law, courts, and departmental regulations protecting citizen rights; officers often feel they are "damned if they do and damned if they don't." The result is illegal behavior, including violence and deceit by officers, and collusion to hide such behavior from the public and from supervisors to avoid discipline and/or prosecution.[7]

5. The use and abuse of police discretion is extensively discussed in the literature: see Goldstein (1960); LaFave (1965); Skolnick (1966); Wilson (1973); and Davis (1975).

6. Neither the courts nor the jails could survive a policy of a "full enforcement" of the laws. Nor would the public tolerate such a policy as evidenced by the pressures not to enforce certain statutes, and the public outcries that arise with increased traffic law enforcement.

7. In addition to the veil of secrecy surrounding police activities there are institu-

All this has resulted in a set of cognitive and behavioral responses, characteristic of police officers, which have been termed their "working personality" (Skolnick, 1967) as well as in a cohesive, closed social group with certain collective ends, norms, and sanctions.

Shaping the officers' "working personality" (i.e., "their distinctive cognitive tendencies as an occupational grouping" [Skolnick, 1967:42]) is a unique combination of elements in their social environment: danger and authority combined with organizational pressures for efficiency. While danger is characteristic of many occupations, in few has it become a part of the occupational ideology as it has in policing, with its lore about risk, force, and heroic episodes. Other occupations are more dangerous,[8] and "dangerous" activities represent less than 10 percent of police patrol time and less than 1 percent of citizen-initiated complaints (Black, 1968:tables 2 and 18).

Police work, however, differs from other occupations in that injury and death may result at any time from the willful behavior of another human being, rather than from a quirk of nature or a mechanical failure. Because danger and the potential for violence come from humans and the work requires the officer to be attentive to potential violence and law breaking, officers develop a perceptual shorthand for identifying certain kinds of people as "dangerous" and focus on "the symbolic assailant" and the dangerous scene (Skolnick, 1967). The police officer, as an occupational necessity, becomes a suspicious person. Yet this suspiciousness may produce behavior that antagonizes the citizen, and makes the officer's work more difficult. Particularly in order-maintenance situations, where the officer depends on citizen cooperation, an officer's questions and suspicious manner may appear hostile, and produce anger, animosity and an uncooperative citizen response. This, in turn, leads to further suspicion on the part of the officer, resulting in a spiral of antagonisms (see Wilson, 1968:20).

---

tionalized practices that include lying to "cover your ass" and the use of "covering charges" to mask police brutality. These tend to arise in instances when an officer stops a citizen on a minor infraction, the person questioned does not display respect, resistance to the officer's attempts at control leads to violence and a "covering charge" of resisting arrest is added to any other charges arising from the situation. See Chevigny (1969); Van Maanen (1974); and Manning (1977).

8. The President's Crime Commission Task Force Report: The Police (1967:189) reported that a 1963 study found that the rate of police fatalities on duty, including accidents, was 33 per 100,000, less than the rate for mining (94), agriculture (55), construction (76), and transportation (44).

Danger isolates the officer not only from the "criminal element" but from the "respectables" in the community as well; the latter seek to avoid exposure to danger and potential violence that has been made the responsibility of the police.[9]

Authority contributes to the social isolation of the police, because whether directing traffic or keeping order at the site of an accident, officers are called on to control citizens, who may resent the restraint on their freedoms. In addition, exercising authority puts the officer in the uncomfortable position of being the enforcer of society's puritanical public morality which many citizens, and officers, neither believe in nor adhere to. In these instances the role of enforcer opens the police officer to the charge of hypocrisy, and leads to avoidance of the potential "punisher" and denial of his or her authority.

Set apart from the larger world, the police officer turns to his or her occupational community for support, solidarity, and social identity. For workers in many occupations the work group is the basis of their social life; for police officers the work group is much more. Regarding the public as hostile and facing uncertain danger, officers are highly dependent on each other for mutual support and physical protection. Their sense of social isolation from others and dependence on each other spill over into their off-duty activities, so that friendships and socializing center around other police officers. The job becomes a way of life, and the occupational group and its norms provide an occupational morality and occupational self-conception (see Westley, 1970).

Officers' solidarity and mutual dependence is increased by internal factors as well. Because police work vests in the officer power over our society's highest values—life, freedom, and physical integrity—and this power may be corrupted or abused, since their inception in the nineteenth century police departments have sought to closely control officers' behavior. They have done so by adopting a paramilitary model of organization with a hierarchical and bureaucratic structure. Detailed rules of conduct govern not only behavior toward citizens but the minutiae of officers' appearance; the officer is considered "on duty" twenty-four hours a day, kept under close and punitive super-

9. Skolnick (1967:54) notes, "The citizen prefers to see the policeman as an automaton because once the policeman's humanity is recognized, the citizen necessarily becomes implicated in the policeman's work, which is, after all, sometimes dirty and dangerous. What the policeman typically fails to realize is the extent he becomes tainted by the character of the work he performs."

vision (and subject to departmental discipline) in an attempt to enforce the rules. But since no officer can follow all the rules and adequately perform the job, officers are constantly susceptible to disciplinary action. To protect themselves from supervisors as well as the public, therefore, officers have informally adopted several basic strategies that guide behavior and elevate the interests of the group above those of the individual officer.

The principal norms of policing include the rule of silence, and the use of the silent treatment for offenders; the requirement that an officer physically back up another officer or face rejection as a partner; the rule of maintaining respect for the police, and the use of ridicule to punish violators; and the belief that the means justify the ends in the apprehension of a felon. Secrecy is necessary to shield the police from the public who, by definition, do not understand the need to frequently violate procedural regulations, and use violence. Secrecy also shields the officers from supervisors' scrutiny, and minimizes punishments for violations of the rules. Thus, regardless of what action another officer takes, a policeman (or policewoman) must remain silent and demonstrate his or her loyalty to the group in the face of a hostile world. The officer who "squeals" risks being ostracized by colleagues, cut off from informal sources of information vital to his or her work, and harassed by officials who may suddenly decide to strictly enforce the rules. Closely related to the rule of silence is the obligation of officers to come to the immediate aid of another officer in any physical confrontation. An "officer in trouble" radio call receives the highest priority. The police officer who fails to come rapidly to the aid of fellow officers gets labeled "shaky" and is shunned as a partner because he or she cannot be relied on in a crisis situation.

The demand for respect arises from the officers' uncertain authority, the public's resistance to it, and the tendency in the officers' minds to merge the office which they hold with their sense of self, or personal identity. Officers come to regard a citizen's challenge to their definition of the situation as a sign of disrespect not only for the law of which they are the representative, but for their person and the group with which they are so strongly identified. The importance of respect to police is indicated by Westley's (1970) finding that 39 percent of the officers he interviewed expressed willingness to use force illegally to maintain respect for the police. A new officer quickly learns that he or she must not back down but instead must attempt to control a situation, by force if necessary, or face severe informal sanctions by fellow officers, such as ostracism, negative labels, and unfavorable assignments.

To assure adherence to the norms and maintain group solidarity, the police have adopted entrance requirements and recruitment mechanisms that select a homogeneous group of people likely to fit into the existing group. Homogeneity is desirable because the unpredictable nature of the work makes trustworthy coworkers imperative, and trust involves speaking the same language and sharing values so that miscommunication and misunderstanding are reduced, and choices of action become more predictable. People tend to trust individuals similar to themselves, and the police have historically recruited from a narrow segment of the population: working-class and lower-middle-class white males (McNamara, 1967; Neiderhoffer, 1969; Westley, 1970; and Hahn, 1974). Only with these "like selves," who must also be tested and proved loyal, can police officers feel free to do the job.

The recruitment process used by many police departments simultaneously operates at three levels to meet the needs of the legal system, the formal police organization, and the informal culture. "Outsiders" are first eliminated by physical requirements (women) and written tests and/or educational requirements (blacks). Background investigations and, finally, personal interviews further screen prospective officers. Interviews assure that candidates not only meet the needs of the legal system for mature, emotionally stable, technically competent people and the organization's need for officers who express the "correct" predispositions toward certain values, including a willingness to use force, the acceptance of personal risk, and a high regard for authority and group solidarity. An additional quality, labeled by Gray (1975) "the mark of affinity" (i.e., a predisposition to adhere to a distinctive set of sentiments) is also required by the informal work group. This "mark of affinity," demonstrated by subtle cues during the screening interview, is the candidate's conception of masculinity. For this reason, Gray concluded, women are viewed as "inappropriate" candidates for police work and would, if hired for patrol, "undercut the basis of male solidarity" (1975:52). Since male solidarity and shared understandings as men are central features of the informal work group's cohesiveness, and the group is so important to the officers, resistance to the entrance of women is predictable. The "mark of affinity" standard makes selecting policewomen difficult, for they can be measured neither in terms of their concept of their masculinity, nor of their femininity.

In sum, the unique occupational subculture, and singularly cohesive informal work group found among police have evolved from both the nature of the work and the police organization. Police officers' diverse responsibilities are tied together by the potential for violence and the authority to use force if necessary. Danger and the authority invested in the office isolate the police officer from the community and foster strong bonds of solidarity among the police. Departmental organization contributes to ties of interdependence, and the resultant informally enforced but potent work norms. Recruitment, too, typically sustains this closed, homogeneous group of policemen who share their view of their masculinity, work, and the world.

MASCULINITY

An examination of masculinity and its particular meaning for policemen is necessary because of the close association of police work with masculinity, and the manner in which occupational role norms and sex role norms overlap and mutually reinforce one another. Being male is biologically determined but "being a man" means fulfilling a socially defined role, and displaying a set of behavioral attributes that varies among societies and even between ethnic and social groups within a society. In the U.S., despite subcultural variations, the core dimensions of the male sex role include four basic themes: the avoidance of anything vaguely feminine; the attainment of success and social status; a less easily defined "manly" air of toughness, confidence and self-reliance; and an aura of aggressiveness, daring and violence (David and Brannon, 1976). To be a man means to embody these qualities in a variety of ways.

The avoidance of anything vaguely feminine begins quite early as young boys are socialized to transfer their initial identification with a woman (i.e, mother) to a male object. A little boy learns not to be like a little girl, and never to display the feminine characteristics of a "sissy." Gradually he learns that women stereotypically are weak and unassertive, so he must be strong and dominant; that women are fearful, so he must be brave; and that women are emotional, so he must inhibit his expression of emotions, including squeamishness when confronted with something shocking or distasteful and his feelings of affection, particularly toward other males except in ritualized gestures that are "safe." He is encouraged to participate in sports, to "stand up for himself" in a fight, and particularly in adolescence, to develop the physical superiority which distinguishes him as a "man." Later he can avoid the taint of things feminine and increase his sense of manliness by selecting an occupation that places him safely in a man's world, far from things that might interest a woman.

To attain success and social status there may be a number of routes: wealth and fame; being the world's (or the neighborhood's) "greatest" in whatever pursuit is undertaken; being the family breadwinner. In whatever route the man pursues, he seeks to have others look up to him so that he is metaphorically if not physically larger than others and, therefore, more important.

To be manly means to exude an air of toughness, confidence, self-reliance, courage (both physical and moral), and sexual competence. Though the components of "toughness" vary, the core of toughness includes a refusal to compromise oneself in the face of opposition or adversity. It may also include, but does not necessarily rest on, physical strength and athletic prowess.

A final component of masculinity is aggressiveness (which may mean either the tendency to attack first or the tendency to act with energy and vigor) and violence (the exertion of physical force to injure or abuse another). These qualities, in part, stem from the need to win at any cost. But even if he is not actually violent or aggressive, it enhances a man's masculinity to be thought to possess such qualities. The extreme idealization of aggression and violence is the Latin cult of machismo, which highly esteems the man who will use force at the slightest excuse. While machismo is not an original part of the American culture, the aura of violence is institutionalized in our association of maleness with both violent contact sports, and with the sexual attractiveness attributed to the man who presents the image of primitive, untamed sexuality.

Although these core traits make up the generally shared conception of masculinity in our culture, there are class and ethnic differences of emphasis. For men of all classes, work is a primary source of status and success, and thus a means by which they may affirm their manhood (or fail to do so, which often leads to frustration and displaced anger). For blue-collar men, whose jobs often do not provide high incomes or great social prestige, other aspects of the work, including certain "manly" features, take on enormous importance as a means through which they confirm their sex role identity. Work that entails responsibility, control, use of a skill, initiative, and which permits the use of strength and/or physical agility characteristic of males is highly valued not only for its own sake but for its symbolic significance. Similarly, working in an all-male environment reinforces the notion that they are doing "men's work" and is a highly prized fringe benefit of a job.

Most policemen come from working-class backgrounds (see note 7 to chapter 3). Even those who do not bring working-class social attitudes and values to the job tend to adopt a working-class perspective toward the meaning of masculinity as a result of the recruitment process, the nature of their work and the frequent interaction with working- and lower-class citizens—the primary users of police services and the targets of patrol efforts. Officers must adjust to the values of the citizens they police in order to work effectively and thus come to be influenced by the "focal concerns" of the members of the lower classes.[10] One of these concerns is "toughness," a composite of physical prowess demonstrated by strength, endurance, and athletic skills; the absence of sentimentality and the conceptualization of women as conquest objects; and bravery in the face of physical threats. The models of the tough guy are the movie cowboy, the gangster, and the private eye. The police share with such males an emphasis on toughness, and seek to be smarter and tougher than the "street dudes" whose values and postures they often mirror.[11]

Although security is a frequently stated reason for joining the police, for many men the excitement, danger, occasional demand for physical strength and courage, and the camaraderie of the (formerly) all-male group—all of which reinforce their sense of masculine identity—are attractive features of police work that offset its mediocre social status and income, and the social isolation that results from the job.

THE EFFECT OF POLICEWOMEN
ON THE WORK NORMS

The entry of policewomen on patrol threatens to alter the division of labor, and the norms according to which police officers work; to

10. Miller (1959) in an article examining lower-class culture as a generating milieu for urban gang delinquency observed that among a wide segment of the urban lower class there is a distinctive patterning of issues that command persistent attention and emotional involvement which differs from the patterns of issues and concerns found among the middle and upper classes. These lower-class focal concerns include trouble, toughness, smartness, excitement, fate, and autonomy.

11. In certain respects the police officer is a combination of the cowboy and the private eye. Police talk about an officer having a "John Wayne syndrome" or a "Wyatt Earp complex." One noted that the city is "the last frontier" to conquer. Officers, like the private eye, do detective work and in their work culture highly esteem the "good pinch" and "crime-fighting" aspects of their job.

disrupt the bonds of group solidarity; and to undermine the definition of police work as men's work. As a result, policemen have reacted to female patrol officers with strong opposition, which arises from both their general working-class perspective on sexual integration in the workplace and the specific impact of women on police work.

One of the objections to policewomen most frequently voiced by policemen is that because women are physically smaller and weaker than men, they are less able to perform the job. In a world in which a man's body as a primary tool in shaping the world has become nearly obsolete, and social distinctions among men are no longer based on physical differences, police work is one of the few remaining occupations in which strength and/or physical ability still are required for the work—if only occasionally. While working-class men generally concede that women are equally as intelligent as men, they demand recognition of their own physical superiority, particularly where it may be a valuable asset on the job. The utilization of women on patrol implies either that the men's unique asset—physical superiority—is irrelevant, or that the man working with a policewoman will be at a disadvantage he would not face working with a male partner in a physical confrontation.

Both of these suggestions are distressing to the men in this study. The emotional volatility of the issue is indicated by the vehemence of the men's arguments, and the fact that they tended to argue in extreme terms. "How can a five-foot woman possibly handle a man who's six-foot-five and weighs 250 pounds?" they ask, ignoring the fact that the average policewoman is not five feet tall and that most policemen cannot handle such a large citizen alone either. One policeman noted,

> Policing is men's work. The only woman I'd feel comfortable with is built like an Amazon. I prefer the muscle of a man. . . . A woman's nice to have in a family argument call but she's not physically able to do the job.

Women's disadvantage in a fight is a frequently raised issue. As one policeman stated:

> Women can't hold up their own end in fights. I'm no babysitter. Equal pays means an equal amount of work. No woman performs the same way or amount as a male. . . . Women are physically inadequate . . . not mentally but physically and this job is both mental and physical.

Women are viewed as unacceptable for patrol not only because they provide less "muscle" to a partner but because the men feel that they cannot be relied on to behave appropriately during a physical confrontation. The author of an article in *Police Chief* (Vastola, 1977:64) stated:

> A policewoman when faced with an incident of this nature [intervening in a bar brawl] is without specific social guidance for her new role. As a woman she probably has not been socialized to engage in physical violence with fighting men. As a police officer, who is expected to share equal roles with her male colleagues, she is required in some way to mediate the incident. The policewoman may, because of conflicting social expectations, unconsciously revert to her female role by standing by, not intervening in the fight. On the other hand, she may react to her police role by attempting to quell the fighting and in so doing, exhibit behavior inappropriate in such a situation, e.g., draw her revolver or cry.

The author never considers the possibility that the policewoman will act in an appropriate manner—neither overreacting nor failing to act. In a similar vein, one policeman who proudly noted that he is frequently in fights stated his objection to policewomen:

> I don't think they should be on this job, not in uniform, not working with me. I want somebody who can back me up. . . . I don't want someone I have to back up. There's only one woman I'd work with in this district . . . 'cause she's meaner than most guys I've seen on the street. . . . When I get into fights it's usually several against me and I'd rather be by myself. That way I don't have to watch out for her.

The men's view that in a physically dangerous situation female officers are unreliable and unable to defend themselves, or their partners, affects their patrol behavior. They state that with a female partner they become more cautious, are less likely to go all out, and will take fewer risks in apprehending a lawbreaker. Whether they believe this improves the way they police by forcing themselves to act with greater restraint, or detracts from their police work, the men agreed on the restraining influence of female officers on their own patrol behavior.

Police partners rely very heavily on each other for protection. While dependence on another man, when properly masked, is part of the "male camaraderie" that binds males together, to depend on a woman (except for sexual and domestic services) is felt to be unmanly, and humiliating. Instead, a "man" protects women by adhering to the code of chivalry strongly embedded in the values of most male officers. As one policeman observed:

> I kind of look down on any type of female who wants to do this job. I don't think it's a woman's place. I've been taught that women should be treated as queens and I try to treat any woman who rides with me as a queen. Anything we come upon, I take the aggressive initiative. In most cases it is almost mandatory that I do so. . . . Females usually shun being aggressive.

Taught to treat women with respect, which includes their physical protection, a self-fulfilling prophecy is created. If the male officer treats the policewoman like a "queen," the woman "sits back," acting like a queen—and thereby performs inadequately as a police officer. Her behavior reinforces his sense that she must be treated differently from male partners, making his job harder but preserving his sense of manliness. If, on the other hand, the woman chooses not to act like a queen, she becomes a threat to his ego; he wants to be able to depend on a partner but does not want to depend on a woman.

Many male officers spoke of having to protect their female partners from danger without mentioning the role that a female partner seems to play in cooling down angry male citizens (who also adhere to the code of chivalry and thus are restrained from hitting or cursing at a woman). Only when pressed did one officer admit that his female partner (whom he characterized as "tough") had kept him from being injured on several occasions. But he expressed indignation at another policewoman who had intervened and prevented him from coming to blows with an irate citizen. The extent to which women threaten the core of masculinity was most clearly articulated by one officer:

> Why did the women choose this job? I don't know. . . . I have respect for policewomen but they should do a less demanding job than they do here. Sure there's some stuff that women can do like type, but they shouldn't jump into fights or be on murders or cutting scenes with naked bodies and blood. . . . I don't know how their husbands put up with it. It takes his masculinity away when a woman is trying to do a man's job.

The men are caught in a bind: they want a partner who will be "tough," fight, and back them up and whom, in turn, they are willing to back up. But women are not supposed to fight, be tough or protect a man. The more a female partner acts like a police officer, the less she behaves like a woman. On the other hand, the more she behaves like a woman, the less protection she provides, the less adequate she is as a partner—although such behavior preserves the man's sense of masculinity. The way out of the bind is simple: keep women out of patrol work.

The rule of maintaining respect is also threatened by patrolwomen. Maintaining respect is central to police work yet, as many recognize, the authority of the uniform and the office are often insufficient; the officer's personal authority and manner of conveying it are involved in gaining citizen compliance. Many policewomen are viewed as insufficiently assertive and authoritative, permitting citizens to "get away" with certain behavior; this ultimately undermines the authority of all officers.

In this society men, including policemen, have been socialized to the view that women are objects to be used and/or dominated, rather than authority figures to be feared, respected or obeyed. They perceive that women possess little power and are frequently inexperienced in its exercise. Although women in certain social roles are to be treated with the chivalrous deference owed to a "lady," or the dutiful respect paid to a wife or mother, the status of women and the authority, power, and prestige that accompany it, in general, are lower than those of men. A woman in authority is a threat to social domination by men, and policemen emotionally share the resistance of men in the street to a woman with authority over men, and are often hostile to policewomen who are assertive. At the same time they fear that male citizens' denial of policewomen's authority will "rub off" on the police in general. Voicing the concerns of many others, one policeman asked,

> Who's going to listen to a small woman? Small men are different. The men on the street know he means business and will put them in jail. He has a masculine way of conveying authority.

Many policemen fear that they will become laughingstocks in the eyes of criminals; objects of derision instead of feared adversaries.[12] Other officers, indicating the threat that policewomen represent to their own identities, projected themselves into the role of male citizens:

> Any man I've talked to doesn't like being told what to do by a woman so this may lead to a bad situation, especially a hot tempered woman who tries to exercise more authority than she has. . . . She's an insult to his manhood.

---

12. Analogously, those opposed to women in the military, particularly in combat assignments, argue that other countries will misinterpret the women's presence, seeing it as a sign of weakness signaling the imminent collapse of the U.S. military strength rather than a principled action.

> If I was a robber and a policewoman came up to me, I wouldn't take her seriously. . . . If she persisted, I'd split and she'd never take me.

For many policemen the most telling criticism of policewomen is not their lack of physical strength, but the allegation that some female officers fail to assert the authority of their office and, instead, "back off." Yet in attempting to determine the frequency of such occurrences, the men's factual statements quickly became shrill and derisive, and displayed a marked tendency to exaggerate, indicating the strength of the emotional reaction that policewomen arouse.

At the same time that the men criticize some women's timidity, assertive women get labeled bossy and unfeminine. One policewoman, the target of such criticism, was labeled a "hotdog" (a police department term for a "rate buster" who aggressively out-performs and thereby shows up other officers); the men predicted that she would soon "get her ass kicked" by a citizen, an event they anticipated with pleasure rather than distress.[13]

A less frequently articulated but strongly felt objection to policewomen is that women will undermine the essential core of police work: the emphasis on crime fighting and the masculine image that accompanies it. Because of the association of women with service occupations and with the less desirable "feminine" service aspects of policing, entry of women into the male world of patrol highlights these "feminine" peacekeeping and service elements which most policemen prefer to hide from public view and their own consciousness.

Finally, the "crime-fighting" performance of most policewomen is taken to indicate their inappropriateness for patrol work. Policewomen have a lower arrest rate than male officers (Bloch et al., 1973a and b; Bloch and Anderson, 1974a and b; Sherman, 1975; Sichel et al., 1977). Even though many policemen are critical of departmental pressures for a high arrest rate, and of fellow officers who make "hummers" (avoidable arrests for behavior that offended the officer rather than violated the law in any but a minor and/or technical sense) the consistently lower arrest rate of the female officers "confirms" the conviction of the men that women either do not adhere to the group norms or cannot fulfill them. In either case, the effect is a reduction in

13. Similar criticism and dire predictions were directed at a male officer as well, but unlike the policewoman he went about patrol work with a hostile, chip-on-the-shoulder attitude. The female officer merely was too active, assertive, and enthusiastic for an experienced officer—particularly a woman.

the crime-fighting emphasis in the work which is psychologically distressing to many of the men and undermines group solidarity— based as it is, in part, on the willingness to use any means (including violence) to apprehend the offender.

IMPLICATIONS OF POLICEWOMEN FOR THE WORK GROUP

Effects on Group Solidarity

Relations among officers and group solidarity, binding policemen into a close brotherhood, are also affected by policewomen. As previously noted, police work becomes virtually a way of life for policemen, who form a cohesive community. Bonds of manhood strengthen the work-related ties among the men; the presence of women changes the rules of the group, and threatens its existence. For example, the ways by which the men resolve differences are affected. Among their peers the predominantly working-class policemen may opt to demonstrate their toughness and win a point by resorting to physical rather than verbal means. Although force is rarely used it has symbolic importance; it is acceptable for a man to use threats or, if necessary, fists to settle an argument. Middle-class men have other resources and have been strongly socialized to use them, rather than resorting to violence, in resolving an argument. Several policemen reported they respond to "harassment" by other officers with threats to settle the matter "behind the stationhouse." One sergeant indicated that he learned to look at another male and size him up, thinking, "Can I take him (physically)?" The policemen's emphasis on the physical makes the entry of women problematic. A man cannot fight a woman and gain status; the code of chivalry prohibits such a physical engagement. Policewomen alter the rules of the game among officers; the men who cope with threats and challenges by counterthreats or a fist fight must learn to deal in another way, and most resent giving up their reliance on physical prowess.

The rules governing males' emotional reserve, and acceptable displays of dependence and affection, too, are threatened by females. Police partners, dependent on each other, develop strong feelings of attachment as they work together. Some men acknowledge that they not only spend more time with a male partner than with their wives, but that they feel closer to them as well. One officer said of his partner, "We're so close that if I'm hurt he'd bleed and vice versa." Another stated (Milton et al., 1974:42):

> I've been working with my partner now for two and one-half years. I think I know more about him than his wife does. . . . He knows everything about me. . . . I think you get a certain relationship when you work together with a partner. . . . There's an attachment. . . . If my partner were a female, I would have married him a long time ago.

Because masculinity demands it, the men mask their feelings of affection and dependency. They guard themselves from the emotionally wrenching situations they face with slogans like "don't let it get to you" and seek acceptable manly outlets such as heavy drinking, cursing, sexual exploits, fast driving and other dangerous sports, and displacing anger onto others. When failures of emotional control occur they remain hidden.

The presence of women threatens to expose the men's occasional emotional failures and sentimentality. When I was working with a male and female team one evening, their conversation turned to traffic enforcement. The policewoman stated vehemently, "I'm hell on drunk drivers" and spoke about several incidents. Her partner said, "You get too involved. You'd never survive the first month in traffic division" and proceeded to explain how he had become hardened to that assignment. Later, when he got out of the car the policewoman turned to me and said, "Don't believe [it] when he talks like a hardnosed policeman. He's just keeping up with the guys, acting like nothing gets to him."

Social-class patterns of interaction, as well as the unusually close relationship that normally develops between patrol partners, magnify the disruption that policewomen introduce in the men's lives. Working-class parents tend to draw sharper distinctions than middle-class parents between the social roles of boys and girls (Kohn, 1959). As children become adults the social gulf between the sexes becomes an abyss. Blue-collar men work, socialize, and live in an almost exclusively male world cut off from close interpersonal ties with women. Even in marriage, companionship and open communication are often neither expected, desired, nor observed. Particularly characteristic of policemen's marriages is the avoidance of any discussion of their job with their wives. For men who are unaccustomed to working with or sharing their feelings with women, the presence of policewomen can threaten their social world.

Policemen tend to have common interests. They enjoy such male pursuits as hunting, sports, and working on their cars in their leisure time. In the station, lockerroom and scout car, conversation focuses on sports, women, and sex. These interests bind men together; since women are not expected to have these interests (and those who do are considered unfeminine) the male officers ask themselves, "What can I talk about with a female partner?" One officer remarked, "I found when riding with a policewoman I had nothing in common with her and I had nothing to talk to her about." A woman not interested in sports is a bore; a woman who is knowledgeable about them challenges the man's notions of masculinity and femininity.[14]

Separating the sexes in work and leisure is closely related to working-class attitudes regarding human nature and sexuality; the sexual double standard remains strong. The prevailing view is that a man and woman cannot be friends; a close relationship inevitably ends in bed. As one policeman stated, "Friendship between men and women doesn't work. Ultimately all men want is to get into a woman's pants." An emotional defense against heterosexual friendship, such a view creates a self-fulfilling prophecy; the men tend to flirt with or avoid the women who, in turn, find it very difficult to establish a close but non-sexual relationship with male coworkers. Given this view of heterosexual relationships and the fact that police partners work for long periods of time together, share intensely emotional situations, and develop very strong attachments to each other, the presence of policewomen raises the spectre of sexual intimacy between partners. Such bonds are feared, however, because they threaten the solidarity of the work group by fostering competition among the men for the women, and a competing set of loyalties.

Cultural taboos prohibiting homosexuality are intensified among the police, rechanneling the "unacceptable feelings" policemen develop for each other into acceptable bonds of brotherhood based on shared manly interests and activities, and strong loyalty to the all-male group. No similar clear set of social controls or taboos regulates work relationships between male and female partners. Such situations had been avoided by sex segregation; when they occur, as with the

---

14. The author of an article in *Police Chief* (Weldy, 1976) observed that the presence of policewomen improved the work of male officers who trained recruits, noting that when men worked together they talked about sports, sex and politics, and criticized police management. Rarely did male partners talk about police work. With a female partner, however, the conversation took a new course, since the men could not talk about sex in the accustomed way, were less likely to discuss sports, and tended to find political conversations boring. With such limitations on their conversation, the talk gradually drifted toward police work—the common ground. By talking and thinking about police work and seeking to impress the female trainees with their knowledge and occupational behavior, the policemen's work was improved.

introduction of patrolwomen, a situation arises for which no norms exist. How are men supposed to act with female coworkers? The only models that society provides for a heterosexual relationship are inadequate; neither the mother-son nor the sexually intimate model "fits."

Sexual intimacy, in particular, creates problems because it disrupts group bonds. Where there is no intimacy, the presence of a woman in the group nevertheless leads to competition among the men for her attention. Since the woman is the object of the men's pursuits—the hunted rather than the hunter—she cannot freely join in the men's sexual activities. If she is sexually active she becomes an object of contempt (because she denies the man the sense of conquest which enhances his sense of masculinity) and/or fear (because she might talk about the individuals with whom she has had relations and expose the exaggerations and tall tales). Although most policemen work with women with whom there is no romantic or sexual tie, they nevertheless treat the situation as sexually charged, engaging in displays of virility and ego-enhancing flirtation which complicate serious work situations by distracting attention from the work at hand.[15]

The presence of women disturbs the informal distribution of rewards based on the "buddy system," in which all compete on the same basis. The men become upset by the fact that women can—and a few policewomen do—gain exemptions and favorable assignments by taking "unfair advantage" of their sex (i.e., using something that the men cannot use to gain favor thus changing the rules of competition). That some men do not follow the rules and play fair is ignored; it is their apparent disadvantage as a class that is so upsetting.

The ambitious woman who attains a good assignment or evaluation creates problems for male officers who are unused to competing with a woman, and feel devastated if they are outdone by one. Such a woman becomes the subject of rumors which focus on how and why she got

15. In working with a large number of policemen on various tours of duty, I observed the frequent displays of virility and attempts at flirtation that were most characteristic of policemen whose opposition to policewomen on patrol was strongest. Their behavior (including exaggerated "door ceremonies," remarks about my appearance, and questions such as "Are you SURE you're happily married?") constantly reminded me that as a woman I was expected to appreciate them as virile males. In retrospect I observed that my language and behavior became more "ladylike" in these instances. In addition, these officers treated the tour of duty with me as a sort of "date"; they were quite chatty (rather than hostile as I had expected) but at the same time made clear that while I was present they could hardly be expected to do any "real" police work.

"favored" treatment. The implication is that such successes must have been the result of using female advantage (performing sexual favors) rather than by superior accomplishment (following the rules of the game and out-performing the men). An old academy classmate asked one policewoman, "Who'd you sleep with to get Sunday and Monday off?" Another woman defensively noted that despite what "they" may say, she earned the high efficiency rating that she had received.

The presence of women also disrupts male solidarity by inhibiting off-color stories and tales of physical and sexual prowess. Policemen have refined the "art" of cursing; such language is considered inappropriate for female ears and binds males who use it. In the presence of women the men either act like "gentlemen" and resentfully avoid the use of such language, or loudly curse, making clear that the women are guests in the men's world by pointedly exercising their masculine prerogatives of swearing, then apologizing to the women. Objecting to the patrolwomen, they said:

> I curse a great deal and with a woman I can't curse like I need to. There are certain words I avoid even if she uses them.

> The women want equal rights and responsibilities and equal money. . . .
> O.K., I'll show them no favoritism including my use of language. I expect them to act like a man in any situation.

When I worked with the second officer he self-consciously refrained from using his usual language although he clearly resented the inhibition.

Not only do the men resent having to behave differently (or feel self-conscious about cursing) when women are around, they are bothered by women using "men's language." Several remarked that the policewomen "talk like truckdrivers" and use language that embarrasses them. Thus, the women not only cramp the men's style, they have incorporated their male colleagues' traits into their own behavior, which blurs the distinction between the sexes that enables men to be men.

Effects on Policemen's Social Status

Policemen's status insecurity intensifies their opposition to sexual integration of their work place. Traditionally male occupations that seek out women recruits frequently suffer a decline in prestige, while traditionally female occupations become more prestigious following the entry of males. A high-prestige occupation such as law or medicine can afford to admit women without suffering much decline in status.

Among "status-anxious" blue-collar men there is less margin for status loss, so that "the battle between the sexes" is more intense and divisive than in the white-collar world (Shostak, 1969). Like other blue-collar men, many policemen believe a woman's place is in the home, and that her presence on the job jeopardizes the well-being of her children, undermines the self-esteem of her husband, and displaces men from their natural work roles.

Police have profound doubts about their social status; unsure whether they belong to the working or middle class, they strongly desire acceptance in the latter (Bayley and Mendelson, 1968). National surveys examining the relative prestige of ninety occupations, in 1947 and 1963, indicated that the relative position of police officers had improved more than any other group except nuclear physicists, but their 1963 rank of forty-seventh confirms the mediocre social status of police (Hodge, Siegel and Rossi, 1966). Despite the fact that the officer has power over our highest social values (life and honor, liberty and justice) policing remains a tainted occupation, and the officer is regarded as someone who does society's dirty work (Skolnick, 1967; Bittner, 1970; Manning, 1977). Public ambivalence toward the police leads officers to feel undervalued and denied the professional status they believe they deserve. Convinced that their status has fallen recently as a result of the social upheavals and mass protests of the late 1960's, they perceive a general decline in respect for law and order, particularly among juveniles and minorities, which they feel makes their job harder and their position in the community more isolated.

Although many officers recognize that their public standing can be improved by professional, honest, intelligent, and racially unbiased conduct and by avoiding adventurous, glamorous, and pugnacious behavior (i.e., "being a 'man's man'") many are emotionally resistant to changing their ways (Bayley and Mendelsohn, 1968). While they recognize that the incorporation of policewomen is likely to improve the public image of the police (a desired goal) by portraying the police as increasingly community oriented and self-restrained, at another level they are distressed by the fact that patrolwomen will reduce the "macho" image of the police. Many of the men spoke nostalgically about "the good old days" before outsiders disrupted the group's solidarity, the courts imposed legal restraints on their behavior, and departments sought to professionalize the police. In those days at least if he was not regarded as a professional, the policeman was viewed as an object of fear, someone with authority, a man to be reckoned with.

DIVERSITY OF OPINION AMONG THE MEN

As a result of a number of changes (see pages 57-59), a growing number of officers in the Metropolitan Police Department are challenging the prevailing police norms and practices, including the traditional opposition to women on patrol. These maverick officers lack unity, are still a minority, and are politically weak, due to their lack of seniority and status within the informal social structure; but they are present and visible, nevertheless.

Washington's male officers fit into one of three general categories with respect to policewomen: traditionals, moderates, and moderns. (This typology is based on the attitudes policemen expressed during my participant observation phase, on interview responses to a direct question about the assignment of women to patrol work, and on my observation of their behavior toward female officers.) A traditional policeman expresses the belief that women do not belong on patrol and that those on patrol should be protected and treated as junior partners. A modern officer expresses willingness and shows the ability to work with a female officer as an equal. The moderate expresses neither strongly negative nor strongly positive feelings toward policewomen or displays ambivalence about their use on patrol.

The men's attitudes ranged from strong opposition to the use of women in any aspect of police work (except clerical tasks) to strong support for the assignment of policewomen to all police duties; most men fall somewhere toward the former end of the continuum. Their attitudes regarding the role of women in policing appear to be closely associated with a number of other attitudes, including their evaluation of the women currently in the department and district; a more general view of the "appropriate" social role for women; their degree of acceptance of widespread changes in sex role norms; and their conception of the police officer's role.

Traditionals

The traditional men are tied emotionally and politically to the police subculture. They emphasize the adversarial and enforcement aspects of the role, and value "good" arrests and aggressive policing. This increases the dangerous, physically demanding aspects of the work and reinforces the subcultural stress on trust and cooperation. Since women are physically weaker and "different" from men, their presence on patrol is strongly opposed. The traditionals object to the women's lack of aggressiveness, undependability, low arrest rate, and physical weakness.

Beneath their rational arguments is a view of men and women that emphasizes their dissimilarities, and the men's desire to remain in a "man's world," keeping women "in their place." Policewomen threaten this world, and the men's perceptions of themselves, leading to frustration and diffuse anger expressed by one policeman in the following terms:

> The women want special treatment, special assignments. . . . They're not as good as the males. The majority are not as aggressive. . . . It's not just fighting. . . . They don't want to do too much. The majority do the least they can . . . which is not different from the young male officers.
>
> The output today is no comparison with what it was five years ago. Then they did twice as much work. . . . I had to work to get a car; it wasn't given on seniority.
>
> The police department hasn't paid the price for policewomen yet; they'll pay it before it's over with. . . . Why do they have a women's coordinator for their problems? They are policemen; why are they different? Why don't they have a coordinator for me? Why are they different? 'Cause they found out that they're not working.

The traditional policemen are on the defensive. They see their subculture, values, and manner of policing threatened by changes. They are angry and resentful at both the sexual and racial integration of the police department, which they feel have resulted in lowered standards and status for the police.[16] They resent the presence of "outsiders" who disrupt their world, and cannot be integrated into the existing group. When white traditionals are assigned to work with black females (in accordance with the department's integration policy) their anger sometimes appears doubled.

These members of the old guard lament the "deterioration" of the department and the passing of the "good old days." They look back ruefully to the time they could get into a "good" fight without fearing charges of police brutality. Several traditionals were critical not only of the women, but of the newer male officers as well, whom they labeled "part men" because they are not inclined to fight like the older generation.

Most of the traditionals are white officers with at least several years of experience in the department. For some black policemen, the job

---

16. Alex (1976) observed this anger in New York's white male officers.

enhances their sense of manhood to such an extent that they, too, strongly oppose women in policing as a threat to their work role and occupational self-image. But a much smaller percentage of black officers are traditionals because the blacks tend to be the newer, younger officers, and also because blacks, generally excluded from the police subcultural world, have adopted a somewhat different, less adversarial, view of the police role and the officers' relationship to the community. Those with a more service-oriented concept of police work see it as more appropriate for women.

Moderns

At the opposite end of the spectrum are the modern policemen who react favorably to the presence of policewomen. They appear to feel little need to prove their manhood by heroic feats and, like many men who came of age in the late 1960's, include in their definition of masculinity, sensitivity to the needs of individuals and the community. They agree with the traditionals that policewomen are less aggressive in many situations but rather than viewing this as a liability, regard aggressiveness as undesirable in many situations. They attribute policewomen's lack of assertiveness to a lack of self-confidence, opportunity, and experience, all of which can be overcome in time. One noted, "After several months women learn how things work and handle things as well as a male officer . . . or better, although it takes more time for them to adapt."

Several moderns have sought out female partners because they believe that the women are more empathetic and tactful with citizens and, at the same time, will act as a restraining influence on their own behavior. One officer who has frequently worked with two police-women, either of whom he would welcome as a permanent partner, said:

> Working with women has taught me to talk with people rather than fight because in certain situations, where it seemed we might have to fight, I'd be more inclined to keep talking to avoid getting my rear end kicked.

Another modern, addressing the often heard argument that police-women are physically unfit for the job, noted, "The physical aspect of this job is overblown. . . . Most of police work is writing reports and talking to citizens, not moving pianos." In a similar vein, an official noted that he welcomed policewomen because they were helping to eliminate the old stereotype of the police officer who was "long on brawn and short on brains."

Other moderns, while not outspoken advocates of policewomen, displayed an openness to and acceptance of female officers on an individual basis. Less rigid in their sex role attitudes and apparently more secure in their manhood than traditionals, they tended to accept the principles of equality of opportunity and were inclined to judge an officer on performance regardless of sex:

> Some women should and some women shouldn't [be on patrol]. Some are here only for the money, although that's one of my primary interests. Many are lazy. A few can handle their own share. . . . I judge each woman on her merits. It depends on the individual woman. If a new one came in tomorrow, I'd have to get my opinion of her first hand.

> If a policewoman can't pull her share of the weight, I don't want to deal with her. If any officer doesn't carry his share I feel the same way. . . . A person doesn't have to be big to fight . . . but if the opportunity arises it is important to show that you'll go to war if necessary. The women have a stick, mace and gun same as I have and they should be able to use them effectively . . . and if they do I don't have to worry. . . . I don't want to single women out; men panic under stress situations and don't act.

Related to a modern sex role perspective is the officer's view of civil rights. Many of the blacks who are racially militant support the inclusion of policewomen as a matter of principle, maintaining that everyone should have the opportunity to hold any job for which they are qualified. While some were critical of the women's performance, they supported their right to be on patrol. One man supported the inclusion of females as an expedient for accelerating the achievement of racial equality in the department. Another noted:

> I'm in a minority so I know how it feels to face discrimination and be disliked. I can't see myself denying someone the same right and opportunity I've been fighting for. It's in the Constitution and someone finally had enough sense to understand it. . . . As far as confidence in whether she'd back me up, I have the same confidence in a female as I do in a male. I don't trust too many people. I rely on myself. I don't look for people to back me up. . . .
>
> Some women function well; others don't. . . . That's not discrimination because it's the same with men. . . . I go out of my way to show I do not discriminate.

Most moderns believe that women will foster desirable changes in the police role (e.g., less hostility to the community and less aggressive policing); in the public image of the police; and in the department (breaking down patterns of discrimination and subcultural solidarity resting on the "buddy system"). Other moderns are open to change, including changing sex role behavior, without advocating major departmental changes; they are willing and able to accept women as coworkers on an equal basis, without threat, and appear less concerned with a disruption of the group since they are less tied to it, emotionally and politically, either out of choice or out of newness.

Moderns typically are the junior male officers who joined the department subsequent to the use of patrolwoman. Some regard the presence of policewomen as a matter of course. They include both black and white officers in their ranks, although the proportion of blacks who are moderns is greater. A small group, several are vocal and outspoken mavericks on several departmental questions, including the policewomen issue, and thus have visibility beyond their actual numbers.

Moderates

The moderates are a larger group than the moderns, and consist of two variant types. One has accepted, in principle, women's right to equality of opportunity in policing, but is uncomfortable with policewomen performing patrol duties. The other openly expresses dislike of policewomen, but willingly accepts some women whom they staunchly support under certain circumstances.

The feelings of the first type of moderate are ambivalent:

> Obviously women can do the same as men but aren't as strong. This does not disqualify them because most of the time it's not physical. Most of the time we're social workers and marriage counselors and so on, so women should be just as able to do the work as the men. . . . I've never had a bad encounter with a woman [never gotten into a fight while working with a female partner]. . . .At heart I'm a chavinist. . . . I still feel that women might get hurt before a man although I say they're capable of performing the same job.

> A woman has a right to work anywhere she feels capable of working. . . . If a woman feels she can be a policewoman, she has the right to do so, irregardless, although there is a realistic side to anything. . . . In a one-on-one situation we all know that there's no woman who can really best a man and therefore I think that in districts where you have a lot of fights . . . [audible sigh] . . . I don't know. . . . I think it would be very

difficult for a woman . . . but I still think if she thinks she can handle it, she has the right to have a job. There are a lot of sorry guys out here . . . guys who can't handle themselves, so it's just a matter—it's a job —you have a right to it—and I will do everything I can with any woman to see that she enjoys her right to work where she wants to. . . . When I work with women I treat them as equals straight down the line. . . . The men harass them and make them feel uneasy. . . . I sympathize with the women and make an extra effort to . . . make them feel needed in the car. . . . I try to teach them what to do and all I know.

Both of these men are experienced, service-oriented, black officers who desire a change in the police relationship to the community and are not part of the police subculture's "in group."

The other type of moderate displayed the "Pygmalion effect": while highly critical of policewomen in general, he was favorably disposed to and complimentary toward specific protégés whom he viewed as outstanding or exceptional officers. For example, one man said:

Women can learn to act decisively if they have a good teacher . . . someone with their interests really at heart and if they have that desire and do not distinguish between the sexes on the job [ask for special consideration because they're female]. For that reason C—— is the best woman on the department. I taught her—trained her by riding that kid real hard; now no policewoman can hold a candle to her. . . . The average woman on the department is not much good. . . . All the girls I had were good; I trained them.

It is likely that a number of the men whose statements appear "modern" share the moderates' reservations about patrolwomen but responded with an "acceptable" answer rather than expressing their feelings or discussing their actual behavior; it was not possible for me to observe their behavior in the lockerroom, or among "the boys" who dominate the informal social structure, since I was an outsider both as a female and as a reserve. Nonetheless the male officers no longer speak with a single voice, and some, particularly the department's critics and younger men with an altered view of masculinity and femininity, express greater willingness to accept women as patrol officers and work colleagues.

SUMMARY

Traditionally the police have developed a well-defined work ethos and closed occupational brotherhood with an emphasis on solidarity and interdependence—based in large part on their shared sense of masculinity. As a result, policewomen face staunch opposition as they seek to enter the ranks of patrol officers. The men's opposition to the sexual integration of the workplace is magnified by the physical aspects of the work, the need to act with authority, the predominantly working-class views of male and female social roles, and the status insecurity prevalent among policemen.

The entry of female officers threatens to disrupt both the prevalent norms and the group solidarity of the policemen. Physical differences between the sexes become a central focus of concern. Underlying the arguments about women's physical characteristics, however, is the men's fear that women will fail to uphold the norms of policing, thus making their work more difficult and dangerous, and less rewarding. Yet they also fear that if women do fulfill the norms, the meaning of masculinity and femininity become blurred. If women can perform in the role of "policeman" (a word which blends occupational and sex roles) the defining social characteristics of an officer and a man are no longer exclusively his; women threaten the men's sense of their own masculine identity.

Female officers also threaten the cohesiveness of the work group by altering the rules by which officers relate to and compete with each other; affecting the expressive use of "male" language; raising the spectre of bonds of sexual intimacy between officers, which would compete with the demands of loyalty to the group; and forcing the men to relate to women in unfamiliar ways.

Although there is growing diversity of opinion among the policemen with regard to patrolwomen, most officers today hold traditional views of sex role norms which make policing a "wrong" occupation for women. A number of policemen, nevertheless, have "modern" or "moderate" views of policewomen. While most are not anxious to work with women, a number, particularly the black men, accept an ideology—equality of opportunity—which cannot be denied to women; others support policewomen as a means to accelerate desired changes in the department.

Chapter 5

Structural Barriers: Socialization and Departmental Policies and Their Implications for Policewomen

How do the official policies of the police department and the informal practices of policemen create opportunities for or throw up barriers to the integration of women into police work? This chapter and the next examine, respectively, the structural or organizational, and the interpersonal factors that make "breaking and entering" different for male and female officers, so that functioning effectively as an officer is more difficult for women. The focus of this chapter is the impact of organizational policies on the socialization of new officers, and the distribution of assignments, both of which affect an officer's opportunities for success. These issues illustrate two important problems faced not only by police departments but many institutions in our society: How to recognize that women are different from men without implying that the former are inferior, and how to meet the needs of both male and female officers while assuring equality of opportunity for all.

Since late 1971 when the first policewomen were assigned to patrol, the Metropolitan Police Department has officially adhered to a policy of treating female and male officers the same. The attempt to minimize or ignore sex and sex differences, including "irreducible" differences (physical and physiological) between men and women, was viewed as both legally correct and the most expedient way of assimilating female officers into patrol.

This policy has had mixed results. Many of the problems initially encountered by the new policewomen have been eliminated and major strides toward their assimilation have been made. At the same time, the policy which appears to be sex neutral in fact puts the burden for being different on the women. By treating them exactly the same as the men (without any change in the manner in which men are treated) the department has failed to recognize and directly confront both a number of deeply entrenched sex-differentiated patterns of behavior that are widespread in our society, and the few irreducible differences between the sexes. In adopting an assimilation model the department implies that the women must be like the men and where there are differences, it is the women who must change to overcome the handicaps imposed by their prior experience, the men's attitudes, and department policy.

WOMEN ON PATROL:
THE EXPERIMENTAL PHASE

Between 1918 and 1967 all policewomen in Washington, D.C., were assigned to the Women's Bureau. In 1967 Congress reorganized the department and combined the women with the male officers of the Juvenile Bureau into the newly formed Youth Division.[1] The reorganization and attendant loss of female leadership and organizational autonomy produced a strong negative reaction among the female officers. Many newer policewomen resigned; those eligible to retire did so.[2]

In 1969 the newly appointed chief, Jerry Wilson, indicated his determination to utilize policewomen throughout the department, including the patrol division. Over the next two years, approximately one hundred new female officers were hired and assigned to all units but patrol. During that period all entrance requirements were equalized and guidelines for the interchangeable assignment of male and female officers were issued. Early in 1971, however, when it became apparent that implementation of the policewomen's program was lagging, the chief made its implementation a policy of highest priority (Wilson, 1975) and soon appointed a new policewomen's coordinator to oversee the fulfillment of his policy.

1. The rationale of Congress in disbanding the Women's Bureau was "to free policewomen from duties which are the responsibility of other agencies" (Milton, 1972:9).

2. By 1971 only eight of the thirty-five women in the Women's Bureau at the time of reorganization remained in the department.

When the women's long-awaited uniforms arrived in December 1971, about thirty women were reassigned to patrol[3] They were given the choice of a patrol assignment in the district where they had been working, or in one of the two "experimental" districts to which all new policewomen were initially assigned. The only special preparation for women reassigned to patrol work was a week of retraining at the academy.

Because Chief Wilson viewed the assignment of women to patrol as an experiment, he arranged for an evaluation study of the women's performance by the Urban Institute (see Bloch and Anderson, 1974a and 1974b and Bloch et al., 1973a and 1973b) and deferred merging entry lists for men and women until the women's performance had been evaluated. The chief authorized the recruitment of one hundred additional policewomen, and between April and October 1972, eighty-six were hired for patrol duties.

Recruiters were instructed to be "brutally honest" to effect self-screening among applicants. No special training was offered to the newly hired women beyond what all rookies received at the academy.[4] Following training, the new female recruits were assigned to the two "experimental" districts: an equal number of male rookies were assigned to two "comparison" districts for purposes of evaluation. In April 1972, as the women began to enter the districts, the chief issued clear new guidelines requiring equal assignments for male and female officers.

Implementation of the equal treatment policy was left in the hands of district supervisors, some of whom were strongly opposed to the use of women on patrol and who permitted their subordinates to un-

3. One factor that hindered the assignment of policewomen to patrol until late 1971 was their lack of a uniform. Chief Wilson noted, "Exemplifying the tendency of minutiae to become substance, more time was spent on the selection of a proper uniform for policewomen than any other aspect of the program" (Wilson, 1975:188). In 1969 a committee of policewomen selected a design for a uniform which was rejected by the chief because it resembled that of an airlines stewardess and was not practical for street patrol. Instead, the chief had the department's property division order a WAVE-type uniform which took months to arrive.

4. It is not clear why no additional training either for the women or their male supervisors or coworkers was instituted; sensitivity training seminars were used when a policy of racial integration of scout cars was adopted. It may be that the policewomen's coordinator did not view such training as necessary or advisable. In retrospect, however, she noted that the lack of special training was the major shortcoming of the policewomen's program.

dermine the guidelines. Obvious attempts to treat policewomen differently from male officers were immediately apparent and corrected by the chief's office;[5] other practices were more subtle and went undetected or uncorrected. From their examination of departmental assignment records, Bloch and Anderson (1974a:11) found that the guidelines were "reasonably well observed during the first six to eight months of the program." Several "experimental" policewomen, however, noted that in reality the women often did not receive the same initial on-the-job instruction as male officers, that their assignments were changed during a tour of duty, and that they faced a great deal of informal opposition and harassment.[6] Discriminatory practices and harassment often did not come to the attention of higher ranking officials because many of the women feared complaining to their immediate supervisors (who often were discriminatory themselves):

> In those days if you were denied something and you wanted to challenge it, you didn't. . . . You didn't dare question or say anything . . . there was no union, no EEO officer. . . . Oh, you could say what you wanted but who'd investigate? Who was there to do anything? . . . Besides, I didn't say anything about lots of situations because I couldn't afford any kind of labels; not as a chicken, not as a complainer or crybaby, or anything.

In February 1973, the Urban Institute issued its preliminary finding, on the basis of an average of four months of patrol experience for the new women and the comparison group of men, concluding that while there were some differences in the performance of female and male rookies, the women were functioning adequately (Bloch et al.,

5. An example of such differential treatment was the practice of informing the dispatcher that a police car was "10-4w" (i.e., a two-officer car with one woman officer) rather than simply "10-4" (i.e., a two-officer car).

6. One policewoman in one of the experimental districts noted that she had not been assigned to work in a scout car, or instructed by a training officer during her certification period in the same way as were male rookies in the district. On occasions she was assigned to a footbeat with a partner, but after 45 minutes of walking the sergeant would invite her partner to ride in the sergeant's car for the rest of the day, while she remained on the footbeat, sometimes alone, sometimes with a new partner. On other occasions she was assigned to work alone on the patrol wagon transporting prisoners despite departmental rules that two officers must be assigned to the wagon. Other women in the experimental group reported having been assigned to work with officers who refused to speak with them during their eight-hour shift. Generally, they observed that a few "favored" women got regular station assignments; the majority were left to "sink or swim" on the street with little instruction or assistance. Similar complaints about discrimination in assignments, hostile partners, and some harassment were reported when the scout cars were racially integrated.

1973b).[7] As a result of this report the chief merged eligibility lists and declared that the policewomen on patrol experiment had been successful.[8] In April 1973 the minimum height requirement was lowered from five feet seven inches to five feet, expanding the pool of eligible female recruits, as a new generation of policewomen was hired and assigned to patrol duties in all districts.

Although the experimental stage ended with a declaration of the success of the first generation of policewomen, an increase in the number of female officers, and a grudging acceptance of their presence as a "fact of life," a number of problems for the women, their male coworkers and the department have persisted.

Many of these problems emanate from the nature of the work, which calls for behavior characterized as "masculine" and the ambiguous and often contradictory expectations facing the women. On the one hand, the department officially treats the female officers like male officers which, in certain instances, overlooks obvious differences between men and women. On the other hand, the women do not act like the men, nor do the male officers have the same expectations of them or treat them as they treat male officers.

7. The initial report found that the women got substantially the same assignments and same types of calls as the comparison men. They made about the same number of felony arrests, but more new policewomen than comparison men had made no felony arrests. The women made fewer misdemeanor arrests and issued fewer moving-violation tickets than comparison men. In addition, the new women were more likely to be given instructions by partners and were less likely to "take charge" at an incident. From the limited number of situations involving violence or the potential for violence there appeared to be no difference in the performance of the new male and female officers. Nevertheless, in an anonymous survey of officials, the women were rated as less competent than the men.

8. The Urban Institute continued to gather data on the policewomen program until August 1973 and issued its final report in May 1974. That report, supporting the preliminary findings of the previous year, stated, "The study shows that sex is not a bona fide occupational qualification for doing patrol work" (Bloch and Anderson, 1974:3). The report looked at assignments, performance and attitudes. Specifically, it found that the new women were less frequently assigned to patrol, less often put in one-officer cars, and more often given station duty. It found many performance similarities between the new women and comparison men, including the results of their handling angry or violent citizens, level of respect officers displayed toward citizens, use of sick leave, and resignation rate. The men had higher rates of felony and misdemeanor arrests and issued more traffic citations; higher performance ratings in handling various violent situations and in general competence to perform street patrol; and more frequent charges of serious unbecoming conduct. The report also found that most patrolwomen felt their patrol skills were as good as patrolmen's, but that the men and the officials doubted that women were equal to the men in most patrol skills.

SOCIALIZATION

Becoming a police officer is a gradual process consisting of several stages during which individuals are socialized, i.e., acquire values, attitudes, interests, skills, and knowledge. Among the stages of socialization for new officers are a preliminary period of "anticipatory socialization," including recruitment; formal training at the police academy; a period of certification, during which the rookie enters a district and faces the "reality shock" of street patrol; and a final "metamorphosis" as he or she gradually adopts the attitudes and behaviors of the seasoned officers, which usually occurs by the sixth month of street experience (Van Maanen, 1975).

Anticipatory Socialization

Anticipatory socialization is a process in which one "tries on" a role and/or adopts the values of the group to which he or she aspires but does not belong. It is important, since it permits individuals to enter an occupational training program or role with some understanding (and some misconceptions) about the role and group to which they aspire; aids movement into the group; and eases adjustments to it. The amount and kind of anticipatory socialization an individual experiences prior to entry into policing (or another occupation) varies widely. Van Maanen (1975), for example, found that fully 80 percent of the trainees in his sample had a good friend or relative already in police work. These experienced officers provided information and encouragement and served as role models to some prospective officers; lengthy acquaintance probably permitted considerable anticipatory socialization so that the "reality shock" of the academy and street patrol were reduced, and adjustment to the role was eased.

Among the officers in the present study only twelve of twenty-eight women and twelve of twenty-seven men had relatives or friends who provided information about policing, or encouraged them to join the police department. For all of the women, these acquaintances were males, and several were men they were dating. For some, their tales of bravado and adventure stimulated interest in police work; one woman noted that her boyfriend had bought her a police radio, but opposed her plan to apply for a job in the department, since "he has no use for policewomen." One other female officer said she was influenced by a policewoman who spoke at her high school. The woman became her role model but was not a personal acquaintance.

The anticipatory socialization of policewomen is generally less lengthy and intense than that of the men. While many little boys play "cops and robbers," few girls do. Similarly, teenage fantasies of heroism, courage, and physical combat are more common among boys, who usually spend more time considering occupational options, including policing. Neither actual nor media role models of female officers were available to young women until the mid-1970's, whereas the policeman has long been a visible media hero. The greater number of females than males who entered policing with "indifferent" occupational role perspectives (see chapter 3) points to this lack of anticipatory socialization for women entering policing.

Their prior work experience had better prepared the men for police work; seven of the twenty-seven men in the sample, but none of the women, had served in the military, and thereby gained experience with military discipline, chain of command, and definition of themselves as "men's men." Several other male recruits worked in "men's jobs," such as construction and truckdriving, and if they were unfamiliar with policing, they had become acquainted with the work and values of blue-collar men. The women came from the white-collar world of the female officer-worker.

The system of recruitment, too, has traditionally selected men who possess the "mark of affinity," a particular view of their own masculinity that enables them to immediately "fit" into the informal social world of police. As yet there are no comparably clear standards for the female recruit since, by definition, women do not "fit." Thus, men and women enter the police academy not only with different degrees of anticipatory socialization, but with different work experiences, skills, and personal characteristics—which, as will be shown, gives the male recruit a clear-cut early advantage.

The Training Academy

Officers' formal socialization to police work begins at the training academy. There, in addition to instruction in the law, departmental regulations, official standards of morality, and technical police procedures, officers encounter the covert curriculum which exposes them to actual police standards and values, paramilitary discipline, and the importance of group solidarity. The training is geared to stripping the newcomers of old attitudes and impressing them with their new identity as a member of the police fraternity. While not as total an experience as military basic training, the police academy shares with basic training its functions as a rite of passage, and a carefully executed process intended to break down civilian patterns and perceptions. It also begins replacing them with the goals and perspectives of the new organization, including a strong emphasis on social solidarity with the group and the shaping of "male" officers whose sex role identity fits the organizational image.

How does the training process differentially affect men and women who enter the academy? How do prior life experiences benefit male and handicap female recruits? Women, particularly those from working-class backgrounds, have been socialized to be "little ladies." While they may be experienced in verbal manipulation, most have neither learned to be physically assertive, nor had experience in defending themselves. As children, boys learn how to defend themselves in the face of threats both on and off the playing field; those who do not are "sissies." Girls are more likely to turn to a protector (usually a parent, brother, or teacher), employ tears or other manipulative devices, or rely on the other's respect for themselves as "ladies" when they are physically threatened. In male-female relationships girls learn to follow rather than lead, and suggest rather than command. They learn to speak politely and avoid challenging or insulting others wherever possible.

For an adolescent male, a car and a gun are especially revered objects because of their close association with manhood. Boys are more likely than girls to have tinkered with cars and developed driving skills, and to have gone hunting and used firearms. Such prior experiences make the acquisition of driving and shooting skills easier and more "natural" for male recruits, and may explain the greater length of time required by female recruits to qualify in these "manly" activities.

Prior athletic and body-building experiences magnify the obvious biological differences between the sexes. Participation in a contact sport such as football, for example, introduces males to many of the elements found in the police subculture: controlled use of violence, teamwork and group loyalty, memorization of codes, uniform behavior, experience with personal pain, a willingness to inflict pain on others, "dirty tricks," and authoritarianism (Gray, 1975). Few of the females in the study who had participated in athletics were involved in contact sports (several mentioned gymnastics and others track). During adolescence, female popularity is not associated with being an athlete, but with leading others in cheering for the male athletes, or being the girlfriend of the sports hero. Smallness and delicacy are esteemed female qualities; boys are admired if they are big and strong. Adolescent social development magnifies adolescent physical development and increases the differences between the sexes. This places women entering the police academy at a disadvantage, and later affects several facets of police work.

Differences in skeletal structure and body tissues enable the average man to run faster, jump higher, and lift heavier weights than the average woman, making the development of a training program that would be equitable for all officers very difficult. In recent years the department has changed its physical training standards several times in an attempt to develop a program that is relevant to the job, rigorous enough for both sexes, and does not disqualify women.

Although it has moved to a modular system of individual academic instruction (a device which permits recruits with widely varied reading and writing skills to move at their own pace, ostensibly maintains standards, and eases some of the tensions of racial integration), there has been little or no alteration in the overall content of the training program and no effort to gear it to the areas of knowledge and ignorance of the new recruits.

Training may foster inequality in a number of subtle ways. Some women encourage coddling or seek exemptions, and are passed on to the next stage because the instructors are either protective or unable to deal with some of the women's manipulative efforts to avoid meeting physical standards. When the women cry, whine, flirt, say "I can't," or claim a medical exemption, many instructors "let them slide." As a result, rather than learning the lesson of group loyalty and "suffering in silence" which builds solidarity, some women are permitted to be "different," leading to further resentment of their presence on the force.

The general failure of police training programs to focus on and develop interpersonal skills so necessary in police work also negatively affects women rookies. Training neither builds on, nor calls attention in a positive way to those skills in which women often surpass men. Failure to provide an opportunity to recognize and alter the ways in which officers' attitudes, feelings, and habits of interaction affect their work perpetuates tension and hostility, directed at the female officers. When the department racially integrated scout cars it recognized that many stereotypes, myths, and misunderstandings prevailed in race relations, and initiated a training program to confront such issues. No analogous attempt to overcome the barriers to male-female understanding occurred when women entered patrol work.

Because males and females grow up together and live together in what appears to be a sex-integrated society, it is assumed that they share knowledge and understanding of each other. Evidence increasingly suggests, however, that there are different male and female worlds and that each sex perceives and experiences life differently (Bernard, 1978). Policewomen entering male turf are expected to do so in male terms, yet the problems they face in assimilating and the strengths they bring from their own world and experiences are ignored.

There was almost unanimous agreement among officers that the academic aspects of the academy training were unbiased presumably because an individualized module system was used. In physical training, however, the men and women performed differently and, as a result, were treated differently. This created a cycle of differing expectations which led in circular fashion to different behavior, which again reinforced different expectations—thus handicapping policewomen from the start.

Currently all rookies run, swim, exercise, and take self-defense training together. The present requirements for men and women differ in that women do modified push-ups, fewer pull-ups, and are given more time to run the obstacle course. (The initial group of female patrol officers had to fulfill the same physical requirements as the men.)

Physical training is problematic for several reasons: the training standards are ambiguous; what constitutes valid job-related training and how much general "conditioning" is necessary are unclear (particularly in view of the department's failure to maintain physical standards, except a weight maximum, after officers leave the academy); and some women seek and receive exemptions from departmental requirements. The training policy has divided policewomen into two groups. One, feeling that the requirements are set too high and are unrelated to street patrol duties, seeks exemptions. The other, determined to fulfill all the requirements (even if they are arbitrary), is angry at the women who seek lower standards. The women's performance in physical training undermines the confidence of some male recruits in their female colleagues' ability to carry out patrol duties, and adhere to all-important norms of group loyalty and backing-up a partner.

The women disagreed about the standards that should be applied, those that actually were applied when they were in the academy, and the appropriate behavior of female recruits during the training at the academy. Some of the female recruits expected preferential training:

> They wanted us to do men's style push-ups. That's ridiculous! J—— wanted to compete with the men but we couldn't so it didn't bother me not to keep up. I could be counted on to bring up the rear—five minutes behind everyone—in running. . . . We weren't physically able to do what was required of us.

Other women were angry that some women sought and received exemptions. They felt a greater obligation to "carry the standard" and prove that the exemption seekers were the exceptions:

> In p.t. women got off easier but four women in my class refused to accept different standards for women. We proved we could keep up with the standards they expected for the men. We refused to hang back in running. The recruits had to run a mile a day. The women pretended they couldn't run it, that they were feeble. They said they couldn't keep the pace so they were allowed to run behind. We thought, "that's a bunch of crap." I felt that if I could do it, and I was smoking a pack a day, there was no reason any other women couldn't keep up with me. . . . Every one of them should have been able to.

> Some women tried to be treated differently in p.t. That pissed me off because it reflected on me. I tried to keep up with the men. I can't run but I kept trying. The other women were angry at me because they wanted an excuse for not trying and didn't want any woman to excel because they'd lose their excuse.

Several male officers complained that in the academy their female partners resented their roughness during self-defense exercises: they said they were merely preparing themselves and their partner for the realities of street fighting. Were they deliberately being rougher with female partners to hurt or embarrass them, as some women alleged, or were they acting as they would with a male partner? Were the women complaining about particularly rough, or "normal" treatment, from which they expected to be excused? The answers are impossible to determine, but it is clear that such situations led to tension, misunderstanding, complaints, and divisiveness—rather than the sense of group solidarity and shared masculine toughness that other recruits got from the police academy (Harris, 1973; Van Maanen, 1975), or basic training in the armed forces (Arkin and Dobrovsky, 1978).

The men who had difficulties meeting the physical requirements were silent, probably embarrassed, and treated as individuals rather than as typical of any class or group. Women who had similar difficulties, in many cases, were permitted to exert less effort and/or were passed on without meeting the requirements; they were perceived to be typical of women and were criticized as females rather than as individuals. At the same time, instructors who believed that they were helping the women by permitting some to manipulate and whine their way around requirements perpetuated a reliance on traditional female behavior, employed a double standard, and fostered (although they did not create) a division among the women over appropriate occupational role behavior and attitudes.

Issues related to physical differences, including the maintenance of physical fitness and athletic participation, continue to have significance beyond the academy. The department makes the academy gym and facilities available to all officers and has established rooms for weight-lifting in the stationhouses. In addition, within each district and division there are seasonal athletic teams and intra- and inter-unit leagues. Policewomen are ambivalent about athletic participation and the use of the weight rooms. An attempt to organize a women's softball league failed, despite the high proportion of interested women, due to the small number of women in one district and difficulties in scheduling practices and games. Although in some instances women have been permitted to join the men's teams, those few that did so found themselves warming the bench. One woman commented:

> The guys don't want the women to play. . . . It's very competitive and they want to win. . . . Women play a different calibre of ball and should have their own teams . . . after all, I want to win sometimes, too.

Making the team (not all men who try out do) enhances a man's status within the department, strengthening interpersonal ties and one's reputation as a team player, as well as someone whose physical abilities are "certified." Since athletic achievement is esteemed as a sign of masculinity, participation contributes to a man's sense of male identity.

The use of the weight rooms similarly causes discomfort for the women but not the men. These rooms are even more clearly "male turf" than the stationhouse itself. In lifting weights a woman may gain a sense of physical well-being and enhance her physical skills as an officer, but she does so at the expense of "womanliness" since a muscular woman is viewed as unfeminine. For a man, in addition to occupational benefits, there are social rewards. Within the department, and the society, the ability to press two hundred pounds is a source of pride, and the muscular build that results is valued as sexually attractive.

Certification and Street Patrol

Following the completion of the academy training rookies, assigned to a district, face the "reality shock" of street patrol. In the Metropolitan Police Department they begin an apprenticeship period known as certification, during which they are trained by seasoned officers before being permitted to patrol alone. During this period, usually between eight and fourteen weeks, rookies learn the basic norms and values of policing. They discover that the best way to survive is to stay out of trouble ("don't make waves") and to express acceptance of the organization. They learn when and how to cut corners and evade certain rules; they begin to view citizens as hostile and the police as an oppressed minority.

The early months in the district are very important to the fledgling officer because the reputation made during the first months on the job will follow an officer for the rest of his or her career. A rookie who shows good judgment and takes initiative will win the confidence of trainers and peers, who will increasingly provide feedback on her or his performance, and impart the tricks of the trade. Rookies who do not appear to be "police material," including those who are shy or self-conscious, those who do not follow the norms, and those who acquire reputations as complainers, are not likely to get adequate instruction. Those who avoid making mistakes or causing problems by policing passively are quickly regarded as unreliable, stupid, or disinterested in the work and receive little assistance from more experienced officers. For a rookie the road to success is to ask a question rather than remain silent, and to do something, even if it is wrong, rather than do nothing.

The assignments a new officer receives and the training officers with whom the rookie works during certification are important in creating opportunities for learning and gaining self-confidence. Insufficient instruction or opportunities to learn have a multiplier effect, because once established, habits and reputations are difficult to change. If an officer feels limited by discrimination (whether real or not) or rejected by those with whom he or she must work, the result will be ego-protective indifference, demoralization, and demotivation for the majority, and a redoubling of effort on the part of a few.

Westley (1970) found that the rookies were surprised and pleased by the warm reception they received upon entering the district. This accelerated their assimilation of the attitudes and behaviors of experienced officers. In this study the majority of the men were quite positive about their initial training. Most worked with a variety of officers, felt free to ask questions, and got little or no hazing; after an initial period of watching and listening rather passively, they "found" their own style, selecting what they admired from the training officers and gaining self-confidence from actually handling a variety of situations. Several mentioned fights or arrests that occurred during the first weeks in the district which had enabled them to prove themselves. None said he had been told to remain in the scout car when a problem arose, although several were critical of officers who taught them little or nothing. Only one mentioned hostility from training officers, which was directed at rookies in general. Several who characterized themselves as "shy" noted that they had received inadequate feedback on their performance, inadequate instruction, and had felt unhappy because they had initially been regarded as disinterested or aloof, making acceptance difficult. One male officer noted that his certification period had been extended, a signal of initial failure, and explained:

> I'm shy and wouldn't speak out or say I wanted to handle a situation. If they'd ask me I'd say "yes" but I figured they knew what I was there for. . . . I waited for instructions; they waited for my questions. I didn't know what was going on and if they didn't take any action . . . I went along with them. Now I know better. I missed a lot of things because I wasn't exposed to them. I worked with the sergeant for a while and asked questions about little things but the guys I worked with didn't bring lots of little things to my attention.

The initial reception of the women appears to have been less accepting, compounding the other obstacles and disadvantages faced by the women as a group. These included a lack of prior experience with street life; smaller size and less strength; the openly negative attitudes of male coworkers and supervisors; the "performance pressure" of being highly visible representatives of a group whose success depended on their ability to do well; and a double standard of behavior and evaluation.

While all officers must gain familiarity with new work situations and tasks, street patrol poses a greater hurdle for women since it is more of a leap into the unknown. Often sheltered from the violence and danger of street life, policewomen find themselves thrust into situations where they enter "tough" unfamiliar neighborhoods, deal with new kinds of people; they have to exercise their new authority to control unruly citizens. While such activities are both frightening and exciting, the job may initially appear to be overwhelming for an officer with little or no experience.

Cultural norms dictate that men must hide their fear of a frightening situation. Not permitted to whine "I'm scared" or "I don't want to do that" to a superior, they must remain silent, swallow hard and act. Otherwise they face humiliation for failure to "act like a man." Women, on the other hand, have been permitted a greater range of self-expression, and are allowed and expected to show fear. They are permitted to whine or cry and gain an exemption from duties felt to be too difficult or too fearful—as is sometimes said, "they're only girls." They are permitted and often encouraged to be helpless.

When confronted with self-doubts, the normative patterns for men's and women's behavior are different: men are more inclined to act; women to avoid. A police officer by definition cannot refuse to act out of fear although some do. The job demands that the officer deal with threatening situations that others cannot legally handle themselves. New policewomen must therefore learn new patterns of behavior. Those like Ann (see chapter 1) who grew up in the inner city, and had experienced unpleasant, terrifying incidents during her childhood, tended to have an easier adjustment than those who had never previously encountered such situations.

The men's opposition to female patrol officers compounds the women's other difficulties; it probably most strongly affects a new, often fearful woman officer. The men's attitudes pressure the women and effect a double standard; the performance of female rookies receives extra scrutiny, and any policewoman's failure is generalized to all women. One rookie male working with a new female officer insisted on driving because "she seemed nervous," assumed responsibility because "she messed up several radio runs," and noted, "the situation became a male-female thing." With male partners, the criticism is specific (i.e., the rookie male officer does not make a judgment about other males on the basis of a bad partner); with the female officer, however, it is generalized to all women. As with the policewoman's previous partners, the male officer in question prevented her assuming any responsibility, thus perpetuating her incompetence.

Several police officers noted the double standard for male and female competence and incompetence. One woman, referring to the practice of identifying officers who seem unsuited for the job, noted,

> a woman does not have to be as bad as a man for them to say she's no good. . . . With a man, he has to be a real dummy before they'll run him out. . . . They're more hesitant because they feel he has family responsibilities and his job is more important to him. . . . As if I didn't have to support myself and my son!

Conversely, as Ann noted:

> If you're a man and a police officer, it's accepted that you can do it. Nobody's watching to see if you can. . . . But if you're a woman, everybody's watching . . . and you have to do twice as much.

The competent woman, too, faces difficulties. Men often prefer to work with an incompetent woman rather than a capable one, because

> Men don't know how to deal with you when you're doing your job competently. They expect nothing from you and that's tolerated but if you do something, they don't know how to deal with or evaluate you.

In discussing their initial training period, the women's perceptions of their experiences varied widely. Some felt they were coddled and/or protected and resented it; others acknowledged a double standard and were appreciative. A few felt the initial treatment they received was, if anything, less sheltered than that of the men. Several of the more assertive female officers complained that they were initially over-protected. One noted that because she was "sick and tired of being babied" and not permitted to work alone, she obtained a transfer to the scooter squad where she was able to work independently, develop self-reliance, and pursue her own cases. Another woman, assigned to work alone in a scout car prior to certification due to a shortage of patrol officers, handled this solo assignment competently; but still had to repeatedly tell male officers not to respond when the radio sent her on a call unless she requested assistance.

The training officer's attitude toward women was mentioned by one female officer as an important factor during certification. Working with one particular male officer who had sought a female partner was much easier than with the others, because she knew "he didn't mind working with me. With the others you could feel the tension." She noted, too, that when she made arrests with an unsympathetic male partner, she would not get her share of the credit; the men took all the cases.

Other women were more accepting, and perhaps appreciative, of male protection, and did not try to change these interactions. Several indicated that they had been told by male partners to remain in the scout car during specific confrontation situations, and had done so. One woman's probationary year evaluation stated that she was "hesitant to take aggressive action," which she attributed to male partners' reluctance to permit her to assume an active police role. Even after complaining to her sergeant, who advised her to speak up and take more responsibility, the men expected little of her and she remained unassertive. She explained,

> When I ride with those veteran male officers and we walk up on a scene, they always take the action. As a matter of fact, when there was a fight going on . . . one hollered for me to stay in the car.

She noted that working with another woman was easier because they shared the work, and working alone was important because "that's where you gain your confidence . . . when you handle calls on your own and start using that authority." She added that since receiving the negative probationary year evaluation, "when I'm working with a veteran I try to get out of the car first and take the aggressive action before he does"; despite this effort on her part, the men continue to view her as a pleasant but far too unassertive officer.

This woman acted "naturally" for a woman by failing to "take aggressive action." For her and other policewomen, however, violating sex role norms is particularly difficult when they are compounded by norms regulating relations with respect to age and race as well as sex, as they were in this case.

ASSIGNMENTS

Evidence of Sex Discrimination

The assignments a rookie officer receives have a great impact on role learning; although the majority of officers have the same rank, work conditions and specific policing activities vary greatly. Officers' assignments strongly affect their attitudes toward work, the department, and themselves. Assignments have two different but related aspects: daily assignments, which are made during the roll call preceding each shift; and permanent assignments to a specific scout car, footbeat area, or a special nonpatrol unit such as a crime prevention unit or community relations.

Daily Assignments. When women were assigned to patrol duties in early 1972, the chief's guidelines (in effect until the end of 1972) forbade distinction by sex regarding assignments. Bloch and Anderson (1974b:11) found that for six to eight months, women were assigned to station duty about twice as frequently as a comparison group of men; for other types of assignments no differences were found. By mid-1973, when the guidelines were no longer in effect, new policewomen were assigned less frequently to two-officer or one-officer scout cars; they were more often assigned to station duty and to one-officer footbeats than the men (Bloch and Anderson, 1974b). Considered least desirable by police officers, such assignments offer fewer opportunities to handle the varied situations patrol officers must learn to cope with, and yield fewer arrests, an important criterion of officer productivity. One woman's description of her experience in the experimental district adds a qualitative dimension to Bloch's statistics:

> I had to walk all the time. I've been in situations when we were on midnights and it was ten degrees below zero, and I was made to walk even though there may have been only one guy in a scout car. . . . There were times I could have worked a scout car but I was denied that because the officer in the car didn't want to work with me . . . sometimes because I was black, others because I was a woman. . . . I had to always hope and pray that they'd work with me.

Although no assignment statistics were available for the district during my observation period, many officers indicated that a pattern similar to that found by Bloch and Anderson exists: women get more than their share of station duty and footbeat assignments, and only infrequent assignments to one-person scout cars compared with men of the same seniority.[9] When women are assigned to scout cars, they patrol beats in the quieter parts of the district rather than the higher crime areas. A recent study commissioned by the department con-

9. While some women are virtually never assigned to the station, a substantial proportion are regularly assigned there. Men outnumber women in the department by more than ten to one; if there are five officers assigned to the station (there tend to be four or five officers there each shift) and one is a woman, then women would do twice as much station duty as men—in practice at least one female officer is assigned to the station at all times.

firmed this observation and concluded that assignment patterns imply an unofficial attitude that "the women's place is in the stationhouse" (Coleman, 1978).[10]

The sergeants who make the daily assignments feel caught in a bind. On the one hand they are reluctant to assign policewomen to scout cars either alone or together and hesitate to put women in the more dangerous areas of the district. They rationalize their reluctance to put women together by saying it would be "bad deployment of personnel" and state their belief that women would face citizen harassment and greater danger. They are loathe to assign a policewoman to work alone in a busy scout car out of concern for her personal safety. (The less aggressive male officers are also put in quieter cars but are treated as individuals rather than as members of a larger group.) At the same time, the sergeants are obligated to treat the women no differently from the men and feel that since female officers receive the same pay as male officers, they should be assigned equal work. Expressing the sergeants' dilemma, one commented:

> I wish I could say I don't treat them differently. I try not to but I suppose I do unconsciously. I tend not to put them by themselves for everybody's good, so they won't get hurt. They're not as good on the street so I put them with more experienced officers.

Another said:

> I try to be as impartial as possible. Women are getting the same pay, they should be doing the same amount and type of work . . . but there are times when we all look out for a girl in a car by herself more than a male. . . . She's still a woman even if she's two hundred pounds and all muscle. She's still a woman. . . . She should be holding her end up but most can't.

Support for, or opposition to policewomen is not a determining factor in a sergeant's assignment policy. One sergeant, strongly opposed to policewomen on patrol, stated:

> I put those broads in the worst assignments; anywhere I'd put a man . . . and I'd put two together although I don't think too much of police-

10. A July 1978 study prepared for the department found that, although women comprise 8 percent of the officers assigned to the patrol districts, they receive 25 percent of the station assignments. The study also found a disproportionate number of white officers assigned to the district with a white middle-class neighborhood and black officers disproportionately assigned to districts with poor black populations. Women were distributed equally among the districts (Coleman, 1978).

women. . . . Most of them sit on the passenger side of the car and just look out the window.

For weeks during my period of observation one woman worked evening and midnight shifts alone on a footbeat in a high crime area, while two male officers patrolled a lower crime rate beat together. This continued until several officers complained about it to the lieutenant. The policewoman's assignments resulted from personal hostility on the part of one sergeant, who insisted that since men walk alone, this woman could do the same. Other officers, however, observed that men generally did not walk alone on that particular beat.

In assessing discrimination in assignments one must examine the subjective aspects of a specific assignment, as well as the number of times an officer is put in the station or a busy scout car. Station duty, for example, may be used to punish the overly aggressive, very lazy, or incompetent street officer. Conversely, some officers may desire such duty. Part of Jane's complaint of discrimination (see chapter 1) is related to her own perceptions of her assignments; she did not get those that she desires while others with the same seniority were more frequently rewarded with assignments of their choice.

Permanent Assignments. Bloch and Anderson (1974b:12) observed that by August 1973 only 45 percent of the new women, but 71 percent of the comparison new male officers, remained on regular uniformed patrol. Thirty-one percent of the new women, but only 12 percent of the men, were given inside assignments (clerical, youth, or community relations duties). In addition, 12 percent of the women but only 4 percent of the men had other street assignments including scooter, morals, and tactical squads. In this respect, then, women had greater mobility within the organization, since all changes of assignment result from the officer's applying (or being strongly encouraged to apply) for a position. At the same time, the fact that the majority of the patrolwomen were transferred could indicate that they felt unwelcome and uncomfortable on patrol, and sought less dangerous assignments where the intensity of partnerships was reduced, where they could be more easily integrated into the work group. (Without interviewing the initial group of policewomen it would be difficult to determine their motivations.)

Currently some units have no women and others have disproportionately few. In both the districts and central headquarters, policewomen tend to be overrepresented in administrative, community relations, and youth service units (see table 5 in chapter 3). They are rare in the detective, vice, and casual clothes units of the seven police districts; traffic and special operations divisions; inspectional services; and in several investigative units. There are no women in the canine units or the robbery squad. In the latter two cases, female applicants were told that they could not handle the assignments: in the canine unit because the dogs are too big and rough; in the robbery squad because the work involves confrontations with violent criminals, and the male officers believe that inadequate back-up by policewomen would jeopardize their own safety.

The Impact of Assignments and Training on Policewomen's Performance

All officers undergo a "reality shock" when, beginning patrol work, they face unfamiliar and unpredictable situations on the street. In successfully taking action and overcoming their fears, most officers gain confidence as they develop policing skills. The ability to cope with the paperwork, the law, the courts, and, most importantly, with the citizens they encounter all bolster confidence. Self-confidence also grows when peers say "good job" since such comments are the looking glass in which a new officer sees himself or herself. The officer who does not have or take the opportunity to develop street patrol skills as a result of limiting assignments, inadequate instruction, or overprotection is likely to act hesitantly or fail to act in a confrontation. Because an incompetent officer is regarded by colleagues as a potential danger to themselves as well as to the officer in question, they are anxious to get such an officer off the street or minimize his or her street activities, thus perpetuating the cycle of incompetence on patrol.

The cycles of success and failure in learning the patrol role are illustrated by Tim and Jane (see chapter 1). Tim immediately seemed to fit in. He handled scout car work well and was rewarded for being an effective officer with assignments to busy cars. His subsequent assignments not only offered opportunities for success, but indicated his superiors' satisfaction with his performance and encouraged him to take advantage of the opportunities that arose.

Jane, small and shy, did not initially appear to be "police material" and her subsequent behavior and performance record did little to reverse this initial assessment. She was assigned more often than Tim to a quiet footbeat or the stationhouse, and when in a scout car worked with assertive male partners with whom she interacted in a subordinate manner "appropriate" for a young black woman. She feels that she is the victim of assignment discrimination which has fostered a "do nothing" attitude toward policing. Her resultant performance and attitude have contributed both to the view that she is not a promising officer, and to her reputation as a complainer. She is caught in a spiral of demotivation and failure. The view that "she can't" has led in circular fashion to "I can't" to "I don't want to," and back again to "See, she can't," and makes it unlikely that she will attain the detective status she desires.

While self-confidence and willingness to face the unknown are not sex-linked attributes, dissimilar patterns of socialization (both prior to entry into policing and on the job) and differential expectations influence the way in which male and female rookies respond to their new roles. Unless the timidity of many policewomen, and the men's protectiveness in making assignments and in patrol behavior are consciously reversed, a self-fulfilling prophecy becomes a reality. Presumed unable to handle situations, women are given less opportunity to prove themselves. Without the necessary opportunities for learning to act with decisiveness and confidence—neither overprotected nor underinstructed—women "prove" thier incapacity for patrol work. They adapt in traditionally female ways, manipulating others' expectations rather than altering their own behavior. One policewoman explained that the situation was less the fault of either the male or female officers, as individuals, than the result of learned social patterns and the department's failure to do anything about the situation. She noted that women have learned to whine, manipulate, and cry and men to permit women's tears to win them exemptions. As a supervisor of women, she never saw women cry over their assignment. With male supervisors, however, she observed a difference:

> I saw women I didn't even know had tears, crying. I guess they knew that crying wouldn't do any good with me whereas with the man they knew it might do some good. . . .
>
> A woman comes to a male sergeant after he's given her an assignment and maybe she is afraid or doesn't feel good and she cries. Men give in to her. This puts men on the spot. Society has reared men to be protectors of women. . . . Women come and say "I want to do this job equally but I'm scared." . . . The men are not conditioned or trained to say, "You have to do it." Most of the officials I've spoken to admit that if a woman came to them and said she was scared of an assignment they could not make her go. What would they do if a man said that? The officials would tell him to get out there but they can't do that to a

woman. . . . Some of the men fear sending a woman out because they think, "Suppose she gets hurt, am I to blame?" The men feel guilty.

On the basis of fairly limited evidence, it appears that young black women from working class families are most disadvantaged in adapting to patrol in comparison with women with other characteristics. Policewomen from very deprived backgrounds are more confident on the street, presumably because they have greater familiarity with ghetto life. Middle-class women have had more opportunity to speak up and act in an assertive "unladylike" manner as children (Kohn, 1959) and, as officers, tend to be more outspoken and ambitious. The older women, who generally have had more work experience, tend to be more mature and comfortable in interacting with the experienced male officers and officials, and are less frequently treated as "little girls." The white policewomen are able to use departmental policies to their advantage, can participate in the informal politicking within the department, since 75 percent of the district officials are white and racial politics are still important, and often have adopted feminist attitudes which permit them to comfortably compete with the men. Women from "poor but respectable" backgrounds, however, tend to be uncomfortable on street patrol, behave like ladies, hesitate to assert themselves, and regard their job as a white-collar one. They "put in their time" on patrol for the $12,890 starting salary but hope to find inside assignments or leave policing in a few years. Black women face an additional problem imposed by the burden of racial etiquette since most of their male partners are white. Many feel discounted both as women and blacks.

The department is caught on the horns of a dilemma. To single women out for special training is likely to be both illegal and resented by many of the men (and some of the women who do not believe women should have special treatment). To ignore the differences that affect performance, however, perpetuates the difficulties many policewomen experience as patrol officers.

The impact of assignments on women's policing skills is illustrated by two unusual situations: undercover work and prostitution assignments. From my limited sample it appears that women who initially were assigned to the undercover unit went on to subsequent patrol activities with great knowledge and self-confidence; undercover work forced them to take the initiative and develop independence, habits which were carried over to patrol work. It should be noted, however, that since an undercover assignment is voluntary, the women who sought this work were probably self-confident and/or ambitious to begin with.

Similarly, policewomen as a group greatly benefited when the department undertook a "crackdown" on prostitution in the summer of 1974. The twenty-three women assigned to the plainclothes detail worked together and discovered they could physically defend themselves and make arrests on their own. Abrecht (1976) noted that the formation of this detail was a "turning point" for the women. Its commanding officer, in his report to the chief, indicated its serendipitous value:

> The operation was beneficial to the policewomen. . . . These officers discovered that they could work together . . . demonstrated they could be self-reliant, utilize their own judgments, and make their own decisions. Self-confidence and maturity . . . increased with each officer as the detail extended in time.
>
> They also earned the respect of their male counterparts. Numerous comments were made by male police officers who were very impressed with the many strengths displayed by the policewomen. It is felt that because of the operation an improved relationship between male and female officers . . . will be observed in the future . . . in which female officers will be accepted as full partners and not a fragile body that has to be "coddled and kept out of the way."

OTHER SYMBOLIC ISSUES

In addition to training and assignment policies, both of which have direct and substantive consequences on those entering policing, two other issues have symbolic significance—uniforms and health services. Both are illustrative of the manner in which a departmental policy without any discriminatory intent can differentially affect male and female officers.

Uniforms

A police officer's uniform sets her or him off from other citizens and assumes symbolic importance both to the public and to the officers themselves. When in uniform the officer is visible and "different"; he or she is invested with authority that ordinary citizens lack. Many officials emphasize that proper appearance is an important characteristic of a good officer. They are quick to criticize those whose appearance does not convey pride in "wearing the blue." Many officers note that citizens, perhaps unconsciously, regard the appearance of the officer on the street as an important behavioral cue. Police officers who look neat and polished are assumed to know what they are doing, and be concerned with their work; sloppy officers give the impression of disinterest and incompetence.

If she is unable to move freely or to withstand the cold, the policewoman's ability to perform her job is impaired. Already at a psychological disadvantage due to her smaller size, a policewoman in an ill-fitting uniform conveys even less authority. When female officers were initially assigned to patrol they were outfitted in skirts, medium heels, and pocketbooks for their guns. When the policewomen complained about the cold, they were temporarily removed from street duty since no other uniform was available. The long-awaited uniforms for patrolwomen arrived in 1972. During the time my research was conducted the women wore men's hats, shirts, ties, and raincoats, which were generally too large and without shape. In addition, the pants and light jackets lacked pockets, present in similar men's wear, and the pants were too short in the crotch for many of the women.[11] The women's request for changes in their uniforms engendered protests of favoritism and discrimination. The women responded,

> changes in the uniforms . . . don't make them better or worse, merely fit for the women. . . . For example, my shirt is designed for a man's chest. . . . We should be given a shirt with darts for the bust. . . . Is that favoritism? If we get one designed for women, is that so bad?

> Why can't we be a little different from the guys? Just because we look a little neater out there doesn't mean it takes away from our job or what we do. The men say, "they want everything around here" when women asked for some changes in the uniform but everything now is for the men. We wear men's shirts, hats, and ties. It won't take away from our job performance to have a neat-looking uniform.

As with many other issues the female officers divided over the uniform issue. While most wanted some change, the more career-oriented women, who sought to minimize the differences between the sexes, regarded it as unimportant. One female officer wanted rear pockets on pants, which many other women opposed, saying they would make the wearer look "fat." She stated emphatically:

> We're not out there to look pretty. We want to deemphasize . . . the feminine role when we're in command of situations that are somewhat

11. Several months after completion of my research the department purchased new hats and ties for female officers.

volatile. Some street dudes don't think it's right that a woman is telling them what to do to begin with. You want to neutralize that, not call attention to it. You don't want to convey the idea that some sweet, pretty little thing is telling him how to behave in front of people.

Health Services

Another area in which "nondiscrimination" by the department negatively affects the policewomen is health services. Health care and facilities are important to police since they have a high rate of job-related injury; a non-job-related injury can also prevent them from working as patrol officers. Officers who are sick or injured may go to the department clinic; those who have been sick for more than three days, or have been out on leave or placed on light-duty status due to an injury, must go there before returning to work.

The clinic had no obstetrical or gynecological services until 1977. To many women the absence of a trained gynecologist was a symbolic slap in the face, a denial of their "special" needs, and a way in which the department conveyed to them the message: "You're in a man's job and will be treated like a man." One woman's statement illustrates the symbolic importance attached to this issue:

> A lot of the women want a gynecologist at the clinic. I guess the women
> have a right to one. I wouldn't go to him but many other women would
> and if just one wants a gynecologist I think she has a right to have one.

Like many others, this woman has her own private physician and would not use the one at the clinic. Nevertheless she believes health services which meet the particular needs of women should be provided by the department.

The department's policy on pregnancy became a hotly debated issue during the time I was a participant-observer. To save money, the department abolished light-duty status for all officers except pregnant women in the summer of 1975, which evoked considerable anger and led to a lawsuit. As a result, the department also abolished light duty for pregnant women in January 1976. Upon becoming pregnant a woman was to notify the clinic and would be put on extended administrative leave until after her delivery. She was prohibited from accepting any other full-time employment for the nearly one-year period during which she was on leave. Light duty has since been restored for all officers unable to perform street duties for more than five days (including pregnant policewomen) but the department's vacillating pregnancy policy angered many officers.

POLICEWOMEN IN ACTION

Some of the initial obstacles to the full integration of women into policework have disappeared; other problems have arisen or have become chronic as succeeding waves of female recruits entering the department remained "tokens" but were no longer viewed as "pioneers." The department ignored the initial storm warnings until a "tornado" hit in the fall of 1975, when several women made allegations of sexual harassment by male officers. Rather than submitting complaints through official channels the female officers went to the local newspapers. The department was then forced to deal with "the policewomen problem," but focused only on sexual harassment— which many female officers believed was "wrong," or at least a secondary issue (see chapter 6).

As a result of public and internal pressures, the new police chief investigated the allegations, which were later shown to be unsubstantiated; appointed two policewomen to conduct a six-month in-house study of the policewomen's problems; authorized a series of one-day seminars which all policewomen were required to attend, but from which male officers were barred; and supported the establishment of Policewomen in Action, an intra-departmental organization for the female officers. The recommendations of the in-house study had not been made public as of December 1977, and no major policy changes occurred as a result of the study.[12]

The establishment of Policewomen in Action (PIA) was not supported by a number of female officers, particularly the most assertive and street-oriented women. They questioned its goals and generally mistrusted an organization sponsored and nurtured by departmental leadership. Several stated they did not vote in the election of district representatives and did not plan to join the organization.

Currently PIA functions more as a social outlet than as a politically active voice for policewomen. It had a successful fashion show to raise money for the police boys' club but failed to make a statement or take an official position when the police trial board convicted a sergeant for sexually harassing a policewoman while on duty.[13]

12. Following the seminars minor changes in the women's uniforms, including a different hat and tie, were adopted and a gynecologist was hired for the police clinic. Although both of these changes were recommended at the seminars, some of the female officers suspected that they were in the works before the seminars were held and were gestures to "cool" the women.

13. In November 1977 a sergeant was found guilty by the departmental trial board of "amorous verbal and physical advances" toward one of his subordinates on duty and

SUMMARY AND CONCLUSIONS

Many of the problems women face entering police patrol work are related to the structure of the work system and the manner in which they are socialized to it. These problems arise neither from individual policemen's opposition to the women's presence nor from conscious attempts on the part of departmental leaders to undermine or limit women's opportunities. Rather, they emanate from a combination of factors, including the nature of patrol work, the socialization of boys and girls which leads to the development of different skills and patterns of behavior (which male and female recruits bring to the department), and the manner in which police officers are recruited and trained for the police role. These, in turn, have resulted in different expectations of and different experiences for male and female rookie officers leading, in many cases, to cycles of demotivation and failure on the part of policewomen.

Although departmental policy cannot eliminate the negative attitudes or sex role stereotypes or alter the cultural patterns of male-female interaction that handicap patrolwomen, it can prohibit discrimination against and harassment of policewomen, actively enforce that prohibition by assuring channels for complaint and redress in the event of violations, and directly confront officers' attitudes through initial and in-service training programs. In addition, as the Crime Commission report and other examinations of the police in our society have made clear, there is a need to reconsider the nature, goals and organization of policing, to reshape the role of the patrol officer, and to alter officers' training to fit the new role requirements. It would be idealistic to expect a police department to do all these things but it is important to note that these structural or organizational changes are both possible and desirable and would greatly facilitate the integration of women into policing.

The Metropolitan Police Department since 1969 has been a pioneer in the assignment of women to patrol; it introduced women into patrol voluntarily without being able to draw on the experience of other departments and, since 1972, has stood firm in its official policy of equality of opportunity and treatment for female officers. Never-

fined $2,000—$1,000 for the offense and $1,000 for lying to officials about the incident. This was the first time in recent years a policeman had been disciplined for making advances toward a policewoman. Although PIA was invited to protest about the punishment (some women felt the sergeant should be stripped of his rank) and bring an EEO complaint, it remained silent.

theless, at times its leaders have been both insensitive to the problems of the women and naive about the extent and nature of woman's difficulties and the men's resistance to their presence. Its policy of assimilating the women without making any other changes has put the burden of differentness on the women. Departmental recognition of the problems facing many female officers came only after public allegations by several policewomen caused both the department and the female officers embarrassment. Since that time the department has fostered the establishment of a policewomen's organization that has yet to unify the women, gain their support or effect significant changes in training or assignment patterns. But a women's organization within the department cannot be expected to make the changes that are needed. A far more active effort is required to break down the structural barriers that hamper the work performance of many policewomen.

Chapter 6

Interactional Barriers:
The World of the Stationhouse

Richmond, Va. (UPI)—A Richmond policewoman says her back was injured by a male superior who spanked her because she "needed a man to teach her a thing or two," police said.

The male officer was suspended for four days and fined $200, police sources said Wednesday.

Police said the incident occurred Saturday during an argument between policewoman Annette Kidwell and investigator Charles W. Patterson over filing a report.

Witnesses said Patterson lifted the policewoman onto his lap and spanked her. Then Patterson's chair toppled and both fell onto the floor. (*Detroit Free Press*, March 31, 1978)

While incidents this extreme are rare enough to be newsworthy, the news item highlights the theme of this chapter: the pervasive "sexual politics" that affect interactions among male and female officers, and place the women at a disadvantage. As Henley and Freeman (1975:391) observed:

Social interaction is the battlefield where the daily war between the sexes is fought. It is here that women are constantly reminded where their "place" is and here that they are put back in their place, should they venture out. Thus social interaction is the most common means of social control employed against women. By being continually reminded of their inferior status by their interactions with others, and continually compelled to acknowledge that status in their own patterns of behavior, women learn to internalize society's definition of them as inferior.

Obstacles to effective occupational role performance are posed by the patterns of social interactions among police officers. Behavior in the "backstage" regions of police work (i.e., the roll call room, the scout car, and the police station) involves frequently overlooked ways in which men and women interact—particularly with respect to sexuality—which serve to keep policewomen "in their place."

THE PROBLEM

Policewomen face interactional dilemmas because they are both police officers, expected to behave according to the norms governing relations among peers, and women who are expected to adhere to the norms governing male-female relations. The former set of norms calls for symmetrical interaction among status equals; the latter for asymmetrical relations between superordinates (males) and subordinates (females) with the additional complications posed by sexuality.

While all individuals simultaneously hold several statuses, certain statuses tend to cluster; this is regarded as appropriate in certain circumstances. Among work colleagues,

> expectations concerning appropriate auxiliary characteristics are worked most intricately into sentiment and conduct. They become, in fact, the basis of the colleague group's definition of its common interests, of its informal code, and of selection of those who will become the inner fraternity. (Hughes, 1944:355)

Those who have a "wrong" auxiliary status in their status set tend to make others feel uncomfortable; more importantly, others focus on this irrelevant status which has associated with it a set of assumptions about people of that type. Thus the irrelevant, auxiliary status becomes the salient status in interaction (Epstein, 1970:88) and the minority individual automatically becomes a representative of her or his ascribed category to the majority group. In the case of policewomen, for example, their being female is salient and the norms governing male-female interactions, rather than those guiding peer relationships, are followed. This interferes with their ability to work effectively and poses interactional dilemmas.

While they face the dilemmas characteristic of tokens in an organization, policewomen must also cope with the particular norms that place them at a disadvantage in male-female interaction. Among policemen the norms governing equals in the (male) police world apply. With women, the men follow a different set of interpersonal norms. The entry of women into policing thus introduces the problem of deciding which rules apply when. When does a man treat a female officer like a peer? On the street? In the station? In the scout car? Does this mean she is treated as "one of the boys"? The result is confusion and contradiction in their interactions: a difficult situation for the men and an even more uncomfortable one for the women.

The men behave according to the cultural rules governing male-female interaction as much as possible—maintaining their superiority as men—although it frequently makes their work more difficult. They engage in interaction rituals and ceremonies to convey male dominance, and interact on an asymmetrical male-female basis, with negative consequences for female officers' occupational self-image and behavior. The men enforce the "handicap rule" that in such interaction, females must play with a handicap.[1]

Many of the dilemmas men and women experience in working together revolve around their sexuality (i.e., how they see themselves as sexual beings and how each responds to the sexuality of a coworker of the other sex).[2] Male-female interaction on the job has a sexual component even when sexual attraction is not involved. "Being influenced and responding either consciously or unconsciously to the sexuality of the other is the primary way men and women have learned to relate to each other" (Bradford et al., 1975:46). Whether he is attracted to her or not, a male, as a man, expects to "protect" a woman. Such patterns carry over to the workplace, lead to a set of reciprocal roles with a semi-sexual basis that limit the behavioral repertoire of all, and are particularly dysfunctional for women's occupational success.

A variety of cues in social interaction are employed to maintain women's handicap, emphasize sex in the workplace, and assure their

1. Normally games are played according to rules which have equal application to all players. If they decide to substitute a handicap (i.e., a rule that places some players at a disadvantage), it is usually determined by the nature of the game and the players' ability rather than some arbitrary criterion. In most games the handicap is explicit; hidden advantages are considered cheating. In male-female interaction, however, females are required to play with an arbitrarily imposed handicap. Spradley and Mann (1975:37) note that "it is as if all the players in the game made a tacit agreement that women must play by different rules than men. Even a suggestion to make these rules the same arouses male anger."

2. Bradford et al. (1975) distinguish four aspects of sexuality: sexual messages underlying male-female interactions; the manner in which men measure their masculinity and women measure their femininity, and the relation of these self-images to work success; the likelihood that the introduction of women into a male work environment will disrupt male ways of interrelating; and mutual attraction leading to sexual intercourse.

subordinate status. These include verbal cues: the use of language, terms of address, swearing and joking behavior, and gossip. Nonverbal techniques of control include touch, eye contact, "door ceremonies," and other rituals. In addition, messages are transmitted by general environmental indicators of place and status.

ENVIRONMENTAL CUES

"Environmental cues set the stage on which the power relationships of the sexes are acted out and the assigned status of each sex is reinforced" (Henley and Freeman, 1975:392). Territorial arrangements reflect the basic definitions of gender roles: there are male places and female places. When women enter "male turf" they find they attract attention and are regarded either as deviant or having a special (service or sexual) function. While the streets are common territory by day, at night they "belong" to men, and policewomen are reminded that they are "out of place" by the almost total absence of women at certain hours. Police are expected to make "business checks" into many "male" establishments such as bars, barber shops, and pool halls. When a policewoman enters, the attention she attracts may cause great discomfort. She must learn how to act in places with which many men are familiar and how to direct attention away from her sex in order to function as an officer.

Police stations often reflect the fact that they are a male sanctuary: several in Washington, D.C., lack adequate lockerroom or lavatory facilities for female officers, and even in the new stations such rooms are significantly smaller than the male facilities. This suggests not only the current low numbers of policewomen, but also departmental expectations of future recruitment.

VERBAL CUES: LANGUAGE AND WOMEN

The language used to describe a person conveys important messages regarding that person's status and the behavior others expect of her or him. When a word is associated with something people don't want to face up to, they substitute other words to avoid their discomfort; "woman" is frequently replaced by "lady," "broad," "girl," and "bitch," each of which by connotation denies equality or full humanity to women. Associated with these terms are stereotypic roles into which women are cast, and counterroles assumed by men. The policemen's limited view of female officers was vividly illustrated when the "Women" sign came off the bathroom door in the officers' section of a police station and was temporarily replaced by a three-by-five inch card bearing the word "Ladies," which was altered in the manner illustrated:

What are the connotations of these alternative expressions? And how do they affect policewomen? A "lady" is expected to be dainty, demure and proper in language, manners and sexual behavior. Put on a pedestal (sexually unavailable and also removed from "the action") a lady is shown deference and displays of respect. She is permitted to exercise moral power in return for which she abdicates responsibility for herself and control of her destiny. She is dominated and protected by men, who expect her to do little work.

The term "broad" conveys a view of women as sexual objects since it denies the emotional side of male-female relations. It permits the user to overlook the personal qualities of the woman and eases the discomfort that arises in treating a person as a thing. Broads, too, are denied full control of their lives and fate since they cannot be treated as peers or equals. Pursued sexually, they are derided when they attempt to be taken seriously.

"Girl" replaces the sexual connotation with the idea of youth, but implies frivolity and irresponsibility. A girl is teased affectionately, not taken very seriously, and given little power since one can hardly expect a "girl" to do a woman's job.

Women who do not fit into these categories are labeled "lesbian" or "bitch," particularly when they are unresponsive to sexual invitations. Upset at their inability to control such women, the men assume there is something wrong—with the women—and express this through derogatory labels.

The policewomen's use of language reminds the women how they are perceived by peers and supervisors, indicates the limits of female officers' acceptable behavior—which denies a central aspect of them-

A policewoman at the court liaison office, preparing legal papers following an arrest. Officers spend many hours in court in addition to street patrol duties.

Police officers now rely on computer technology for rapid checks on personal identities and motor vehicle registration information; the crime analysis unit in each district uses the computer for analyses of crime patterns and trends.

At the police academy learning is based on an individualized module system which permits recruits to progress at their own pace. Most complete their academy training in sixteen weeks.

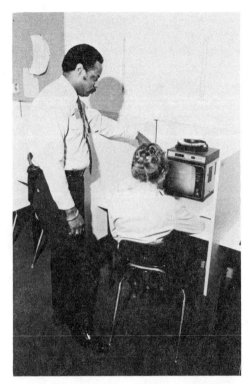

Recruits such as these are sworn in at the Metropolitan Police Department prior to the commencement of training.

Female training instructors at the police academy can serve as role models for
rookie policewomen.

Policewomen receive training in the use of a variety of firearms. Here they are on a field training exercise for Civil Defense Unit duties (including riot control).

The work of officers assigned to a district scooter squad includes crime prevention and traffic control.

The policewoman (on the left) searching a suspect is a member of the check and fraud squad of the Criminal Investigations Division.

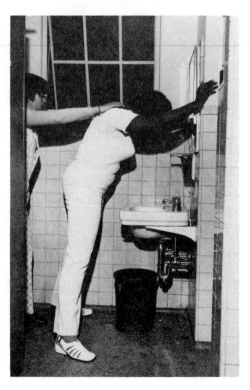

Officers patrol on foot in all parts of the city.

Members of the the executive board of Policewomen in Action stop to pose for a photograph.

Officers Marilyn Hershey and Dorothy Cobey are the first pair of police-women in Washington, D.C., assigned to work in a scout car together. Recently Officer Hershey became a sergeant.

selves—and keeps them subordinate to the men. One male spoke of supervising women in this manner:

> Treat them differently? Nope, I put them *broads* . . . anywhere I put a *man*. . . . As far as the street is concerned, there isn't a *woman* in thirty who is worth her salt as a street *policeman*, er—*woman*. . . . I have one in my squad and I have no problems with that *girl*. I come in contact with the other *gals* only occasionally.

Another sergeant said:

> I give the *girls* in this district credit. Those *girls* earn their pay . . . although they're not doing the job a *man* would do. Ask the *men*, deep down they're looking out for the *girls*. . . . There's one *woman* we've come down hard on [by strong discipline]. She's been *woman* enough to take her lumps.

The latter official makes clear the distinction in his expectations of a "woman" and a "girl." The former spoke about policewomen in terms that indicate his difficulty in treating them as peers.

The terms by which an individual is addressed indicate status. A superior can first-name the status inferior in situations where the latter must use the superior's title and last name. The superior may initiate or increase intimacy in the relationship, giving him or her greater control; policemen sometimes keep policewomen "in their place" with the use of terms of endearment, or first names. One policewoman remarked that she had quickly acquired a reputation as "stuck up"; when one officer called, "hey, baby, how'ya doing?" she replied, "you don't know me that well. When I tell you my name is 'baby' and ask you to address me that way, O.K. Until then my name is Officer J——."

Another policewoman observed that one way to behave in a "professional" manner and maintain respect is to avoid being on a first-name basis with other officers. However, this makes the police-woman "different" since the men are on an informal first-name basis with each other. Policemen I had never met addressed me as "sweetheart" and "dear." By the end of one tour of duty one officer was calling me "hon" and others called me "Suzie" although I had introduced myself as Susan. Several of the men got quite upset when, in response to their question as to whether I was Miss or Mrs. Martin, I replied that "I'm Ms. Martin." They were unable to relate to me comfortably until they knew whether I was "taken" or "available," assuming that unmarried meant available.

Just as the men face a "language dilemma" with respect to cursing in the presence of women, policewomen encounter problems choosing between men's language and their own. When women curse, many men become offended and withdraw the deference and respect they give to "ladies" or condemn the women's behavior by calling attention to the use of certain words rather than their meaning. For example, a policewoman working in the station with two male officers noted that she had "fucked up" a particular task. "Did you hear what she said?" asked one of the officers. "Sure I did," said the other, "but I'm pretending I didn't. I know she didn't mean to say a thing like that." The first man added that he guessed he could forgive her "accidental" slip into crude language. Conversation about police business ceased as the men focused on the woman's use of the tabooed word.

The alternative approach (the avoidance of foul language) results in female officers making less emphatic statements that others take less seriously, insofar as they depart from the male norms, and leads to a search for other means of expressing strong feelings. Women have traditionally repressed such feelings or expressed them by crying, which implicitly reduces a person to the status of an impotent child. Several female officers reported that they left the room when the men persisted in cursing despite requests that they stop; their departure permitted the men to dominate, and gave them the "victory" of driving the women out which was probably part of the reason for their cursing. Other women are more tolerant of the men. One said:

> I let them talk gross; it shows their immaturity but I stop it before it gets
> to the point of upsetting me. . . . They're like schoolboys who try to dip
> the girls' braids in the inkwell to get a reaction.

In structured relationships tension or conflict may be partially resolved by institutionalized behavior; a "joking relationship" is one in which a person by custom is permitted (and in some instances required) to tease or make fun of the other who, in turn, must take no offense. It is a relationship of "permitted disrespect" (Radcliffe-Brown, 1965:90-91) which is restricted to certain participants in limited settings, involves ritual insults and sexual topics, and is a public encounter. It is asymmetrical—men are permitted to joke about a woman's anatomical features which have sexual connotations, but women do not conversely joke about men since it would be seen as "crude."

Such joking can frequently be observed among police officers. A male and female officer who were not working partners had been assigned together for a tour of duty; throughout the tour, the male told his partner to walk three paces behind him.

Male officers frequently told me "that uniform does nothing for you," although it obviously conveyed an authority on the street that I lacked in civilian clothes. What was meant, of course, was that it was not sexually alluring and that I would be more attractive if I were not wearing a man's uniform and doing "men's work." Others commented on my appearance out of uniform; when I wore a dress for a court appearance, I received a stream of compliments. I wore a skirt to the station one summer day; while waiting for the officer whom I was to interview, he and a sergeant discussed my legs. Their remarks made me self-conscious; I had become an object to be discussed rather than a professional person there to do a job. Several policewomen remarked that they rarely wear skirts or halter tops to the station, even on the hottest days, in order to avoid the men's attention and humiliating comments.

Even more upsetting was the situation that one female officer had faced as a trainee. She and several other students at the academy were assigned to a special detail to protect a visiting foreign dignitary's hotel. A sergeant, in front of the other recruits, said to her, "Come on, I have a room. I want a header." She was shocked and dismayed, less at the suggestion of the sexual act than at the fact that it was made in front of others and was calculated to humiliate her. She added, "He was just pulling my leg and not at all serious, but no matter what I said I looked worse and worse!"

One female officer reported that when signing out, several officers looked at her chest and remarked, "How long do you think she can float?" as others stood chuckling. She noted, "I know this is sexism and I try to put them in their place, but if I get snippy they'll get me for insubordination." Other women are less concerned with reprisals. One was greeted as a newcomer to the district by the comment: "Officer, I don't mean any harm but I just want you to know that you have the biggest breasts I've ever seen on a policewoman." She reportedly replied:

> Officer, I don't mean any harm but I just want you to know that you don't comment on my anatomy in any shape, form, or manner unless I comment on yours. . . . When you see me coming just act like you don't see anything. Don't speak to me and I won't speak to you.

The result was that he was humiliated in front of his peers and she acquired a reputation for being "stuck up, snotty and evil—even being a lesbian." But, she added, "I preferred it that way. Then they'd leave me alone."

A policewoman who had applied for a special assignment asked one of the men if he had heard whether the selection had been made. The policeman asked the woman, "What did you have to offer to the lieutenant to get the job?" To her angry reply the man protested that she had a "dirty mind," but his conversation had a decidedly sexual tone. The woman commented that this was typical of the constant sexual teasing to which policewomen are subjected.

During roll call and in the scout car policewomen are constantly reminded that they are females and should stay in their place. In one roll call the captain read a letter from a female citizen who complained about police service, and then invited officers to drop by any time after 6 P.M. The captain added, "I won't make any further comments since there are ladies present" amid the snickers of the men. At another roll call, following an airing of officers' gripes about supporting services including helicopters and dispatchers, one male piped up, "That female dispatcher is not designed for what she's being used for either." During one roll call my request to work with a particular female officer led to the sergeant's comment, "Put two females together? I can't allow that . . . no way." He quickly added that he was joking, but it was at the expense of the women.

Although these are three seemingly minor incidents, if one substitutes black or Negro for female or lady the disparagement becomes clear. Such racial expressions would not be tolerated; sexist remarks, however, still produce laughter and are a source of embarrassment to the women.

Even on duty in scout cars women are subjected to negative reminders of their female status, and to sexual invitation. When I banged my knee on the edge of the car radio, which resulted in a large bruise, and exclaimed "ouch" my partner replied, "What did you do, dear, break a fingernail?" In another instance my partner and I had hiked down and up a steep hill chasing a purse-snatcher. The man, who smoked heavily, was panting and when I observed he was "out of shape," he replied, "too bad I can't see your shape with that raincoat on."

Another form of verbal interaction that affects policewomen's behavior is gossip. Workers usually gossip about each other, the supervisors, and the work. This has several functions; it is a key mechanism of group control over the behavior of its members, provides feedback on performance, limits competition, is a source of vital information about work-related matters, and is a medium of exchange among the workers. The struggle to both be "in the know" and maintain one's privacy affects all officers, but poses unique problems for policewomen because they are excluded from much of the information exchange but, at the same time, are a primary subject of the gossip.

When work is a matter of life and death, as it is for the patrol officer, the need to know if one can rely on a colleague is intense, and the grapevine becomes an important social institution of worker control. An important norm among police is that one officer does not complain about or "squeal" on another officer to an official. When a partner fails to provide adequate back-up it is generally dealt with through whispers among the officers or by direct confrontation. When two men have a disagreement or one is highly critical of the other's performance they have a "man to man" talk or even, on rare occasions, physically fight. When the men have complaints about a woman they whisper among themselves or complain to a sergeant who is left to handle the problem without revealing names, rather than directly confronting her as they might if she were male. In this way, policewomen are deprived of an important source of feedback which, particularly for a new officer, serves as a form of informal socialization.

Police officers are in competition for the system's limited rewards: better days off; a scout car and other desirable assignments; high evaluations for promotion; and ultimately, control of the department. Competition for rewards, however, must be tempered due to the need for teamwork. Gossip checks those who would compete "unfairly," leading to control over their behavior by ostracism and ridicule. Because the men are fearful that women will gain exemptions and favorable assignments by taking "unfair advantage" of their sex (using something that men cannot use to gain favor) gossip about ambitious women or those who are given good assignments is intense, and may limit the mobility aspirations of some women.

The few openings in desirable units often are not well publicized. The grapevine is an important source of information, enabling an officer to be in the right place at the right time. To gain access to valuable data, however, an officer must be tied into the gossip exchange network through friendship and alliances and be willing to play by the rules. Information may be traded for favors between patrol officers and others in strategic positions. The more one is an "insider" with ties to those with information, the more he or she is able to exchange gossip with others. Thus close ties to powerful individuals are vital in gaining information and assignments. While these ties may develop merely through working together, they are generally cultivated through informal socializing. One policeman caught the eye of the district inspector when they both participated in the intra-district softball league. Another was told that to gain a promotion he should get into the habit of coming into the station well before roll call and "hanging around," chatting with the officials, and making himself visible. Women are excluded from playing on the men's teams and often are self-conscious about "hanging around" because their presence may be misinterpreted. As Jane observed (see chapter 1), while men often seek to be friendly with the officials,

> I don't talk to them. I don't know what to say and don't want them to know my personal business. If . . . I'm friendly, being female, they'll approach me for a date, taking what I do or say the wrong way. . . . To avoid any problems I just don't act too friendly with them and take my chances about assignments.

Thus excluded from access to inside information and lacking personal ties to influential members of the department, women remain outsiders in the informal exchange network.

Policework facilitates gossip. In court and the scout car, like housewives "with nothing to do but gossip," they pass the time talking. Twice daily workers in one section meet in the lockerroom away from the public, officials, and members of the other sex. The women's lockerroom is quiet and relatively empty with only two to seven occupants at any time. The men's lockerroom, on the other hand, buzzes with chatter about sexual exploits, grumbles about officials, gossip about officers' personal lives, and stories about an officer's work if it does not conform to group norms.[3] Women are unable to challenge, confront, or rebut the gossip. They are unable to

3. As a female I had no access to the male lockerroom; I only heard the raucous laughter and loud noise emanating from it. In both interviews and informal discussion with officers, however, a number of the men pointed out their discomfort at the questioning, teasing and gossip that occurs there. One man stated, "In the lockerroom they have daily gab-ins. They talk about the women and try to guess about their personal life. . . . If someone finds something out, it's talked of there and spreads all over." He noted that when he attended a department social affair with a date (which he had previously refused to do) he was the target of much teasing and many questions. Another male stated that he has adopted a rule of avoiding policewomen because after going out for a casual dinner with a woman friend in his section, he had to face a lockerroom gauntlet of questions, remarks and statements of disbelief when he insisted "nothing had happened."

participate in the grapevine in the same way since they are the subjects of much of the gossip as highly visible outsiders, feared competitors, and desired sexual objects. Instead, the women must be concerned with how their words and behavior will be interpreted; and avoid even the appearance of impropriety or face the consequences in public exposure, ridicule, and/or the demeaning treatment meted out to "broads," "whores," and "bitches" for failure to be "ladies." Yet by avoiding interactions that might be viewed as having a sexual connotation, they fail to build close interpersonal relationships that are necessary for sponsorship and protection within the police system.

NONVERBAL MESSAGES

Nonverbal cues of dominance and deference include the use of personal space, and simple interactions such as "door ceremonies." The higher the status, the greater the personal space permitted to the individual. Willis (1966) found that in conversational settings the personal space of women is more likely to be breached than that of men. One such breach is touching, which implies privileged access to another person. The higher status person is more likely to touch a subordinate, since the reverse is considered presumptuous.

Henley (1970) observed that men interpreted a touch by a woman as conveying sexual intent. Because a touch is an indication of either power or intimacy and women are status inferiors who are not supposed to have power over men, it was inconceivable for women to be exerting power. If their behavior could not be given a sexual interpretation, it was assumed that the woman was deviant (unfeminine and castrating). In police work a touch is an important line of demarcation and an indication of superior-subordinate status vis-à-vis citizens. While police today are expected to tolerate verbal insult, a touch, taken to mean an assertion of another's power, is not tolerated and frequently results in criminal charges.[4]

Policewomen are frequently kept in place by unexpected physical contact by male officers. One white woman, who had been detailed to a new assignment for less than a week, responded angrily when one of her sergeants put his arm around her, saying "if you want to put your hands on me, put me under arrest; otherwise, keep your hands off." The sergeant, who was black, interpreted her response as racially

---

4. Technically it constitutes assault on a police officer. Since that charge is difficult to prosecute, officers generally charge disorderly conduct unless they are seriously injured.

motivated. Conversely, a policewoman reported being told by a
sergeant that he thought she was "fresh" because she touches people.
The officer insisted that she was simply friendly and had no sexual
intent, but her behavior was obviously misinterpreted by her male
superior.

Other officers and her prisoner were present when a male officer
came into the station and gave a policewoman who was typing an arrest form a playful kiss on the back of the neck. His behavior was a
reminder, not only to her but also to the man she had arrested, that
even though she had police powers (which she had just exercised) she
was still treated differently as a woman. Further undermining her
authority, the prisoner addressed her by her first name (which I had
made the mistake of using in his presence) rather than Officer L——.
His breach went uncorrected.

In another instance a policewoman called for back-up assistance.
Several cars arrived and broke up an impending group fight. The
woman was angered by the men's handling of the incident and at the
end of the shift, outside the station, discussed the incident with several
of the men. While they were talking, another policeman started
playfully nipping at her ear. His message was clear: I don't want to
hear what you have to say about work. I will treat you as a woman, to
be played with instead.

In one instance, when I was the only woman on patrol in the
district, I was assigned to search a female suspect. Since I had not yet
completed training and did not know how to conduct a search, my
partner gave me hasty instructions. When it came time for him to
demonstrate where and how to run one's hands over a suspect, he was
unable to maintain the definition of the situation. Instead, he gave a
sheepish grin, snickered, and commented that it was unfortunate my
uniform was so bulky.

Off duty, the boundaries of male-female relationships are also
problematic. One policewoman who had struggled for acceptance
noted that she had become a regular member of the group that went
out for beer after work. One evening, sitting with the others in the
park where they usually went, an officer put his arm around her.
Although the other men immediately told him to "stop acting like an
ass" and leave her alone, the damage was done. She dejectedly
reported: "We were all buddies but I happen to be a girl and have to
pay the price of having people make passes at me." It was probably
more a friendly gesture than a pass, but it singled her out as
"different." Men's attempts to assert power over women by touch

undermines the women's attempts to gain equal status as peers. Through nonverbal cues women are reminded that they are both sex objects and subordinates who must accept the limitations imposed by the handicap rule.

Similarly, chivalrous ceremonies and rituals remind women of their subordinate status. One policewoman remarked that when she lit her partner's cigarette while he was driving the scout car, he got upset and insisted that it diminished her femininity. "He wants to treat me like a lady, but I'm not," the woman exclaimed. If she is not permitted to light his cigarette, how much of the police work is she permitted to do?

SEXUALITY AND SEXUAL HARASSMENT

Sex Role Stereotyping

In addition to the joking, gossip, and nonverbal sexual cues directed at the policewomen, several other aspects of sexuality pose problems for them. In interaction on the job, policemen cast female officers into several stereotypic roles which closely reflect their linguistic categories for dealing with women (Kanter, 1974) and place themselves in parallel counterroles (Bradford et al., 1975) which have a semi-sexual basis, limit participants' behavioral options, and are particularly harmful for policewomen's work performance. These role pairs include the seductress and the "macho"; the helpless maiden and the chivalrous knight; the pet and protective father; and the nurturant mother and the tough warrior. Women are pressed to choose among the sexually available seductress ("broad") and the sexually inactive maiden, mother ("lady") and pet ("girl") roles or be labeled lesbian, bitch, or "funny" for their failure to flirt, foster the men's sense of masculinity, or acknowledge men's superiority.

The relationship between the seductress and the "macho" is strongly sexual, including game-playing and flirtation. He is concerned that she sees and values him as a potent male, and constantly emphasizes his sexuality. He affirms her femininity by complimenting her attractiveness, then stresses her incompetence in other areas, which inhibits her expression of occupational skills.

The knight is polite, tolerant, and respectful toward the maiden but expects little in the way of work skills and, therefore, makes few demands on her. He permits or invites her to avoid many work tasks (which he then performs) through feigned (or real) ineptness but angrily resents having to carry more than his share of the workload and his inability to confront her or make unchivalrous demands of her.

The men treat the pet as a daughter or a mascot and expect her only to be their cheerleader. When she does act competently, they make a great fuss over behavior they ordinarily take for granted in a male, illustrating the double standard of expectations for male and female officers. One woman who acknowledged adopting the "kid sister" role explained that she flatters the men, feeds their egos ("I tell them they have pretty green eyes if they have green eyes . . .") and demonstrates a willingness to work at the less physically demanding tasks, and in return gains protection and "respect."

The nurturant mother is the tough man's confidante, valued for her support but unrewarded for independent action. She is thrust into the role of emotional specialist, and then criticized for being emotional.

Women who do not fit into the above categories get labeled "bitch." Their failure to flirt or acknowledge the men's superiority is interpreted as aberrant. The men are uncomfortable with such women and alternately try to flirt, tease, or bully them into "acceptable" behavior. One such woman told me that when she arrests a man and policemen arrive at the scene, they "imply I'm more man than woman," call her "funny" behind her back, and to her face tell her about "the doggish things they do" (i.e., brag about their sexual exploits).

The pressures to act in one of the above mentioned stereotypic roles puts women in a bind; they are criticized for failing to carry their share of the work load at the same time that they are pressured not to develop occupational skills, and may even be prevented from doing so. Those that do not conform get punished with negative labels. Several women, struggling to move beyond stereotypic female behavior, observed that they sometimes find themselves unconsciously reverting to traditional male-female interaction patterns out of habit.

Sexuality Issues

Sexual propositions and harassment also present difficulties for female officers. Harassment, as distinguished from a proposition, occurs when a man in a position of influence over the job or career of a woman attempts to coerce her into sexual relations or punishes her rejection. For policewomen, handling sexual approaches is particularly problematic because of the openness and persistence of the men, the need for a sponsor and the good will of others in doing the work, and the social attitudes of the predominantly working-class officers.

In general new policewomen become objects of the men's attentions and sexual invitations. One policewoman explained the particularly difficult situation she and several women had faced when they were rookies in the district. Due to a labor dispute one officer was assigned around-the-clock to stand at a particular fixed post on the street for four hours at a time. This unpopular duty was frequently given to the rookies. She observed: "They all tried to hit on us when we arrived, to see who could be the first to get one of us. When we had that detail, they'd line up their cars trying to get our phone numbers." This was upsetting to her because she could not leave the post, wanted to do her job, had difficulty tactfully getting rid of the men, felt painfully conspicuous, and discovered many of the men wanting dates were married. She observed that some of the policewomen did date the men but they got a "reputation"; those that refused invitations had to find a way of saying "no" firmly without being insulting. In a number of instances it required bluntness and/or threats of public exposure, tape recordings or telephone calls to wives to make clear their unavailability. Bluntness and coldness, however, make many women uncomfortable. They had to unlearn the lessons of childhood when they found that a tactful refusal was ignored or taken as a sign of encouragement. One single woman pointedly talked endlessly about her boyfriend; another began wearing a wedding ring. A third woman who is married to a policeman said:

> If I'm unfriendly I get labeled a snob . . . which you can't be. If I'm friendly some of them think "she's looking at me." If I act as I generally am [warm and friendly] there are some who figure "she's an easy catch." What you have to do is catch it on the first remark and let them know where you stand. If you laugh it off, it doesn't do any good. . . . They take it as encouragement.

One officer, comparing her situation with that of two female friends who experience little sexual teasing in their middle-class jobs, lamented, "No matter how well they know you, they think the only thing a woman's good for is to have relations with men."

The power of the officials to punish makes the women's situation difficult. A new woman can be assigned to a scout car with a friendly partner or to a footbeat with one who will teach her nothing; she can be protected from minor disciplinary action or face full enforcement of the rules. When there is no relationship, she can be embarrassed by the appearance of one. A woman noted that one sergeant arrived at the scene on all of her radio assignments and frequently called for her location, singling her out for unwanted attention. Two former high school classmates, a male and a female, found that they were in the same class at the police academy. They were talking, before class started, when a sergeant sought to gain the attention of the woman, who ignored him. Within fifteen minutes both officers had dereliction notices in their personnel folders. Although the notices were destroyed at the end of the training period, it was a quick demonstration of the power of the sergeant who made clear the priority of his "hunting rights."

Another female officer complained that when she went into a special unit where the officers were able to choose partners, she was told that she could not work with a particular unmarried male. Her sergeant assigned her a different man to work with because, he said, he wanted to minimize her chances of becoming pregnant.

One policeman found that when he was assigned to work with a policewoman who had been in his class at the academy, one sergeant was frequently "on his back." The sergeant was sexually interested in the female officer; he thought the officer was dating her (he wasn't). The officer requested not to work with the female since he "could feel a dereliction coming." Thus it was the woman who was doubly penalized for being unavailable to the sergeant. Not only was she likely to receive extra disciplinary measures, she was avoided by her friend and coworker who feared for his own welfare.

When a female officer makes her unavailability clear, "eventually the men get the message." "Eventually," however, may seem like a long time to an already insecure and socially isolated rookie, and in the interim it is the woman who pays the price in isolation from others, and gains a reputation for coldness.

One factor adding to the burden of policewomen is the strong feeling shared by both male and female officers that the woman who gets sexually harassed "asked for it" and thus bears the responsibility for what occurs. To paraphrase many policewomen, "It all depends on how a woman carries herself." While some women do act seductively, then turn around and shout "foul play," most do not. Such a generalization, however, automatically places the burden of responsibility on the woman. One policewoman, upset at the behavior of several female officers, said, "If a person cannot deal with their own sexuality, they have no business having a gun, arresting people or making serious decisions about other people." She did not apply this standard, however, to the men. Her anger and that of many police-

women was directed at the women who are available and/or those
who complain of harassment, rather than at the men or at the sex role
ideology that keeps both men and women in stereotypic roles, and
holds women in subordinate yet "responsible" positions.

INFORMAL SOCIALIZING

Policemen tend to form friendships with other officers and socialize
off-duty with them. Policewomen rarely participate in this social
activity. Often the men exclude them; at other times the women
decline the men's invitations to join the group. They explained:

> I avoid socializing [with the men] because they act like little boys and I
> could be the next one they're talking about.

> If I went out for drinks it would be me and a bunch of guys and
> someone might talk about it. It's better not to mix business and
> pleasure.

Others noted that they are parents and do not have the time or interest
to join the men off-duty. Several have jealous husbands who get upset
when their wives do not come straight home from work. Abstinence is
another social inhibitor, particularly for black women with certain
religious beliefs. Since the use of alcohol is an important part of police
social life, these women are set off from the others.

Most policewomen do in fact socialize with policemen at some time
in their careers. A majority said that they had dated an officer at least
once and a number are involved in stable relationships with or are
married to a policeman. These relationships, unlike policemen's
friendships, however, do not cement the bonds of solidarity among
officers or lead to the women's acceptance in the informal social
group. On casual dates, although there may be discussion of work and
sharing of police gossip, conversation is likely to be of a different
nature from that which occurs in the lockerroom or over a drink among
a group of male officers. Dating or romantic relationships may lead to
jealousies and hostility on the part of other male officers due to the
exclusiveness and "possession" of one of the scarce women and the
threat that she, rather than the group, commands his loyalty, time and
attention. The women in stable relationships with policemen do not
socialize with their male colleagues more than do female officers who
are not involved with a male officer. At parties or police social
functions policewomen are forced to be circumspect about their
behavior and demeanor, or they will suffer the consequences of gossip

and rumor about the same behavior that earns a man a reputation for virility (see Goffman, 1978).

While several policewomen involved romantically with a respected male officer found their acceptance by other policemen eased by the relationship, and their "taken" status afforded a degree of protection from sexual advances, vulgarity and teasing from the man, it did not entirely eliminate such problems. Some of these women, too, have been subjected to sexual harassment by an official, strong jealousy on the part of a policeman spouse, and social exclusion from informal social activities. In addition, female officers paired with a policeman, while privy to the information available to the men, often bend over backwards to avoid even the appearance of using their personal relationship to gain advantage or a desired position in the department.

Female officers who date officials, especially when they do derive an occupational benefit from the relationship, are particular objects of resentment and exclusion. One former policewoman from middle-class origins attributed the sexually segregated social patterns found among policemen to their working-class attitudes toward sexuality and human relations. She observed:

> One thing that made me uncomfortable in police work is that the average policeman doesn't have very many categories to put women into. You're either having an affair with someone or you've no relationship whatsoever. I found it very difficult just to develop friendships with the men I worked with. . . . [Going out for a drink after work] was awkward with the guys I worked with because most policemen don't have friends who are women.

This woman, previously married to a policeman assigned to a different district, noted that when she had gone out for a drink with other officers it had been with her husband and the officers from his district, and that in these instances she had been included as his "date" rather than as a fellow officer. At the same time her presence had encouraged several of the other men to call and invite their wives to join the group, thus changing its character.

As a result of these socializing patterns a few women benefit from special ties to higher ranking officials and the sponsorship and protection that their relationship affords. The majority of police-women, however, face informal social disadvantages. The women tend to participate less than the men in much of the informal social activity, and as a result miss out on an important source of information and feedback, and on the opportunity to make contacts, cultivate sponsors, and build alliances that lead to occupational success and power in the department. In addition, their limited informal social participation, which results partly from the men's opposition to their presence and attempts to make them feel uncomfortable and out of place "with the boys," ironically is taken as a sign of the female officers' disinterest, lack of dedication to the job, and thus, their inappropriateness as officers.

SUMMARY AND CONCLUSIONS

The female handicap of status inferiority compounded by the problems resulting from token status result in a difficult work environment for policewomen. Although officially they are expected to fulfill the obligations of an officer and adhere to the norms of interaction among peers, women are subjected to pressures to "stay in their place" by a variety of verbal and nonverbal cues. The terms by which they are addressed and/or described, the "language dilemma," the joking, gossip, touch and door ceremonies, informal social exclusion and sexual harassment—all remind each policewoman that she is not "just another officer." Highly visible, much talked about, and feared as competitors, they are excluded from the information exchange network and the informal social life which is so important in the competition among officers for better assignments and high efficiency ratings. Policewomen's behavior is circumscribed by the sex stereotyped roles into which they are cast. Adding to the discomforts in the work environment is the often sexual atmosphere of the police station, which reminds women that as females they are sex objects, vulnerable to harassment yet held responsible for the outcome of the interaction. The women's interactions with other officers and their informal position within the district and department multiply the stresses they face in performing their duties on the street.

Chapter 7

Police-Citizen Interaction:
Dilemmas of On-the-Street Behavior

> For Tulsa, Oklahoma, policewoman Perri Burnett it started out as a
> routine arrest. A man had run a red light. When she pulled him over she
> discovered he was also under the influence of alcohol. She instructed
> him to sit in the squad car with her while she wrote out the ticket. . . .
> The man started nibbling at her elbow with a series of spontaneous
> kisses. Officer Burnett talked her admirer out of the cruiser, called for a
> backup, and arrested him for assault and battery of a police officer.
> The Tulsa city prosecutor refused to accept the case. So, at the
> insistence of Officer Burnett, it was taken to the county attorney, who
> accepted a no-contest plea from the perpetrator. Why would the city
> attorney . . . not prosecute? Being kissed, he explained, is an occupa-
> tional hazard of being a woman police officer. (*Police*, 1978:2)

As the above news item illustrates, the gender of both police officer
and citizen affect their interactions. Imagine the occurrence of such an
incident, including the prosecutor's reaction, given any other combination of sex statuses of the participants. How might the officer have
handled it? Would the incident be seen as an "amusing" news item? A
policeman similarly accosted by a drunken male citizen probably
would react by physically assaulting the "faggot" or arresting him; in
this situation the prosecutor would not view the incident as a
legitimate "occupational hazard." If a female citizen were to attempt
to kiss a policeman who arrested her, an officer who made a charge of
"assault" would be laughed out of the district. It is hard to imagine
such an incident occurring between a female citizen and female officer.

This episode shows that in addition to the recurrent uncertainties
faced by all officers in dealing with often reluctant citizens, policewomen face contradictory expectations and inappropriate behavior

by citizens. As an officer the policewoman is required to take control and act with authority. As a woman she is expected to act in a different fashion—as a subordinate seeking displays of chivalry and deferential behavior.

Goffman observed that while an individual is enacting a focal role, the demands related to more diffuse roles, including age and sex, remain in effect, modulating the focal role performance. He noted:

> Given the fact that a man in the role of surgeon must act at times during surgery like a male, the question arises as to what capacity he is active in, what role he is playing, when he decides how to allocate his time and action between the two roles. (Goffman, 1961:139)

A similar dilemma arises for all individuals who work, but for the female surgeon there is an additional question. Does the surgeon role require that she also "act like a man," or "act like a woman"? If in the performance of another role we are called upon to act as males or females—and these indeed imply different behaviors—then occupational role interactions of males and females will be different, not because of innate psychological differences, but due to the different habits of the actors and expectations of others. In Goffman's example, acting like a man and acting like a surgeon both imply superordination, and are in many ways compatible. What is the effect of her ascribed female status on the female surgeon's achieved occupational one? How does her acting "like a female" affect interaction in the operating room? Acting "like a female" implies displaying such sexually stereotyped behaviors as emotionalism, dependence, reliance on intuition; relinquishing control of the interaction; and, often, assuming a childlike status (Goffman, 1976). The display of such behavior may directly affect the female surgeon's leadership role in the operating room. Analogous problems arise for policemen and policewomen due to their simultaneous possession of multiple roles. This chapter will examine the problems faced by police officers interacting with citizens and the means by which officers attempt to control these interactions, with particular emphasis on the deference dilemmas of female officers.

POLICE AND THE ASYMMETRICAL STATUS NORM

Police-citizen encounters,[1] although often transient and unplanned, exhibit an orderly structure that arises from the recognition and

1. An encounter occurs when persons are in one another's immediate presence, share

fulfillment of mutual obligations and expectations. Among these mutual expectations are the rules of deference or interpersonal ritual, which establish the ways in which crucial social attributes (age, race, sex, and socioeconomic status) are dealt with during encounters.[2] Deference patterns in our society institutionalize sex differences and impose a "handicap rule" on women,[3] which, as will be noted, affects the focal interaction between police officer and citizen.

In police-citizen encounters, unlike most other interactions, although the police embrace their role (i.e., are seen in terms of its image) and expressively confirm their acceptance of it, citizens do not. Citizens attempt role distance[4] due to their frequent reluctance to be performers; their unfamiliarity with a role only rarely assumed; the fact that they display properties it is important not to display in interaction (such as a lack of self-control or embarrassment); and their projection of a self that they would prefer not to have known. Participants in most encounters can count on each other to help maintain face and project an implicit self-image during the encounter; police, instead, must anticipate citizens' denial of their imputed selves through joking, offering accounts for their behavior, and activating other, irrelevant statuses for themselves (and the officer) to alter the definition of the situation.

Normally interpersonal rituals including gender displays give structure to the interaction. They may, however, be used to undermine or alter the structure by calling attention to a factor that should be disattended during the on-going activity, thus interrupting its orderly flow. Such interruptions can be expected to occur when the norms governing the interaction are ambiguous or when the interaction is particularly unpleasant to one participant. The other then must not only carry on the activity but attempt to control the definition of the situation, and the other actor. A citizen, embarrassed or upset at the

---

a single visual or cognitive focus of attention, attend to each other and their mutual activity in an "ecological huddle" and then disperse (Goffman, 1961).

2. Goffman defines deference as "that component of activity which functions as a symbolic means by which appreciation is regularly conveyed *to* a recipient *of* this recipient, or something for which this recipient is taken as a symbol, extension or agent" (Goffman, 1956:477. Italics in original).

3. Spradley and Mann (1975). See chapter 6, note 1.

4. Role distance is an individual's way of expressing a sense of separateness between the self and a role which is being performed. By displaying role distance the individual disavows the virtual self that is implied in the role for all accepting performers (Goffman, 1961).

definition of self imputed in an interaction with the police, may seek to redefine himself or herself and the situation through ritual displays at inappropriate times: an example is the female driver who seeks to avoid a traffic ticket by tears or flirtation with a policeman.

Under some circumstances the officer may permit or even initiate such a redefinition of the situation to gain citizen compliance. While the officer normally stays in role, relying on the uniform and authority it implies to maintain control, in some instances his or her effectiveness can be increased by reducing the social distance between the self and a citizen. In these cases the officer accepts a different definition of the situation, self and other in a kind of bargaining that permits the officer a little loss of dignity in order to maintain control. At other times, however, to maintain control and/or save a situation the officer must "draw back to the formal position accorded him and exact the full swift measure of his authority" (Goffman, 1961:124). Thus officers need to learn when one can be "a good guy" and when one must be "a dangerous one."[5]

The police-citizen encounter is also regulated by an "asymmetrical status norm" which regulates deference and the maintenance of proper demeanor.[6] The police officer, as a symbol of the law and the sacred in Durkheim's sense, has greater social value and influence than the citizen who is obligated to express deference, particularly when the officer was sought out by the citizen. The law-breaker is expected to show additional deference, not only for his or her "crime," but for

5. Banton (1964:168) observed: "The establishment of uniform and predictable modes of action is not a matter for police alone. They cannot respond in a standard fashion unless they know their behavior will be correctly interpreted by citizens. The officer in the United States is less predictable than his British colleague partly because, in a heterogeneous population, common understandings are less inclusive. The American officer cannot rely on the authority of his uniform but, in dealing with subjects, must establish a personal authority by proving what a good guy he is, or what a dangerous one."

6. In examining police behavior Sykes and Clark noted that most explanations rest on a psychological construct such as "working personality." Seeking an alternative approach, since the psychological explanations neglect "the necessity of actors to organize their activities toward one another not solely on the basis of personality dispositions but by virtue of the positions they occupy" (1975:585), they adopted an interpersonal and normative perspective on police-citizen interaction. They note (1975:586): "Police behavior must be examined in terms of the rules which order their relations with citizens and which are usually mutually acknowledged by both officers and civilians. Among these rules we posit the influence of an interpersonal norm governing police-civilian relations which we shall term an 'asymmetrical status norm' (after Brown, 1965)."

failing to display proper deference to fellow citizens (who were forced
to summon the police). The greater the offense committed, the greater
one's obligation to behave deferentially. The flow of deference
upwards and downwards explains many facets of police-citizen
encounters.

As in other facets of interaction, the operation of the asymmetrical
status norm extends to broader dimensions of the actors' identities
than those peculiar to the legal situation. Since police officers are most
often in contact with lower-class citizens, whose status is below theirs,
they may expect deference to their social position as well as office.
Age, sex, and race may also augment an officer's status superiority, or
they may confound or diminish it.[7]

While Sykes and Clark (1975) found that the deference displayed by
an officer usually was less than that displayed by citizens, their study
was limited to an examination of citizens of different statuses in
interaction with white, male, urban police officers.[8] The officers'
characteristics must also be considered in examining their interactions
with citizens. Of particular interest is the effect of the sex of the officer
on such interactions. While a systematic examination of police-citizen
interaction awaits further research, this study will explore some of the
interactional dilemmas arising from the various combinations with
sex.

Goffman observed one other aspect of the operation of the asymmetrical status norm. Much of the surrounding ritual derives from the
parent-child relationship. This involves a "no contest" interaction
characterized by the exercise of "benign control" which serves to
reduce potential distance, coercion and hostility. He noted (1976:73):

> The superordinate gives something gratis out of supportive identifica-
> tion and the subordinate responds with an outright display of gratitude,

7. The increase in tension and misunderstanding in minority encounters with white
police in the past two decades was explained by Sykes and Clark. Previously the
asymmetrical status norm and the special asymmetrical norm governing ethnic stratification buttressed each other, and called for great deference by black citizens to police.
In seeking upward mobility, blacks have rejected the norm of racial deference. The
result is that in some encounters when an unprejudiced white officer expects general
deference, this may be interpreted by a black citizen as assuming racial superordination.
A black citizen's refusal to express deference is interpreted by the officer as a refusal to
acknowledge the normal social obligations of a citizen.

8. Status included not only race and social class but a distinction between higher
status complainants and lower status violators, and between those whose interaction
involved a request for service or a breach of decorum and those involving crimes against
persons or property.

and if not that, at least an implied submission to the relationship and the definition of the situation that it sustains. . . . However distasteful and humiliating lessers may find these gentle prerogatives to be, they must give second thought to openly expressing displeasure, for whosoever extends benign concern is free to change his tack and show the other side of his power.

While the asymmetrical status norm in general dictates that deference flows upward to the police officer, who has higher status than most citizens with whom he or she interacts, lower status "irrelevant" characteristics of the officer may lead to a reversal of the flow.[9] Although all officers may face such a reversal and find themselves treated like subordinates, such situations continually confront policewomen who must find ways to turn such situations to their advantage, minimize their occurrence, and limit the effects on the officer's control of the situation.[10]

POLICE AND CITIZENS: SEX STATUS AND INTERACTION

In examining the activation of the sex status of the officer and the citizen by either party there are four possible cases that must be examined: male officers interacting with male and female citizens and female officers interacting with male and female citizens. In each case the activation of participants' sex status has different implications. Each combination of participants is governed by different sets of expectations which either conflict with or reinforce the expectations and norms regarding subordination and superordination in the basic police-citizen encounter. While each category of interaction is further complicated by factors such as race, social class, age, and the conditions of the encounter, the first three will not be discussed

9. Analogously a reversal of deference may occur in the case of a black officer dealing with a white citizen and may even have a compounding effect for the black female officer.

10. Goffman illustrated the exercise of "benign control" in two interactions, both of which involved a police officer and a citizen in which the former was subordinate. In one instance a young male officer was patronized by an older middle-class male businessman; in the other a policewoman, having apprehended a shoplifter, found that no call box or scout car was available. To maintain her arrest she resorted to tears as the prisoner chivalrously accompanied her until a scout car could be found. Similarly, a number of officers in this study recognized they were being treated as subordinates, noting that they disliked interactions with "snobs" and with those citizens "who think they own the police department."

TABLE 13
Police Status Expectations in Interactions with Citizens

	Police Officer			
Citizen	Male		Female	
Male	Occupational status	+	Occupational status	+
	Sex status	=	Sex status	−
Female	Occupational status	+	Occupational status	+
	Sex status	+	Sex status	=

further. Table 13 indicates the status expectations in each of the four cases.

Male Officer-Male Citizen

As an officer of the law the policeman has status superiority and the right to exercise his authority over citizens who, in turn, are obligated to defer and comply. As men, however, the citizen and policeman are status equals (leaving aside other statuses for the moment). Activation of the sex status by either officer or citizen thus implies a leveling or reduction of social distance. In such a case the officer is acting as "good guy," giving a little to gain compliance or cooperation or overlooking a citizen's presumptuous behavior because it appears to be irrelevant to the officer's control of the situation.

In some instances the officer will initiate the activation of the citizen's sex status. Generally it is to the citizen's advantage and he will accept the invitation which says, in effect, "Act like a man, control yourself, and I won't have to exert my authority as an officer and humiliate you" thereby preserving the citizen's dignity. It may imply, too, that the male citizen is acting like "less than a man" (i.e., like a child or bully who has lost self-control). Such appeals to a citizen's manhood occur frequently in dealing with drunks and with domestic disputes.

Two incidents illustrate the officer's appeal to a male citizen's masculinity to gain compliance. A man, separated from his wife, was to take his son out for the afternoon. The boy was living with the mother, and the father did not arrive until 10 P.M., drunk, to pick him up. The mother would not let the boy leave and summoned the police, who permitted the father to talk with his son but would not allow him to accompany the father. After nearly a half hour, they sent the son back into the apartment and urged the man to leave. The father threatened to fight, and in an attempt to assert his manhood, urged the police to lock him up for disorderly conduct. One officer indicated that he had children and understood how the man wanted to see his son, but patiently explained that he would have to come back sober the next day. In discussing the incident with my male partner he indicated that he had clearly empathized with the man and had done all he could, including mentioning his own parental status, to maintain the citizen's self-respect and get him to exercise self-control.

In another incident an officer stopped a man for speeding. As he approached the car he heard the man's wife say to him, "I told you not to go so fast." The officer did not give the driver a ticket but merely said, "Your wife has something to say to you." He later explained his behavior saying that the man had been humbled enough merely by being stopped by the police and chastised by his wife, so he spared him any further assaults on his manhood.

Black officers appear to be particularly sensitive to threats to the "manhood" of male citizens that an interaction with the police implies. Several illustrated the tactics they adopt, including occasional appeals to "brotherhood" (sometimes on the basis of race but also implying a male solidarity) to get a man to act with respect for the officer and himself. In addition, in handling groups a number of officers selected one member of the group, asked him to step aside and talked with him privately. The officer thus created a one-versus-one situation, isolating the man from his peers and avoiding humiliating him before his friends.

In other instances involving male officers and citizens, the result of the activation of participants' sex status may be a "duel of manhood." The assertion of equality as men, which may be seen as a denial of deference to the officer when initiated by the citizen, implies a leveling that the officer may reject. Such situations often occur in interracial interactions and appear as racial tension, but underlying the situation is the assertion of status equality as men by blacks, which may or may not be accepted by white officers.

Some officers appear to be so unsure about their own masculinity that they use the authority of their office in virtually all interactions to assert superiority. Their hostile, offensive postures threaten the citizen's sense of manhood, create a definition of the situation which is intolerable to the citizen's sense of self, and lead to an escalation of hostilities—not merely a citizen's challenge to the law or the officer's authority, but a "duel of manhood." Two officers' behavior most clearly illustrate this phenomenon. One officer, noting that his father had initially opposed his joining the department, but that he "now thinks more of me than my brother who is a lieutenant in the navy," proudly reported arresting his father. The arrest, the officer stated, occurred when he accidentally found his father drunk in the district. The son arrested him for disorderly conduct, despite the fact that he recognized his father was not acting disorderly, in order to "get him off the street" and refused to permit the father to post the ten dollars collateral at the time of his arrest. The father spent the night in jail and the son paid the ten dollars the next morning, reporting that he thought that he had taught his father a lesson because "he had no business in town." In telling this unusual tale the officer made it clear that he had deliberately overstepped the bounds of legality to prove his manliness to his father.

During a single shift another officer was involved in the following incidents:

Incident 1—Waiting in the scout car and hidden from view, the officer spotted a speeding car and pulled it over. On approaching the vehicle he remarked of its driver, "Oh, damn, it's a woman," to whom he only gave a warning because "she had a good attitude."

Incident 2—Cruising down a major thoroughfare in the district, the officer deliberately attempted to run down a citizen who was jay-walking, snarled at the angered citizen (a young male) about how he deserved to be hit, and later commented that he wished he'd hit the pedestrian.

Incident 3—The scout car was dispatched to accompany an ambulance summoned to assist an injured citizen. Upon entering the apartment building, the officer heard music blaring from one apartment. He knocked on the door and in a brusque manner told the male citizen who opened it to turn down the noise. The citizen asked who had complained; the officer replied that it did not matter who had complained since he, the officer, was telling the citizen to turn it down. The citizen got angry, insisting that he paid his rent and could play his music as loud as he wanted. As tempers escalated the man's wife tried to calm her husband down and the officer threatened to lock him up for disorderly conduct. Only the arrival of the ambulance interrupted an increasingly menacing scene. Back in the scout car the officer vented his anger at the "wiseass" citizen who was inconsiderate of his neighbors and justified his own action saying, "they all have guns in that building."

Incident 4—In response to a fire alarm, the officer drove at top speed to the wrong address, saw smoke coming from the rear of the house and instead of going into the alley behind it, attempted (unsuccessfully) to break down the door. Neighbors at the scene informed the officer that the fire was in the alley.

Incident 5—The scout car was sent to a "disorderly" call at a grocery store. The clerk reported that an elderly drunk whom he refused to serve was making a disturbance. The officer found the old man waiting quietly outside the store holding a bag; he said that he had given money to a young man to make a purchase for him at the store. The bag belonged to the young man. The officer demanded the bag and examined its contents: seven pairs of scissors, still in their wrappers from a local chain drug store. When the young man came out of the grocery with the old man's goods the officer started questioning him about the scissors and the whereabouts of his sales slip for them. The young man (whom the officer characterized as a "faggot") reluctantly named a store but produced no sales slip and protested the officer's questions. The officer persisted, however, in his questions and demanded some identification, which the young man produced; the young man objected more loudly that the officer's request was unwarranted police harassment. Contributing to the increasingly confusing scene was the elderly man's claim that the young man had short-changed him and the store clerk's comment that he had previously suspected the young man of "returning" goods purchased at another store. The officer, after seeing to it that the old man received the correct change, told the young man that he believed the scissors were stolen, that he was seizing them as stolen property, and that they could be recovered at the police station if a sales slip could be produced. The young man's identification papers were thereupon returned and the officer left the scene, after admonishing the old man to be more careful with his money. The officer took the scissors to a nearby branch of the drug chain and learned that the store code on the scissors indicated that they were not purchased at the branch named by the young man. Only after returning to the police station to turn in the stolen property did the officer run the man's name through the computer and learn that he was wanted on a bench warrant for petty larceny, and should have been arrested at the scene. In the station house the sergeant told the officer that the young man had called and complained about his behavior; and added that despite the officer's justified suspicion of the man, he had acted illegally by seizing the scissors. Later the officer indicated that he believed that his actions were justified.

In the first incident the officer, more interested in flaunting his authority than enforcing traffic laws, had no interest in challenging a woman; instead, he bolstered his ego by acting in a "chivalrous" manner since she had a "good" (i.e., deferential) attitude. In the others, the officer displayed poor judgment and a chip-on-the-shoulder attitude that in incidents 2, 3, and 5 led to "duels of manhood"—angry verbal exchanges, a complaint of police harassment, and a barely averted physical fight. This type of officer frequently flaunts his authority during interactions with male citizens threatening the citizens' sense of self. He has difficulty separating his formal authority from his personal sense of masculinity and attempts to strengthen his shaky sense of manhood at the expense of others, using the authority of his office to do so.

A variation on the "duel of manhood" theme occurs in domestic disputes, which make them among the most difficult situations for officers to handle. By intervening in a conflict between a man and a woman, a male officer frequently must protect the woman from physical harm. By acting as her protector he threatens the other male's sense of manhood. When this occurs, particularly in those instances where the woman wanted the officer to threaten but take no further action, the perception of aggressive police behavior may unite the conflicting parties against the officer. The policeman then feels that his authority is challenged, the conflict shifts and the officer's control of the situation may be lost.

In other instances citizens will initiate such "duels." Among adolescent boys in particular, baiting or challenging a police officer is a form of recreation. In a sense, it is a proof of manhood to test one's wits and nerve by competing with a policeman. In such cases an officer can draw on his age superiority to assert control. In one instance, an older male onlooker to a police-citizen interaction challenged to officer to take off his gun and uniform and "fight like a real man." The officer refused to rise to the bait, drawing on his formal position of superiority to keep the citizen from interfering with the incident; he avoided putting his own sense of manhood on the line.

Male Officer-Female Citizen

The dilemmas experienced by policemen interacting with female citizens are different, and generally fewer, than those encountered with male citizens, since in most such situations both of his statuses imply superordination and lend him greater control. While he often feels an obligation to grant favors or give deference to a woman, the physical dangers he faces are fewer and he can more easily remain in control of the situation, and thus can "afford" to permit a woman unilateral disrespect. Whether it is his sexual or occupational status that is active, the officer's sense of potency, which is closely associated with his "manhood," is enhanced.

A number of officers stated that they have different expectations and a different set of standards in evaluating the behavior of male and female citizens. They are less suspicious of females, feel less satisfaction in arresting or controlling them, and make fewer deference demands of them—provided that the women "act like ladies" (i.e., indicate a willingness to "stay in their place"). Many officers initiate the activation of the woman's sex status in an interaction in order to gain compliance, particularly when a female citizen is defiant, threatens to misbehave or needs physical force to control her.

I often heard policemen say to female citizens, "If you act like a lady I will treat you like one." In several instances this statement was directed to women who had become "shrill" at the station house; at other times it was directed at prostitutes who initially were reluctant to produce identification demanded by the officer. What the policemen meant by suggesting that the citizen "act like a lady" was that she should behave in a calm, emotionally reserved, dignified and soft-spoken manner and that if she was neither hostile, flirtatious, nor childlike (i.e., neither "bitch," "whore," nor "kid sister") she would be extended courtesies and "exemptions" appropriate to her protected female status. The quid pro quo thus is a promise to exercise gentlemanly benign control in exchange for the implicit recognition of male—and police—superiority.

If this approach is a successful one, the officer has gained control while enhancing his sense of manly generosity. If this strategy fails, as with a woman who had just murdered her boyfriend and who became uncontrollable, foulmouthed, and abusive while handcuffed to her bed in her apartment, a show of force can be applied. In this instance a male officer threatened the woman with his blackjack, then told her that she could only have the cigarette that she had requested if she behaved properly. The combination of threat and promise worked, temporarily, but her unladylike behavior, which included emotional outbursts and sexual insults directed at the officers present, clearly achieved its aim of angering them.

An officer's willingness to activate, or permit the female citizen to activate his sexual status, while generally permitting him to control situations, can also lead to dilemmas. Officers get hurt by women who take advantage of their willingness to grant exemptions and privileges to "ladies." One such instance occurred when a male officer did not handcuff his female prisoner while doing the paperwork on her arrest, only to find that she had quietly walked out of the station house. In other instances men have been injured by women from whom they were not expecting physical violence, or whom they had refrained from hitting because as men they felt it was improper.

Another dilemma involves sexual invitations proferred by female citizens. Many women are attracted to policemen, who are highly visible (their uniforms themselves hold some kind of fascination), well groomed, and physically fit—as well as anxious to live up to their social image of virility. While some policemen accept such sexual invitations, most are aware that there are dangers in such situations whether they accept or not. One male officer reported that while on switchboard duty, particularly on the midnight shift, he had to deal with recurrent female callers who wanted a man to talk to, and sometimes asked for officers to come visit or take a report. When he attempted to discourage such callers or cut them short, he feared the women might file a formal complaint alleging rudeness or neglect of police duties, which would lead to an investigation. Other officers have been embarrassed and/or disciplined as the result of a female citizen's accusations of rape or sexual impropriety. In several instances male officers requested that I ride along with them when they transported an attractive female prisoner to the cell block or receiving home for juveniles, despite the fact that the department protects the officers (and the female prisoners) by having policemen report to the dispatcher the time and mileage at the beginning and end of such trips.

A number of male officers have rigidly stereotyped images both of "appropriate" police behavior and of "masculinity" which create problems in interactions with females who have been physically abused; the men's sometimes patronizing demeanor fails to meet the victim's needs or gain her cooperation. Officers are taught to deal with emotionally charged situations in an impersonal and formal manner. Exposed to the worst in humanity, many policemen adopt a self-protective emotional hardness expressed by the slogan, "don't let it get to you." Adding to their impersonal style is the widely held definition of masculinity that regards inexpressiveness as a sign of "a real man" and outward expression of emotion as undesirable, a sign of femininity. Given both the sex role and occupational role proscriptions against emotion, many policemen have difficulty empathizing with a female citizen victimized by a man. Empathy requires a projection of one's self into the situation of the other and some male officers are threatened by such an exercise, believing that the female victim "asked for it." The discomfort generated by such situations is dealt with by a retreat into formality, a flippant joking manner, and/or assertion of their status superiority—all of which serve to maximize the social distance between officer and citizen, rather than closing the gap and offering the personal warmth and emotional support which the victim needs.

Female Officer-Male Citizen

Interactions between female officers and male citizens are highly problematic because the normative prescriptions and others' expectations are sometimes in direct conflict. By virtue of their office, policewomen expect deference to their position from citizens; by virtue of their female status, they are subordinate to men. Although a policewoman usually is given deference, it is an unstable situation, since the extension of such deference is revocable. It is most likely to be revoked when she acts "unladylike" in fulfilling her occupational role obligations. Since she is physically at a disadvantage, a female officer may have to rely on the deference of males as the best strategy. While some female officers denied that they police any differently from men, others recognized a difference in style. One noted, when on the street,

> I don't think of myself as male or female . . . but my style is different from a male since many of them go in with an "I'm the police" attitude. I don't go in like that. I don't get as loud and boisterous because men can back up their threats and I can't so I won't say anything to get the citizen out of control.

At the same time, almost all the policewomen strongly asserted that women should not and do not rely on the activation of their female status to maintain control. While many noted "there are still some men around who respect you just because you're a woman," most consciously minimize rather than activate their female status, except in very rare instances:

> I use my femininity undercover to get information but not in uniform. I don't want to get hurt being cute.

> I don't use my femininity. . . . The one exception is occasionally with

drunks to get them into the scout car. I don't believe in getting cute with people but sometimes with detox cases I'll kid them and act like we're going on a big date.

Policewomen recognize that men activate their gender to redefine the situation in a way that preserves and reaffirms male status superiority. Where it is also to the officer's benefit (i.e., leads to both deference and compliance) the policewomen permit the redefinition of the situation to stand unchallenged. When it is a direct threat to their authority, some female officers react by asserting the full authority of their office, thus rejecting the attempted redefinition of the situation. Others, through fear, habit or ineptitude, feel they can do little and ignore the situation; they "back off," failing to assert their police authority.

In the majority of encounters male citizens treat policewomen with civility and respect; activation of the male sex status does occur, however, and must then be dealt with by the women.

Comments. The most frequent activation of the policewomen's sex status comes in the form of snickers, smiles, or comments from citizens on the street, calling attention to the fact that the sight of a female officer is unusual. While policewomen become accustomed to receiving gawks, stares, and inappropriate remarks which occasionally are humorous, sometimes good-natured, but often annoying, there is no simple way to eliminate them or the self-consciousness that they cause, although the initial awkwardness that all officers feel at finding themselves highly visible in uniform gradually dissipates. The responses of the women include witty rejoinders, remarks calculated to indicate displeasure or, more frequently, stony silence.

Such remarks as, "Hey baby, do you want to arrest me?" are ignored; several women explained that such comments come from people who have nothing better to do than "mouth off." Rationalizing by "thinking of the source," they can put aside annoyance or anger, being above it all as officers are expected to be with all sorts of citizens' comments. Another policewoman said she jokes back if such remarks are said in jest but responds to "nasty comments" by saying "you wouldn't say that to a male officer, would you?" adding, "they generally get the point."

The potency of sex role stereotyping and the incredulity of citizens at seeing policewomen was illustrated by seven-year-old Marvin. Seeing me in a uniform with an officer who regularly patrols his block and who had taken the boy under his wing, Marvin asked the policeman, "Is that your wife?" Although he surely had been exposed to policewomen patrolling in his neighborhood, on seeing a white male and female working together in the scout car he presumed the policewoman only "belonged" on the scene as the policeman's wife.

Often the activation of female status cross-cuts an encounter and allows it to be disposed of in a way that reaffirms the identities of both the male citizen and female officer without threatening the officer's control. When a male partner and I were in a luncheonette talking to the manager, an older black man entered, looked at me, and said, "I'm drunk. You can lock me up." My partner replied that it was not a crime to be drunk, and since the store was closed he should leave. The man reiterated that I could lock him up and asked to shake my hand. He took it, gallantly planted a kiss on the back of it, and then left the store. In another instance, while waiting for a tow truck to remove a disabled auto from the middle of a busy street, a male passenger in the car attempted to make conversation, asking me, "Is that a wedding ring? What does your husband do?" His assumption of a male prerogative in both initiating a conversation and asking a question about my personal life annoyed me but led only to a remark as to his question's irrelevance.

Another type of activation of the participants' sex status involves citizens who are angry but under control. Their goal is to insult the officer. The most frequent tactic is to make a derogatory remark about the officer's race or sex. When men direct such taunts at policewomen, they are implying that female officers are not "real women" (i.e., not adhering to stereotypically feminine behavior)— much as a female murderer implied that the policemen were not "real men." Other examples include the remarks of one man, "You look like a female but you don't act like one"; the motorist who said to the policewoman who gave him a ticket, "Why don't you go home and cook dinner?"; and the irate citizen who asked a female officer, "Why aren't you home taking care of your kids?"

Occasionally policewomen are the targets of directly sexual remarks or invitations. Other comments that appear sexual are made less as "come on's" than as assertions of male superordination and hostility at "uppity" women. One woman officer registered annoyance that when she is making a routine business check businessmen "want to talk trash to you like asking for your telephone number or inquiring about a date." In another instance when I was with a female partner, she spotted a car occupied by two suspicious men. She followed it and stared at the car and its occupants. When the scout car stopped next to the other car at a traffic light, one of the men asked, "Is it O.K. to admire police ladies?" I coldly replied that we were on duty. The policewoman followed the car until it reached a hotel where one man got out, came over to the scout car, and asked what time we got off duty. The response was a stony silence and refusal to acknowledge his presence, based on indignation at his misinterpretation of occupationally appropriate behavior as a sexual invitation.

On rare occasions, such a situation can be turned to a policewoman's advantage. One female officer reported that when she attempted to break up a fight between two drunks, one said to her, "I'd like to get into your pants." She retorted, "One asshole in these pants is enough," which cooled the situation, and gave her control by humorously putting him down; the man peacefully left, still chuckling.

Verbal and non-verbal cues. Policewomen seek to minimize activation of their sex status through verbal and non-verbal cues including use of their voice, appearance, facial expression, and body posture. Although some women wear make-up on duty, most seek to minimize their "sex appeal." In addition, through the use of facial and body expression they convey the message that despite their small physical stature they are to be taken seriously. Goffman (1976) observed that a smile acts as a mollifier, signaling that nothing hostile is intended or invited, and that women tend to smile more frequently than men in cross-sex encounters, indicating an offering of subordination. Thus a policewoman's smile may effectively "cool" a situation or relax tension signaling, in effect, an intent to listen and calm rather than assert or demand. This may explain why citizens perceive contact with policewomen as more pleasant than with policemen, although at times the woman's smile may be misinterpreted or be inappropriate.[11] To be effective policewomen must learn when not to smile and instead put on the "I-mean-business" face.[12] Many have clearly learned this: when they enter interaction with citizens, their lips tighten and faces harden

11. In a study of police performance in New York City, despite the fact that male and female officers performed similarly, and used the same techniques to gain and maintain control, female officers were judged by civilians to be more competent, pleasant, respectful, and understanding than their male counterparts (Sichel et al., 1977).

12. Both policemen and an occasional citizen remarked that I smiled a lot (i.e., too much) particularly when I first became a reserve officer. Their comments indicated that my behavior was incongruous and/or "inappropriate" for the situation and the role that I was enacting. And, indeed, I was painfully aware of my frequent uncertainty, not only about what to say but how to compose my face, when to smile, and how to "look tough."

like many of the male officers. One woman can only be described as a thundercloud about to emit bolts of lightning—her eyes flash at the slightest resistance to her authority.

In addition to facial expression, body language may clearly convey the intent to act with authority. Head and body angles, and certain postures indicate hesitation or unreadiness, and these are generally more characteristic of women than men. Thus women's body language "naturally" is likely to ease situations, although it can also embolden an aggressive citizen. My own sense of not knowing how to stand, what to do with my hands or how to "look like a police officer" was, most likely, initially shared by many female officers. Many policewomen have learned to alter their nonverbal messages. One woman remarked that her body mannerisms had changed so much that a date remarked on her new posture and carriage. Others have learned to literally "stand up to people." The women judged to be the least successful officers by their peers continue to have girls' facial expressions and body mannerisms.

Women's speech, characterized by modulated tones and a greater tendency to politeness, is both more and less effective in dealing with male citizens. Many men are more responsive and willing to comply with a politely phrased request than a barked command, and female officers appear to have fewer complaints of verbal abuse lodged against them. Lawbreakers sensing hesitation or indecision may seek to take advantage of the policewomen by noncompliance. Sometimes the officer must get "loud" to "get the citizen's attention." Several policewomen observed that they found themselves increasingly "jumping down people's throats," more verbally aggressive and less polite than they were before joining the force.

Altering verbal and nonverbal messages may take longer for the policewomen than the policemen to master because longstanding habits must be broken. If they are learned, however, the women's range of communication may be wider than that of the men, since it includes both "feminine" nonthreatening behaviors and assertive stances, which when coupled with manipulation or utilization of citizens' expectations of them as females permit policewomen to overcome the handicap of their smaller size and physical weakness.

Using Citizens' Expectations. Citizens' expectations can create self-fulfilling prophecies. Expecting policewomen to be "nice" and less threatening than a male officer, men act deferentially, display respect, and offer the policewoman greater opportunity than a male officer to make polite requests rather than issue commands. Even the "police fighter," who made his mark as the "bad" guy on the street, may be forced to alter his approach when he deals with a policewoman. When the loss of freedom as well as his "macho" image are of paramount importance, any law officer attempting to apprehend him faces a difficult problem. Such a citizen may decide that his chances of eluding or overpowering a woman are greater than a male officer and be emboldened to do so. On the other hand, for the "street dude" who aspires to be more manly than a policeman, there is little to be gained by outdoing a female officer. A man who fights or hurts a woman may face greater status loss than one caught without a fight. While the hesitant policewoman may permit defiance, many men will avoid a confrontation with the woman who stands firm. Instead they will assert their masculinity by a display of "macho gallantry" or a "who wants to mess with a woman" attitude.

Policewomen, while not relying on male deference, do take advantage of the accepted norms of deference to a woman. As one noted, "You use any resource you have. I appeal to a man's masculinity in getting him to exercise self-control. I tell him he should have control of the situation because he's so big." Another controls abusive male prisoners saying, "I haven't disrespected you. Why don't you give me a little respect?"; they generally apologize and cooperate. Thus policewomen can chide men about not acting "like men" without getting into "duels of manhood" or a competitive situation. They can appeal to such male citizens to act as superiors and, by activating their sex status, often succeed in gaining compliance.

In other instances, female officers play on the fact that many are terrified of women with guns, believing they are "trigger happy" because "they cannot fight like a man." When a man defiantly says "no broad can lock me up," Ann (see chapter 1) explains,

> "Oh yes I can. The only difference is that this time you're going to get shot." He'll look at me and say, "What you gonna do that for?" and I say, "If a man was locking you up and you gave him trouble, he'd be able to beat you up. But I'm so confident that I couldn't beat you up I'd shoot you if you hit me. . . . I'd probably go berserk and shoot you." And they know I'm so sincere that they get locked up a whole lot easier.

In one of the few instances in which I participated where police officers drew their guns, the policewoman with whom I was riding spotted a car just listed as having been involved in an armed robbery earlier in the day. She followed it, alerting other police units of her location. As several scout cars arrived, she pulled the vehicle in question over, approached the driver with her gun pointed at his face, and arrested him, as other officers with guns drawn arrested a passenger. In the stationhouse the driver repeatedly asked "Why did she put that gun in my face?" whereas the passenger, who encountered policemen with similarly drawn weapons, made no such comment.

Another policewoman stated that she has an advantage over male officers because she does not feel obligated to use her fists to control male citizens. She feels freer to employ the "tools of the trade" which give her a clear physical advantage in such situations. She noted, "If I feel a prisoner is going to try to escape, I'll hold him at gunpoint and though I won't shoot him, he doesn't know that."

Other instances cited by policewomen where their female status can be used to advantage include dealing with domestic disputes and victims of accidents or violent crime. Several observed that men sometimes prefer to talk to a policewoman, who they assume is more willing to listen and will not "put them down." One noted that when she puts on her uniform she generally loses her feminine qualities in the eyes of many citizens but,

> where someone is injured, women . . . can show more compassion whereas men may want to but feel they cannot. For example where you have someone hurt or dying, you can hold them in your arms while a man feels he can't do this . . . because he would be showing a feminine attribute . . . and that's bad.

Female officers can also invoke the parent-child complex to reduce hostility and assume a superordinate position by implicitly assuming a maternal role. The policewoman who turns an encounter into an interaction in which she is cast in the role of "stern mother" chastising her wayward children multiplies the sense of obligation on the part of citizens to comply. Such a tactic reverses the officer's subordinate female status while maintaining "benign control," and is most success-fully employed by several older policewomen whose assumption of the role of "strong matriarch" appears more "natural."

Effective policewomen use their sex status to advantage, but still take police action when necessary.[13] They do not count on citizens

---

13. "Effective" is measured in terms of current police department standards: effective officers are those who were praised by their officials or fellow officers and/or policewomen who received high efficiency ratings or evaluations. Because of the extensive grapevine it was not difficult to get other officers' opinions of female officers.

playing by different rules, although they know some will attempt to do so and as officers take advantage of that fact when possible. While they recognize that they are at a physical disadvantage in a fist fight with a man, they can adopt several coping strategies. Many noted that large male officers have had failures of nerve so that size alone does not determine success (or spell failure) for an officer. They rely more heavily on the use of psychology and their "mental strength" as well as the tools of the trade and the radio to get assistance so that they, too, are able to play by "cop's rules"—fight dirty when necessary, but always win (Rubinstein, 1974). Effective policewomen, who display good judgment in police-citizen interactions and have the ability to control potentially volatile situations and the physical courage and good sense regarding when to fight or use their weapons, enjoy a cycle of success (see chapter 4). They are offered opportunities, by the assignments they get and by the partners with whom they work, to further broaden their policing skills which, in turn, allow them, in an increasing number of situations, to maintain control, achieve their goal, and avoid the use of physical force.

The less effective policewomen expect to be treated deferentially. When citizens act in a hostile or defiant fashion, they become paralyzed. Consciously or unconsciously they convey their hesitancy to citizens, lose control of situations, and fail to take action when compliance with their requests is not forthcoming. One policewoman, Jane (see chapter 1) rationalized such behavior with a double standard for female officers, noting, "I'm not going to break my neck especially if I don't have a radio when I'm walking. . . . I'm not that strong. I can't handle it. A man should be able to sustain an arrest . . . but me, I'm not going to drag myself to a call box." Their physical disadvantage becomes a crutch and reason to adopt a passive policing style. Uncertain about their ability to assert and maintain control, they attempt to avoid situations in which they must take control. One unusually frank policewoman noted that, alone on a footbeat, "I don't really police. I don't go up to people on the street and ask for an ID. I don't investigate anybody. . . . I don't do the job as it should be done. I'm walking like a dummy."

My own judgments of the officers with whom I worked as well as opinions formed as a result of interviews tended to confirm others' views on the willingness of officers to take an "activist" role or practice reactive policing, although it was hard to judge what constituted "backing off."

Female Officer-Female Citizen

Policewomen appear to receive both greater cooperation and more "hassles" than male officers in their interactions with female citizens due to the conflicting expectations policewomen arouse in other women. While their common female status implies a reduction in social distance, it revokes the special consideration and deference given to female citizens by policemen, and for this reason may arouse the citizen's anger at not being able to cry or flirt her way out of a situation. One female officer noted the hostility of a woman driver who had carefully hiked up her skirt anticipating an interaction with a male officer.

Another source of difficulty is the female citizen's greater willingness to fight a policewoman than a policeman. Several women officers said that the only times that they had been assaulted involved interactions with female citizens. One woman explained that she had been assigned to handle a complaint against a woman who was frequently drunk and disorderly. The citizen hit her as she sometimes did the men, but the policewoman, who could not merely contain her, responded by returning the blow.

While women do not engage in "duels of manhood," they frequently view other women as competitors. Such a situation arose when policewomen were assigned to pose as prostitutes during a crackdown on prostitution. The female officers clearly threatened the livelihood of the prostitutes, which led to a series of pitched battles until the policewomen made clear their willingness to fight and their determination to control the street.

While it appears that policewomen encounter more problems with some female citizens who resent another woman's authority, they also receive greater cooperation than policemen in dealing with female citizens, particularly victims of serious crimes. Women, particularly those who have been physically abused by men, often believe that a female officer understands their problems better and activate their mutual female status. Policewomen generally accept the implied equality in these circumstances and frequently gain the cooperation of female citizens who refuse to talk with male officers. One policewoman explained that while responding to a call for "shots fired," the male officer on the scene told her to remain by the elevators in the lobby. Suddenly a wounded woman fell out of the elevator in front of her. The policewoman, held her hands, kept her conscious and she gave me a description of the killers. It made me feel good. . . . She needed me and I needed her. She wouldn't talk to the guys but I kept her awake and got the description out.

With prisoners as well, policewomen may activate their mutual female status to bring a situation under control. In a number of instances a female prisoner, who was upset and behaving wildly when brought into the station by male officers, was calmed by a policewoman, who reassured the prisoner that she would "protect" her from harm on the condition that she act "like a lady." By redefining the situation the policewoman was able to bring the prisoner under control without resort to physical means. The promise of treatment as a "lady" reduced the prisoner's panic about her physical and possible sexual vulnerability and removed the need to resort to another nonsexual role, that of a child having a tantrum.

An appeal to "sex-appropriate behavior" may be employed by both male and female officers with either male and female citizens. While "acting like a man" and "acting like a lady" have quite different connotations (in terms of subordination and superordination) both phrases, when used by officers in police-citizen interactions, imply that in exchange for an exercise of self-control on the part of the citizen, the officer will treat that citizen on the basis of higher status than that currently implied by the interaction.

SUMMARY AND CONCLUSIONS

The manner in which an individual's "irrelevant" statuses affect interaction is poorly understood. As Goffman noted (1961:138):

> Although it is obvious that principles of identity and social organization such as age and sex are always receiving their small due, the reason why we have not constructed an approach that gives appropriate place to them is not as apparent.

In seeking to give a place to sex in police-citizen interaction, my research found that sex does influence the exchange of deference that structures these focal interactions. The norms guiding sex role behavior sometimes reinforce, and in other instances contradict, the norms operative in the basic encounter, which call for greater deference to the police officer than to the citizen. Thus while officers face a number of dilemmas in maintaining control of encounters and limiting the unwanted activation of their sex status, due to the different expectations and norms, the problems differ depending on the gender of the citizen and the officer.

Male officers' interactions with male citizens may lead to an activation of their common sex status or may result in "duels of manhood" marked by competition rather than mutual respect. With female citizens male officers have double status superiority increasing the likelihood of citizens' compliance. In some instances, however, the expectation of male deference to a woman may cause the officer to give too much and he finds he faces a loss of control or embarrassment.

Policewomen face two different but related types of interactional dilemmas. Because they have an unusual complement of statuses in their status set, their "irrelevant" status (i.e., sex) is often made salient and becomes the focus of attention in interaction (see Hughes, 1944; Epstein, 1970; and Kanter, 1977). In addition, they face potential disadvantages and dilemmas, as well as some advantages, as a female officer in their interactions with male and female citizens. In dealing with male citizens policewomen are posed with a contradiction between occupational status superiority and subordinate status as a female, which has several possible results. In instances where officers can control the situation by being "a good guy" because they are believed to be less threatening and more compassionate, female officers diminish the tension in police-citizen interactions and receive an extra measure of deference from male citizens. At times when the officer must be "the dangerous one" the policewoman faces greater challenges to her formal police authority due to the presumption of her physical as well as social inferiority as a woman.

In dealing with these dilemmas policewomen seek to minimize the activation of their sex status by altering both their appearance and verbal cues, and attempt to manipulate citizen expectations of them as females to their advantage to gain compliance and control.

Because they do not give special treatment to female citizens, policewomen may face resistance and hostility. In other instances female officers gain greater cooperation than male officers from female citizens on the basis of their mutual understanding as females. Effective officers of both sexes use their sex status as well as their authority as officers of the law to gain citizen compliance. They are flexible and utilize citizens' expectations and values to their advantage. They are able to draw on mutually shared statuses to diminish social distance; invoke the parent-child complex to increase their informal authority and control; and only when necessary draw on the authority of their office to increase their different "assets" and diminish their "liabilities" in policing. The manner in which they do so, however, differs according to the "irrelevant" statuses of the officer and citizens in the interaction.

Ineffective officers, on the other hand, either too rigidly rely on their formal authority without taking advantage of their other statuses, or cannot transcend the limitations on their behavior posed by adherence to traditional sex role norms. In the case of female officers, this means they fail to use the authority of their office, relying instead on deference to them as women. When this fails, they are unable to act effectively. For male officers the greatest problems arise in the inability to separate their identity as officers from their sense of manhood. Instead they tend to see a challenge to their formal authority as a threat to their personal identity. Flexibility and the ability to use their sex status (as well as other irrelevant statuses) to their advantage, rather than the sex of the officer per se, is a key to an officer's success on patrol.

Part III

Role Options, Dilemmas, and Prospects

Chapter 8

An Examination of the Role Choices and Dilemmas for Policewomen

THE PROBLEM: POLICEWOMEN'S ROLE DILEMMAS

The male officer beginning police work does so as an individual who may choose from among policing styles and perspectives to enact his occupational role. If he proves himself as an officer on the street he is eligible to become "one of the boys" and to enter the mainstream of the district's informal life, affirmed in his occupational identity and as a man doing "men's work." The policewoman, on the other hand, faces a number of dilemmas related to the conflict between the norms of behavior appropriate for women and those appropriate for a police officer. The result is that female officers are forced to choose between two polar patterns of behavior which Hochschild (1973) characterized as "defeminized" and "deprofessionalized." The defeminized woman seeks to overcome the limitations posed by socialization, informal work structures, and the men's attitudes in order to be a peer and "professional," doing the same things as the men under different interactional conditions and with little support. To succeed, such a woman must unlearn many habits, ignore assumptions and expectations of others, overcome frequent discouragement, and deny certain personal and/or special needs. Hochschild (1973:181) notes:

> It is not simply that professional woman must be more dedicated, reliable and productive *than men* to get the same recognition: it is that she must be more dedicated, reliable and productive than what people in general and employers in particular expect *other women* in the professions to be. (Italics in original)

Even with occupational success, however, she remains a sex object and outsider who is reminded of these facts by interaction rituals (see chapter 6).

The deprofessionalized woman, on the other hand, accepts men's invitations to behave as a nominal equal but actually works as a junior partner, receiving treatment and exemptions appropriate for a "lady." She does not threaten the subcultural solidarity of the men by trying to participate in the informal peer group except by invitation as a wife or girlfriend. Her emphasis on femininity on the job leads to accusations that she is unwilling or unable to perform her share of the work or act in a "professional" manner.

A policewoman must choose between defeminization (and its emphasis on occupational role obligations) and deprofessionalization (and emphasis on meeting sex role norms while on the job). Those who adopt the former option I have called *police*women; those who choose the latter, police*women*. Most women fall somewhere along the continuum between the *police*woman and the police*woman* extremes in the way they mesh their roles. This operational model will be used to examine the ways women of each type view their work role, their occupational goals, other policewomen, and their own femininity.

*POLICE*WOMEN

Work Role and Officers' Role Conception

The *police*women, while recognizing and accepting themselves as females, closely adhere to the predominant police norms, including a strong law enforcement orientation. They recognize that they are sometimes at a disadvantage as women on street patrol and as outsiders in the department, but they do not let this deter them from striving to fulfill their occupational role obligations. They adopt a number of coping strategies to maximize their effectiveness as officers, including a strong emphasis on "professionalism," assertiveness, occupational achievement, and loyalty to the department. In viewing herself and her work role, for instance, a policewoman said:

> I know I'm a woman and have different plumbing from the men I work with. . . . Some other women think what they sit on is worth a million dollars and fail to see themselves as human beings. . . . They think all the men want to get into their pants. This is an immature and egotistical attitude. If you act with self-confidence, people treat you as a human

being and you can carry yourself accordingly. . . . The men would rather be protected by a policewoman on duty than screw her afterwards. . . . What they care about is that you do your job.

In seeking to gain acceptance as officers (as peers and partners) the policewomen strongly embrace the role conception prevalent among the male officers, and are enforcement oriented—although most also stress the desirability of displaying empathy, compassion, and a willingness for service. The *police*women strive hard to meet and surpass "production" norms of the department (e.g., maintain a high rate of arrests) and tend to derive satisfaction from law enforcement activities and their outcomes. Several explained their greatest satisfaction as an officer:

I get satisfaction from my narcotics cases and gun cases even more. When I get a gun off the street I feel like I've accomplished something. It makes me feel good.

The greatest satisfaction was when I locked up this pimp. . . . That pimp was best because he was an insult to the law, the morals, the values and the community and he deserved to be locked up more than anyone I've ever seen. He was pimping these two little girls about fourteen years old. . . . I worked sixteen hours that day trying to get him locked up and finally I got a judge to sign a warrant that night. Once I had it I got out of bed and rode around looking for him because I had to have the satisfaction of getting him. He was like a cancer eating at me. We locked him up in front of his whores and about five other pimps. . . . We got him on everything I could think of. It was a twenty-three count indictment. . . . I felt good because he deserved to be belittled like that. I told him . . . "There's a lot of hookers out there. Nobody is bothering them. But you don't put babies out on the street 'cause it's wrong."

My partner and I were shot at and I ran the car through a chain link fence to catch the guy. I jumped on the man and smashed him with my fists. I don't like people shooting at the police.

Several of the *police*women frequently referred to "professionalism" as an important component of their job. One said she had exercised her "professional curiosity" by obtaining special permission to accompany a homicide detective at the autopsy of a homicide victim, and by following up on several sex cases in her spare time. Professionalism also includes doing the job just like another (male) officer and carrying one's share of the load. Several *police*women spoke disdainfully of the role of "junior partner" into which they had been cast and expressed annoyance at what they felt was "overprotection" by the men. When faced with such treatment several sought a new partner or new assignment where they were able to work alone, take initiative, and develop their own cases. Others discouraged male protectiveness by being outspoken, displaying toughness, and acting independently.

Allegations of sexual harassment of women by officials upset all female officers, but the *police*women's primary concern was the damage to their ability to do the job and to their professional reputations rather than their sexual reputations. One said, "These allegations reduce any type of professionalism to being a sex object of your peers. . . . Like that's the only thing you can do."

*Police*women recognize and accept as an unhappy fact of life that to be accepted as an officer, a woman has to try harder. While a new man is assumed to be competent until proven otherwise, a woman is assumed inept, and faces constant tests of her competence and her ability to withstand harassment and teasing. While they do not relish the pressure of constantly being taken as a visible representative of all women, they have accepted this challenge, recognize that they can succeed, and seek to prove themselves as "exceptions." They believe,

> If you want to be treated like a Barbie doll you will be. If you demand to do the job and be treated with respect, they may test you and laugh at you but eventually you'll gain respect.

> I don't try to cut any slack. I don't primp or prance around. I'm fighting to get up front and see what's going on and I think they like that.

As Ann previously noted, she had gained acceptance as an officer by working harmoniously with an officer with whom others feared to work. She said:

> This guy didn't want to work with a woman. After a week together he went and told the sergeants "This is a dynamite officer. I'd rather have her than any guy. She might not be as strong but I know that she'll be right there with me; she's not going to leave me." And getting his seal of approval on me was like getting the Pope's blessing and I stayed in the car with him . . . and the sergeants said there must be something because most guys didn't want to work with him. He'd give you ulcers the way he would go chasing into houses and man-with-gun calls. He'd do anything, but I'm like this. . . . I may be scared but if my partner's going to do something, I'm going to go in there with him, regardless. And whatever happens we'll both get killed or both back out the door

together but he's not going to get killed himself. . . . And that made things really O.K. for me.

The *police*women accept the necessity of fighting and the possibility of getting hurt on duty, knowing that acceptance as an officer hinges on proving oneself on the street. They recognize the significance of the first "battle test." One woman noted that when her first physical confrontation occurred she "went a bit overboard" in her determination to do well. When she arrived in the station with blood on her "it was extra good." Several *police*women expressed great concern with standing by a partner and were highly critical of some female officers who fail to take physical action when necessary. One stated:

> You have to fight the way the people fight out there . . . you fight to win. . . . You've got to be physical. Hit, kick, do what you can . . . and the person who doesn't do that should be disciplined. Often it's the women and they are said to not know any better. But they've been trained; they *do* know better. Generally the women aren't aggressive enough but once you've been punched a couple times, you learn to get the punch in first.

The *police*women exhibit strong loyalty to the department and to the informal system, which they recognize is a prerequisite for acceptance and advancement. They prove their loyalty by accepting the prevailing work norms, staunchly defending the department and its policies in the face of outsider's criticisms, including charges of sex discrimination, and concurring in the men's negative evaluation of policewomen. Many adamantly refused to be women's representatives or coordinator in the district. One woman rather sheepishly explained that she had refused to help a group of women fight an instance of discrimination because she feared being labeled a "women's libber" and was concerned that her efficiency evaluation would suffer. *Police*women also exhibit their loyalty by accepting the system, avoiding complaints, and playing by the rules of the game—however unfair they might be. As Ann (see chapter 1) explained, her strategy for survival included overachievement, low visibility, and strict adherence to the rules of the game. During her rookie year she had proved herself by,

> locking people up, not getting scared in a couple of shootings and getting the chance to be a hero three or four times although I never was on paper. . . . On paper someone else got the arrests but in reality they knew I'd done it. . . .

[Now] very little happens to me that I have reason to question. I proved myself a long time ago so nobody bothers me. . . . In the last few years nobody doubts my competency. They know . . . they can't get to me . . . so they go harass someone else. . . . If you show them that they can't get to you, they'll leave you alone. My attitude is that I'm going to make it, regardless. . . . I don't make waves. I play by the rules. . . . I played by the rules so straight that now if I don't play by the rules nobody seems to notice because it's an accepted thing that I play by the rules. . . . Once you become good, you're good forever.

View of *Police*women

While recognizing the difficult time women have in proving themselves, *police*women minimize the existence of discrimination against women by the department, and blame the female officers themselves for the problems they encounter. One woman said:

There are a lot of feeble women out here where they shouldn't be. . . . Many of the women are flighty and interested only in dating. Many don't seem aggressive enough. You don't have to be superaggressive but I can see why the men dislike the women on the street.

Another perceived a "generation gap"; a member of the first wave of policewomen, she considered the women of her cohort "pioneers" who succeeded in proving that women can do the job even against high odds. The newer generation is a disappointment:

I can't understand the hassles the newer women are complaining about. We were asking for equal rights; they're asking for preferential treatment. . . . They have a continual crybaby attitude and it's the fault of the women that they're having problems. It is unfortunate that women have to put out extra effort all the time but that's the way of the world. New people must prove themselves. . . . In the early days if we got discrimination . . . we took it as a challenge. The new group doesn't have to prove anything because policewomen are here to stay whereas we were on trial. Therefore I think this new group is having problems. They don't have the incentives. We felt we had to do things because we felt it would reflect on us not as police officers but as policewomen. . . . Now the girls say "no, we don't want to do it" about something whereas we didn't want to but we felt compelled to.

Thus the anger of many *police*women is directed at other female officers whom they feel are "resting on the laurels" which their group worked so hard to earn. In a similar vein, another woman stated:

They shouldn't be accepted on the department just because they need a job. . . . They're holding us back. We need people who will take initiative. . . . As long as we have those women who are just "here," we won't make it. Sure there are men like that but there aren't many women so we can't afford to have many of those types. . . . Initially we have to be better. . . . You won't change the men's attitudes by mediocrity. . . . We must bombard these people [opposed to policewomen] to prove they're wrong. Hiring mediocres just leads to worse problems. . . . We're not second-class citizens; we're the same. We should just be treated fair but many want to be treated special. We all fall into that sometimes due to our socialization but we have to try to fight it. . . . Instead they just sit and bitch. . . .

One woman expressed great anger at another policewoman who was complaining about the way male colleagues treated her. She was of the opinion that the woman deserved the treatment she got since she failed to act properly in an emergency situation:

She and her partner stopped a car and the guy dropped a gun under the car. Her partner got out and said to radio for help then chased the guy into the alley. . . . She sat there and all she could do was shout "emergency, emergency" into the mike and not even give her location . . . and she sat there complaining about the man. I have a thing . . . if my partner's chasing someone, I'm right there behind him and if he gets beat up, I'm there. . . . She didn't even know where he was. . . . I'm not going to be "Miss Clean" and here's my partner lying in an alley. I can't see that.

The *police*women who have succeeded as officers, by stepping outside society's assumptions about them as women, are highly critical of the less successful female officers who still act in traditionally feminine ways on the job and accept a limited police role. One even likened the majority of the women on the department to Uncle Toms who are unwilling to give up the protection of familiar stereotyped behavior. On the other hand, she no longer pretends to let the man be superior and has ceased being submissive.

While some of the *police*women have attempted to assist new female officers and have spoken out in behalf of greater opportunities for women in the department, they tend to be hostile to the nascent policewomen's organization; they see it as unnecessary for themselves, and protecting women who are incompetent. Several expressed the opinion that the chief could easily have gathered information about difficulties encountered by female officers and made changes if he had desired to do so previously. They interpret his move to establish a policewoman's organization as a way to "cool out" women's anger without bringing any real change. They are uncomfortable that he permitted women to organize on department time because it appeared that women received special treatment, which the men resented.

On the Street

The *police*woman is comfortable on the street and enjoys patrol. Several have refused transfers, noting that other assignments offer less variety and opportunity to meet people. While none of the women expressed a desire to get into fights as some of the men did, they were willing to face physical confrontations. They do not emphasize their femininity on the street but recognize it as a useful tool along with their gun, nightstick, and mace, which they are also prepared to use when necessary. Their confidence in their street patrol skills has grown from the conviction that the physical aspects of the job are vastly overemphasized, and the knowledge that they have developed the verbal and nonverbal techniques and "mental strength" that are the keys to success on patrol.

Aspirations

*Police*women are ambitious. They aspire to promotion and/or investigative jobs with greater prestige and power in the department. They have confidence in their abilities as officers and feel comfortable with the prospect of supervising male officers. While both *police*women and police*women* date policemen, *police*women are more likely to socialize off duty with groups of male coworkers than are other female officers. Anxious to avoid isolation and gain allies, they are not deterred by the men's sexual jokes and crude language from participating in informal group activities. Most *police*women actively cultivate political friends and sponsors in the department, believing that the system will reward their hard work and political maneuvering.

More than any other attitude, confidence in the likelihood of gaining their share of the system's rewards separates the white and black *police*women. The latter have less faith that the department will treat them fairly or recognize their accomplishments. Sometimes their anger is directed at the white women who they feel are advancing more rapidly than they are. While most of the white women are *police*women, many of the blacks are police*women*. The black *police*women are more reluctant than the white to criticize the police*women* openly because the former perceive some of the white women's criticism as racism. They remain silent or are thrust into the uncomfortable position of defending black women whose work they may feel is inadequate.

Femininity and Gender Identity

The *police*women do not feel that their work threatens their feminine identity. They have adopted the role repertoire of the police officer—including assertiveness and the ability to take control of situations and use their authority—and find it liberating and fulfilling. They stress the fact that the manner they adopt on the job does not affect their off-duty life. One woman said:

> On the job . . . I'm strictly police. Off the job I'm more feminine than I was. I now care more for myself. The men say that stuff [about being unfeminine] because they feel all women should respond to their approaches . . . and if you don't they think you must be "funny."

Another *police*woman noted:

> What's femininity anymore? On the job, I'm an officer. Off duty I'm an average woman. . . . On a date I wear perfume and even a dress occasionally . . . but why wear makeup and stuff on the job? Working is different from being on a date and I can't see any reason to doll up for work.

Several women mentioned that since they began working with many men their sense of femininity has grown. One observed:

> I'd never had contact with so many men before. . . . It's great for the ego. They'll tell you anything. It's not true but it's great for the ego . . . because you seldom get praised by your officials.

Some of the *police*women have adopted the language and manner of most policemen; several others noted that while they are activist, enforcement-oriented officers they have consciously adopted a different style from most of the men. They refuse to curse or use "raunchy" language and seek to avoid "jumping down people's throats."

POLICE*WOMEN*

Role Conception and Work Role

At the opposite end of the spectrum are the police*women*, who have a less clearly articulated approach to their work. Included in this group are: apathetic women who adopt largely traditional feminine behavior and who are disinterested in their work except as a source of income; and women involved in the work but struggling with discrimination, their lack of assertiveness, and the desire to remain "ladies" on the job as well as off. As officers, many police*women* are very uncomfortable having to control citizens' behavior. Most adopt a service-oriented role perspective which is more compatible with their sex role, and which calls for behavior with which they are more familiar. Despite their emphasis on the service aspects of policing, most are not actively allied with male officers working to change policing through departmental policies. Police*women* make few arrests, often stating, "I have nothing to prove," respond to calls to which they are dispatched, but do little else.

Asked about their principal sources of satisfaction, a surprising number related tales involving law enforcement activities. Closer examination showed that it was less "bringing to justice" or enforcement of the law that was satisfying, than the fact that they had proved themselves in situations where others—and probably they themselves —had expected little. For example, one woman explained,

> I was on the street less than a month. We got a run for a burglary in progress. Other units went in the back of the house. I was left in front, praying. . . . The others thought the burglars wouldn't come out that way. Suddenly a man came out the front door. I took my gun and put it in his stomach but didn't shoot. He was scared by a woman with a gun and stopped dead.

The men's limited expectations of her performance were clear, as was this woman's sense of satisfaction in being able to surpass these expectations.

Other service-oriented women derived their greatest satisfaction from an act of service to an individual:

> An old couple called and reported that their German shepherd had been shot. The dog was in the back yard, someone came up through the alley, and shot him. They were so broken up. It was like there was a death in the family. I'm an animal freak. I took their name and told them I would get them another shepherd. I contacted the humane society and

got the name of people who wanted to give away a German shepherd, contacted these people and gave them the name of the old couple. For me that was a big accomplishment.

Another woman recounted several incidents, including her attempt to help a runaway girl who had just begun working as a prostitute. She contacted youth services to see if they could remove the girl from a bad home situation (they could not) and talked extensively with her. The policewoman noted that the second time she arrested the girl she stopped caring about her but felt good that she had tried, since most people do not make an effort to help others. She added:

> I like the good parts of the job. It makes you feel good when you can make someone believe in the police. There's . . . a lot of negative stuff out there but the positive is much more important. I'd rather go in a store and have the owner say, "It's sure nice to have you come through here every day." That makes me happy. Locking people up . . . doesn't. . . . I feel strongly about the role police should play in the community. . . . I guess I should have been a social worker.

Like the *police*women, the police*women* resent the constant tests of competence and loyalty that women face, and the fact that an individual woman is taken as a representative of the whole group. But unlike *police*women who accept the tests as an unpleasant fact of life, police*women*, who often are unable to prove themselves "exceptions." resist the pressure to perform, refuse to exert extra effort, and protest discriminatory treatment. The result is that many become "under-achievers" who fall into a cycle of failure and demotivation. Feeling they cannot succeed on patrol they display little initiative. This leads to lower expectations of them by others, overprotection, fewer opportunities to prove themselves as individuals, the conclusion that "policewomen are not good as patrol officers," and the further reduction of their work effort and career aspirations. They cope with this situation in several ways: protesting discrimination; seeking an alternative type of acceptance; isolating themselves socially; and seeking and often obtaining nonpatrol assignments.

Many police*women* attribute the difficulties they encounter to sex discrimination. They focus on the lack of opportunities for women citing, for example, the few female officers assigned to scout cars.[1]

---

1. The *police*women point out that in the latter case, a fairer comparison would be between men and women with the same amount of seniority rather than overall numbers. Such statistics are not available.

Their complaints range from the frivolous (women should have special hats and should receive special consideration on the first day of their period) to the more serious (such as the lack of good assignments, inadequate training, and sexual harassment).

Rather than seeking acceptance as "one of the boys" or as outstanding policewomen by overachieving as officers, they are content to attain personal acceptance, willingly acquiescing to the stereotypic roles into which they are cast by men. One woman expressed pleasure that her lieutenant calls her his "little girl" and volunteered to be godfather to her baby. Another has become scorekeeper for the men's baseball team. Both have gained acceptance as "pets" or mascots. Others gain personal acceptance as "mother confessor" or through dating male officers, thus fitting into the "seductress" role. Generally the police*women* avoid socializing with a group of male coworkers, however, for fear of gossip and the discomfort of being subjected to the crude language and off-color jokes which become exaggerated in their presence. Rather than face these "tests of loyalty," they avoid social contact with the men outside of work (except in the aforementioned sex-appropriate roles).

On the Street

The police*women* are not happy or comfortable on patrol. They do not like the street and feel ill-equipped to deal with it. Several of the most extreme police*women* stated that they do not feel that women should be on patrol. They said:

> It should be an option. Some can but not all women can function on patrol. . . . There are other parts of the department where women do much better and they should go where they can function best.

> No, I don't think women should be on patrol. . . . I shouldn't be, at least the way they're doing it now. . . . For women to be on patrol they must prove they're as good as a man. . . . In some situations we are but when it comes to tooth and nail we're not physically equipped. . . . The majority are just surviving on good luck. We do the job to the best of our abilities but shouldn't be called on to do something we can't. Patrol is asking us to perform as superwomen. It should be a joint effort; not just one of us out there. . . . When I go out on the footbeat I play a game with myself. . . . I force a mental transition to say I'm not scared. . . . Sergeant S—— said "don't say I can't cause I'm a woman" but it seems obvious to me that I can't. Maybe J—— [another policewoman] can walk ——th Street but I can't. . . . So I don't really police.

No other woman was so blunt although others likely share her feelings. Several with inside jobs said they would sooner quit than return to uniform patrol.

In talking about patrol they emphasize the physical limitations of women. One police*woman* said women do "almost everything" a man can but if they get into a fight they are likely to get hurt and should recognize their limitations. They typically cope with their physical disadvantage by avoiding situations in which they might be injured or relying on a male partner to handle things. One stated:

> I do my share but I'm not interested in doing more, taking risks or going out looking for trouble. I have nothing to prove. I do my job but figure it's just a job. . . . I like living too much to take unnecessary risks. . . . You don't get any more money for doing the job actively than just doing it.

This woman faces multiple disadvantages as a young, new, black female who works with older, more experienced white men. With them she accepts the role of follower into which she is frequently cast, noting that with a male partner, "I don't have to say a thing in many instances because he won't let me." Nor does she seek to reverse the situation. She is content not to take control or pressure her partner for acceptance as an equal. She is rarely in court since she makes arrests only in those cases which fall into her lap. She "puts in her eight hours" and feels that is enough. Her aspirations are tailored to her expectations. She hopes to get an inside job, and sees little chance of promotion, which she does not actively desire.

Femininity and Gender Identity

The police*woman* puts great emphasis on "being a lady," which is difficult to combine with police work. As one explained:

> Although I was a tomboy as a little girl, when I reached maturity, the most important thing was to be a lady, first and above all . . . and this job drains you of that . . . because you have to come up aggressive and take command in situations. Some women naturally can fluctuate between that and femininity, others have to make themselves be aggressive when they put on the uniform. It is *not* a womanly feeling to strap a gun on my hip. It's an everyday battle to be feminine. You can't be feminine on this job and be effective. . . . That's why it is important to me to wear make-up and earrings. . . . I don't want to be looked at as a man but as a woman. I like being a woman. Many people think the women in positions like this are staunch women's libbers but that is not the case with the majority of us.

They are upset by the men's cursing which they see as disrespectful to them. One bitterly commented, "We're regarded as nothing but sex idols so why treat us with respect unless they want to get some?" Another took offense that the men pointedly forget that the policewomen are also wives, sisters, and mothers who are owed respect as women.

View of Police*women*

The police*women* are critical of the *police*women; one wanted to leave the department to disaffiliate herself from the other women's objectionable morals and behavior.

> Some of them try to act like men on the street. They curse and talk and walk mannish. . . . The women on the street swear they are superwomen and they aren't. There are things women can't do.

Another added:

> I reject getting into that macho thing [like some women]. . . . "I'm as good as," "I'll whip your ass" et cetera. . . . I'm not into that.

They feel that *police*women "overdo it" and resent the fact that the latter tend to dismiss their complaints. Several police*women* were highly critical of two *police*women with nonpatrol assignments. They insisted that these two women do not complain because they have "made it" and have turned against other women.

Aspirations

Police*women* generally are less careerist and less interested in promotion than *police*women. They know that promotion leads to a street patrol assignment for most sergeants; do not feel comfortable with the prospect of supervising men; do not want additional responsibility or shift work; view their chances of promotion as slim and, therefore, avoid potential disappointment. Some hope to leave the police department in the next few years; others aspire to gain and/or keep an inside assignment which meshes more harmoniously with their personal life. Taking an assignment calling for administrative or clerical skills (which many have) or one in community relations, they avoid competing with the men on "the men's turf," vastly reduce the chances of having to physically fight or control others, and perform occupational tasks felt appropriate (and which, therefore, are less stressful) for a woman. At the same time the women feel that they can perform such assignments well, and are more certain that their coworkers will also approve of and praise their work. In addition, the women with "inside" assignments are generally teased and harassed much less frequently by male officers, and have either no contact or generally cordial relations with the public, so that their work environment is more comfortable.

CONFLICT BETWEEN OCCUPATIONAL AND FAMILY ROLES

The unique demands of their work create strains on family life for many police officers. Policemen have relatively high rates of divorce, suicide, alcoholism, and stress-related diseases.[2] This is often attributed to both work tensions which get carried into the home, and work demands which conflict with family obligations. It is often impossible for officers to leave at the stationhouse the tensions which emanate from job-related dangers and their exposure to the lowest level of human behavior. Yet when they bring such feelings home they are not verbalized. The male officers have no desire to expose their wives to the seamier side of life and believe that as outsiders, their spouses would be unable to understand such problems. Some of the men said they drive around (or have chosen to commute long distances) to cool off before going home. Others unwind at local bars. Several male officers reported that a supportive spouse who accepts police work and is willing to endure its inconveniences is the key to the survival of their marriages. Others who are divorced or having marital problems pointed to police work as a major contributing factor.[3] All

2. While statistics are limited, police officers tend to have higher rates of stress-related disorders than those in other occupations. Kroes (1974) noted that no occupation exceeded policing in combined standard mortality ratios for coronary heart disease, diabetes mellitus, and suicide. Richard and Fell (1975) found police die from circulatory and digestive disorder and suicide at higher rates than men in other occupations. Although national statistics on rate of divorce by occupation are not available, according to Roberts (1975) those police agencies that have examined the failure rates of police marriages (including Seattle, Los Angeles, and San Jose) yield data indicating divorce rates as high or higher than those found in the population the agency serves. Most officers view their work as a major cause of their marital problems. Hurrell and Kroes (1975) observed that although alcoholism statistics are unavailable, department officials have reported informally that as many as 25 percent of the officers in their respective departments have serious alcohol abuse problems.

3. Cain (1973) found that the wife's acceptance of her husband's work was an important factor in career satisfaction for English rural police officers.

three of the divorced policemen in the interview sample had separated from their wives since joining the department, whereas four of the six divorced policewomen were no longer married when they joined the department.

The conflicts between work and family demands are even greater for policewomen than for policemen because the domestic responsibilities associated with the roles of wife and mother are greater than those of husband and father; the work for a patrol officer is the same regardless of the officer's sex; and the expectations of a husband with respect to his spouse's commitment to work are more limiting for the ambitious female officer than the wife's expectations of her husband's work involvement. Thus policewomen probably get less support for their work from their spouse than do male officers (particularly those married to men in other occupations). While none of the women mentioned difficulties maintaining the house or fulfilling housekeeping responsibilities, several acknowledged that their husband or boyfriend became jealous at the prospect of their working all night with another man, or being continuously in the company of many men. One woman remarked that her boyfriend so strongly opposes the use of women on patrol that he will not talk with her about her work. Another woman, who refused to quit the department when she married, gained her husband's approval only because of the salary she earned ("He does like that paycheck coming in," she noted); he adamantly insists that she come straight home after work. While several men also noted that their wives were not happy about police work, only one mentioned his wife's jealousy.

One way that the women reduce work and family conflicts is by marriage to (or a close relationship with) a fellow officer. While it is too early to determine how successful "police marriages" will be in the long run, such relationships probably decrease role conflicts (Epstein, 1970). Such policewomen tend to get stronger support for their work than women involved with men in other occupations and find that they can discuss their work with someone who understands it.

More serious problems arise for policewomen who are mothers. Changing shifts every two weeks, and frequent court appearances of uncertain length create scheduling problems for all officers. Since the expectations of a woman as a mother (in terms of time and emotional input) are traditionally greater than those of a father, the role strains are correspondingly greater.[4] Policewomen neutralize or minimize

4. Those policemen with correspondingly great child care responsibilities face stresses

these strains by living with kin or having children living with or kept by a relative responsible for childcare; rationalizing the parental guilt by stating "I have to work"; and seeking assignments that reduce the strain by avoiding rotating shifts (optimally, working nine to five Monday through Friday) and limiting their appearances in court.

Twelve of the 28 women interviewed have children; 10 of these women are not currently married. All 10 rely heavily on a boyfriend, relative, or the child's godparents for childcare. The children of four of the women live with relatives while the mother resides nearby and either calls or visits frequently. Two other women live with kin who care for their children during work hours. Without such assistance many of the women could not manage since day care is expensive and unavailable on an around-the-clock basis.

Regular and fixed assignments (preferably day work) is another means of reducing the interrole strain. Four of the 12 mothers have "inside" assignments which they took due to motherhood, and which two want to keep on a permanent basis. One woman sought exemption from assignment to a prostitution detail (working 6 P.M. to 2 A.M.) saying, "I'm watching out for my family now." The attempt of many individual policewomen to ease the strains of patrol work on family life by seeking transfer to a new assignment has had an adverse effect on female officers as a group, since many of the men conclude policewomen are not committed to the job and are therefore unwilling to support or sponsor them.

Several women reported a variety of mechanisms for coping with the fact that they have less time to spend with their children than they previously had in other jobs. One woman said she frequently takes her son with her when she goes out in the evening. Another declared, "I'm not a terrific mother," but added that she rejects the stereotypic mother role and likes her work too much to change. A third woman, who took the job largely to "provide my children with things I didn't have," rationalizes her occupational choice as economic necessity. She added that she has learned not to make promises to them anymore since, frequently delayed, for example by a late arrest, she is unable to

that may be even greater than those of the women, since they get less social support in fulfilling parental responsibilities. The one policeman in the sample who had custody of his children was clearly having problems obtaining adequate paid child care for his children. Another man whose working wife had already left home when the babysitter called in sick one day was severely criticized by his lieutenant when he called in for emergency leave. The official told him that he ought to "shape up" his wife with respect to her domestic responsibilities.

take her children to McDonald's or attend the school play as she has promised.

Only one woman expressed a strong sense of maternal guilt over her absence from her child, saying:

> I know I'm neglecting him with this job but it has to be done. . . . On four-to-twelve I don't see him at all . . . but I make a point to call him once a night. I know I'm not much of a mother but . . . he's with my mother and sister, never left alone. I am guilty about it. On the street people can call me names and that doesn't bother me but if some man says "Why aren't you home taking care of your kids?" that upsets me. . . . I know I really should be home with him but I really know I can't afford it. I want to be able to live my own life. . . . Things are better since I got weekends off.

One policewoman with long experience observed that there would be few women applying to the police department or remaining for twenty years if other jobs provided women the same income. She reasoned that most women still desire to marry and raise a family and that patrol work is particularly difficult to mesh with child-rearing. Because she had been able to work a straight shift for several years (working from four to midnight instead of changing hours every two weeks) she had managed but noted, "I wouldn't have been able to raise the kids and work around the clock."

Given support by a spouse or extended kin, economic necessity, some officers' enthusiasm for their job, and the availability of straight-shift assignments, policewomen cope with the stresses of being both a mother and an officer despite the difficult conditions of the work and the lack of social support.

SUMMARY AND CONCLUSION

The problems and choices that policewomen face, particularly the dilemmas related to the apparent conflict between sex role and occupational role norms, and those emanating from their status as "tokens" and outsiders, include the work itself (and their readiness to perform the control functions); the continuous demands that they prove their competence and loyalty to the group; and their treatment in stereotypic ways rather than as individuals. Their dilemmas lead to two principal patterns of coping behavior: one characteristic of *police*women; the other of police*women*. The former stresses over-achievement and conformity to rules and group norms in order to fulfill the requirements of the occupational role against the odds; the latter emphasizes conformity to sex role norms, has decreased occupational commitment and/or desires to obtain a nonpatrol assignment.

Regardless of which pattern of behavior a policewoman adopts (many make a series of compromises and fall between the extremes of *police*woman and police*woman*) as a woman and an outsider the female officer is handicapped. She faces increased psychological pressure and often expends much energy attaining satisfactory relationships at work. She is excluded from situations where important learning occurs, and is under great pressure to perform and allowed less margin for error. She is treated on the basis of generalizations about women and pressured into stereotypic roles. In addition, many women face conflicts between their domestic and their occupational roles that increase the stress. The result is hardly surprising: many policewomen do not perform well as patrol officers. They fall into cycles of failure and demotivation. Other women overcome the obstacles and are adequate or outstanding officers but they, too, face choices, limitations, and problems as token women doing a "man's job."

Chapter 9

Conclusions

This study has explored a number of the difficulties encountered by women "breaking and entering" into a male-dominated nonprofessional occupation (policing) and the manner in which they cope with the stress of performing their occupational role. Because the cultural norms and behavioral expectations of women conflict with situationally defined behaviors appropriate for police officers, policewomen must find ways to manage the conflict and mesh their occupational and sex roles. In addition, they face problems as newcomers in an organization where they have limited power and opportunity for mobility, and are present in only token numbers. Thus their difficulties in managing the work role emanate both from cultural factors related to the norms governing male-female interaction, and from structural features of the work organization.

Policewomen's difficulties stem in part from the nature of police work which requires an officer to exercise authority and control others, by physical means if necessary. Unused to assertively taking control of situations, wielding power, and acting authoritatively, and rarely perceived by others as conveying personal authority, women must learn a new set of behaviors when they become patrol officers. Initially they are at a disadvantage due to their prior socialization and experience. Departmental training and district assignment patterns often perpetuate the women's adjustment difficulties, while their high visibility, resulting from their presence in only token numbers, magnifies performance pressures. In addition to their occasional conscious sex discrimination, policemen have low expectations of women's work performance; this, combined with their insistence that the women should be treated just like male officers, has a negative impact on the women. It results, for many female officers, in the development of a cycle of dependency and failure. Other women face these contradictory expectations by redoubled effort and prove themselves as patrol officers against the odds.

The informal organization and work culture of policemen also contribute to limited opportunities for policewomen's success. Because they threaten the solidarity of the men's work group, as well as their social world, their already mediocre occupational status, and their self-images as "men's men," the women are not accepted as officers. They are denied information and feedback, friendships, alliances, and sponsorship that are vital to success in the department's informal structure.

Female officers also face dilemmas at the interpersonal level in dealing with peers and citizens. In police-citizen interactions citizen unpredictability is due to conflicting norms, and the deference dilemmas that arise from them. In working with male peers, female officers must contend with the strains of status inferiority as women, compounded by the heightened performance pressures they bear as tokens. They are cast into limiting stereotypic roles in which they are treated either as subordinate "ladies" or as sexual objects and reminded of their status by a variety of verbal and nonverbal cues. These culturally prescribed patterns of male-female interaction constitute the last and perhaps most difficult hurdle for women to overcome because they are learned at an early age, internalized, and pervade male-female relationships. While it often appears that the arrangements between the sexes are based on biological differences and are justified as "natural," as Goffman (1977) has observed it is the institutionalized, culturally prescribed behavioral norms for men and women that magnify and reinforce social perceptions of the relatively minor biological differences between men and women. They form the foundation of many of our social patterns and, therefore, will not be easily eliminated.

Because women are treated as women by male coworkers, they adopt strategies to cope with the strains of their work situation. One group, labeled *police*women, react by overachievement, invisibility, staunch loyalty to the department, and adherence to the rules in order to prove themselves exceptions among the women. Successful as officers, they pay a price in terms of pressure to perform, social isolation, and self-distortion (Hughes, 1944; Jourand, 1964; Kanter,

1977a and b). Police*women*, on the other hand, adopt the stereotypic roles into which they are cast, tend to fail as patrol officers, and thus "prove" women's incapacity for policing. Whichever path a woman takes (and most seek an intermediate solution or a nonpatrol assignment), she is faced with dilemmas not encountered by policemen.

Although these findings arise from a case study of police officers in one district of a single urban police department, and one can generalize with only the greatest caution, the research suggests that a number of the problems encountered by Washington, D.C., policewomen may be common to female officers in other departments as well as to women entering a variety of nontraditional occupations, particularly at the blue-collar level. Similarly, the impact of female patrol officers on the policemen, their informal norms, and the department's policies observed in this study is likely to occur in other police departments and affect policing as an occupation. Indeed, the findings raise a number of questions for traditionally male occupations and for the study of work and occupations as well.

"THE IRREDUCIBLE DIFFERENCE": POLICE-WOMEN AND THE NATURE OF POLICE WORK

One important factor limiting generalizations from the police-women's experience to women "breaking and entering" other non-traditional occupations (particularly at the white-collar and professional level) is the nature of the work itself. Two characteristics make police work "men's work" and, at the same time, make it a unique occupation: the authority vested in the officer to enforce the law, and the right to physically restrain or control others when they violate the law. Because women are thought to convey less authority and are smaller and physically weaker than men, they enter the job with a disadvantage that is both real and symbolic. Goffman (1976) observed that one's social weight (power, authority, rank or office) is echoed expressively in social situations through relative size. The verbal metaphors of "looking up to" and "looking down on" someone indicate the relationship between physical size and social value. Because women are smaller than men, the latter can literally "look down on" policewomen who thus must find alternative means of conveying their authority. Small men, too, have some difficulties in becoming officers and asserting their police authority; but like taller men, they have been socialized to act "like men" when physically challenged; are guided by the imagery (if not the actuality) of combat readiness; have learned how to control conflict situations; and are likely to have adopted a number of mechanisms (including increased verbal aggressiveness and bodybuilding through weight-lifting) to compensate for their disadvantage.

Upon closer scrutiny in recent years, the multitude of "sex differences" has been reduced to a questionable handful (Maccoby and Jacklin, 1974). One difference that remains undeniable (although not unchallenged) is the difference between men and women in size and strength. The objection to patrolwomen on the basis of their physical characteristics is "the bottom line" and, therefore, can be expected to be staunchly upheld. In jobs requiring some physical exertion, such as policing, the pressure to exclude women is based not only on men's desire to preserve their superior social and economic status but, more importantly, to preserve the meaning of "manhood." If the physical differences which are visible, measurable, and the traditional basis of the division of labor are irrelevant, how can other, less tangible differences be significant?

The men's objections to policewomen are magnified by the fact that many occupations, previously assigned only to men due to their physical advantage, have passed into oblivion (e.g., blacksmithing) or been mechanized so that the justification for defining the job as "men's work" disappears. As the pool of legitimately "men's jobs" diminishes, the resistance to women in those that remain becomes a fight for men's shrinking "turf."

Policing is one of the few occupations where the legal right of women to equality of opportunity has been challenged by the claim that sex is a bona fide occupational qualification, on the basis of significant physical differences. While doctors and business executives may not want women as their colleagues and may say they do not perform as well as men, the question of whether women as a class have the ability to perform the work is no longer open. The physical issue, raised to the status of a legal question about women's right to be patrol officers, has generated a number of lawsuits, and is still not resolved in the minds of many male officers, a few policewomen, and some citizens.[1]

The changing division of labor in policing (and other work) poses a

1. Although Bloch et al. (1973a), Bloch and Anderson (1974a and 1974b), Sherman (1975), and Sichel et al. (1977) all found that women were able to perform adequately on patrol, their research does not have legal standing.

direct challenge to the basis of our social order and the cultural values on which it rests. It threatens not only the position of the men but the place of women as well. Recognition of such a threat may explain not only the vocal objections of male officers to patrol women but the hostility of police wives to policewomen on patrol and the behavior of some police*women.*

The nature of the work is a reality with which the women must cope. They must come to terms not only with the physical aspects but the requirement that they command rather than ask, and talk and look "tough" rather than act "ladylike." For most women this means altering longstanding patterns of interaction. For *police*women such changes appear less difficult and less threatening to their sense of identity; many were initially independent and appear to find an androgynous style comfortable and even liberating. Police*women,* however, have greater difficulty coming to terms with patrol work. Some resist adopting new verbal and nonverbal modes of assertiveness. For others, the problem is less being seen as a "lady" than frequently finding themselves in situations in which they do not know what to say or how to act "policelike." One very enthusiastic policewoman noted, "I got by on my personality and hard work. . . . People will say I gave 110% but there's more than willingness to work . . . to succeeding in this job. I lack the right degree of aggressiveness and self-confidence."

SEXUALITY IN THE WORKPLACE

One important aspect of male-female interaction in the workplace is sexuality, which includes both the consequence of individuals' definitions of themselves as masculine or feminine, and job-related sexual joking, pressure, and harassment. These issues have rarely been discussed in the literature on occupations (see Roy, 1974; Bradford et al., 1975; Spradley and Mann, 1975; and Riemer, 1976) although they affect a wide variety of workers.

Sexual conquest, as one facet of their shared masculinity, has long united policemen. It now threatens to divide the male officers who are in competition for a limited number of female officers and to weaken their subcultural solidarity, as some men form bonds with the policewomen.

Sexuality in the workplace, however, has a more divisive and negative effect on the women as a group. The female officers are divided between those few who gain advantages by granting sexual favors and those who do not.[2] The latter find themselves at a competitive disadvantage in relation to other policewomen, as well as to the male officers in the department. In addition, instead of focusing hostility on the male superior who uses his authority for sexual gain, the male officers displace their anger onto the women. All women as members of the group "female" are held responsible for the advantages sought by one of their own group. Finally, the burden of "controlling" those female officers who do not play by the department's formal rules falls on the shoulders of the other women. For example, one of the reasons that the department nurtured the formation of the Policewomen in Action organization was to establish a mechanism allowing female officers to influence those women the department was unwilling or unable to directly challenge over use of their sexuality on the job. On the other hand, policemen's willingness to favor an attractive woman or seek and accept sexual favors from a few policewomen continues to be ignored.

While sexual harassment is an issue of unexplored dimensions, sexual invitations or advances may be seen as less of a problem than other aspects of sexuality by some women, since they are familiar with responding to and dealing with them. The problems arise, according to one female officer, relating to men on other levels: as peers, supervisors, competitors, coworkers, and friends. What are the current "rules of the game"? Several women noted that they had been able to "charm" high-ranking officials into hearing a complaint or listening to an argument that might otherwise have been ignored. Should they put aside "feminine wiles" or the advantages conferred by being female? Could they if they wanted to? Questions regarding how women and men do and should relate to each other and their own sexuality while on the job are arising with increasing frequency as more work places become sexually integrated and sexual norms become more permissive. We still have only traditional models of male-female interaction, however, as a basis on which to evaluate and judge such behavior.

It has been suggested that as women become assimilated into the police world and adopt "liberated" sexual attitudes, they will adopt patterns of sexual behavior similar to those of the men. Although there are some "free spirits" among the policewomen currently, it is clear that liberation and an end to the double standard are not

---

2. The latter group includes women who may have had sexual relations with policemen but who do not exchange sexual intercourse for occupationally related goals.

imminent and are regarded with ambivalence by both men and women.

While greater sexual availability and activity on the part of the women promises a greater variety of partners for the men, it also is quite threatening to them. The sexual double standard has long been an ideological element supporting men's economic and physical control over women (see Collins, 1972). A single standard would not only add an element of reality to lockerroom tales and increase performance pressures on the men, it would also signal greater equalization of the economic and social positions of the sexes.

Women have long used their sexuality as a resource in male-female exchanges. When men controlled virtually all the economic resources, women adopted a strategy of feminine idealization and sexual repression in order to elevate their status and increase their power. They succeeded, but did so by maintaining cultural barriers between men and women; their very idealization kept them confined in a fantasy world, one in which they were protected by men. As women enter the occupational world, gain power and financial resources, the feminine ideal becomes less necessary. Although gains in other spheres permit a relaxation in sexual restraints, widespread promiscuity is unlikely because women have not yet attained equality so that sexuality remains a resource. While policewomen's sexual activity is likely to increase, several factors suggest that most women will not adopt behavior patterns like the men: the complications and implications of sexual activity among work peers increase pressures to limit such activities for the good of the group and its solidarity (which still leaves policewomen free to find partners outside of the department just as most of the men do); and the small numbers and relatively powerless position of female officers within the department suggest that men still define certain activities, and the social meaning attached to them, which will inhibit some women. It is likely that true sexual liberation will occur for most policewomen when there is an equalization of the power between men and women and the bargaining calculus that affects male-female exchange relations is shifted.

ORGANIZATIONAL POLICY
AND CULTURAL CHANGE

The policies of the work organization have a major impact on the way in which women or other newcomers perform their occupational roles. The organization trains the workers and is responsible for creating the environment and opportunities which enable them to learn and perform the work. While it cannot immediately alter stereotypes or cultural patterns of male-female interaction, it can establish effective training programs, actively seek to limit discrimination and harassment, assure channels of complaint, and attempt to correct problems—or it can fail in any or all of these areas.

The entry of women into police work raises many questions related to "affirmative action." In the case of policing, issues related to training (particularly physical training), the socialization of female officers for patrol duties, and assignments that affect subsequent opportunities within the department raise particularly difficult questions. How can a police department adhere to the law requiring equality of opportunity, adopt an evenhanded policy and at the same time meet the needs of both male and female officers? While there is no single or simple answer to the question, the Metropolitan Police Department of Washington, D.C., does not seem to have found a solution to the dilemma. It has taken the first step, prohibiting sex discrimination, but done little else, hoping that time and experience would eliminate the difficulties faced by the first group of women. Unfortunately such has not been the case.

What might the department do to alleviate problems and accelerate sexual integration? Several policy changes might be easily adopted. These changes imply an individual model rather than a structural approach to the situation but as short term suggestions they have some merit. For both new and experienced officers of both sexes, heightening awareness of the ways certain behaviors of each perpetuate traditional behavior patterns that are dysfunctional for effective police work is likely to be beneficial. In a number of instances misunderstandings have occurred and tensions have mounted through failures of a partner of one sex to act in certain ways that were taken for granted by the other. Greater sensitivity to and awareness of how their words and actions are perceived, and the encouragement of open communication about the difficulties that arise can alleviate some of the tensions and problems. It is particularly important that departmental leaders who make policies and enforce them gain greater awareness of the impact of their behavior on policewomen. The human relations aspects of police training have generally been given scant attention; efforts to improve communication between supervisors and officers, between police officers and citizens, and between male and female officers are likely to benefit both the police and the community.

The serendipitous effects of the prostitution detail should be institutionalized through the regular assignment of females to patrol
together. Rather than continuing to discourage female partnerships,
the department should selectively encourage them, since many policewomen act more independently and assertively when working with a
female partner than with a male partner. The use of policewomen as
training officers, particularly for female rookies, should also be
adopted to provide important role models for the latter.

While a structural approach to equal employment opportunity may
involve alteration of the organizational structure and job redefinition,
a more limited suggestion for dealing with the problems emanating
from the token status of policewomen includes a substantial increase
in the number of female officers. This would reduce the isolation and
effects of tokenism, and probably would improve women's position in
the power structure of the department, as well as increase their
opportunities. Similarly, continued support of the nascent Policewomen in Action organization on the part of the department is
beneficial.

None of these suggestions, however, will change the wider cultural
patterns of male-female power relations or eliminate the effects of
interpersonal cues that mirror and perpetuate these relations, which
serve to keep women "in their place" and limit their opportunities for
occupational success. In the long run, structural changes must be
accompanied by altered cultural values and changed interpersonal
patterns of behavior in order to replace the "male only" ethos of the
policemen's world—and the wider social world—with a heterosexual
basis for solidarity among male and female police officers.

MOTIVATION AND COMMITMENT

Motivation and commitment appear to be both a cause and a
consequence of policewomen's position in the work organization, as
well as women's place in the larger society. Women have different
work motivations and aspirations than men (Turner, 1964; Psathas,
1968) and apply a different meaning to success (Laws, 1976). Women
are affected by the sex role ideology that says work is the destiny of
men and marriage the destiny of women. The result is that achievement in the workplace often is viewed as adversely affecting their prospects of marriage thus depressing occupational aspirations.

Although the men and women in this study entered policing for
similar reasons, they displayed differences in aspirations and expec-

tations. These result from both cultural factors and structural features related to the position of women in the work organization. Women's status as tokens and their lack of power and opportunity for mobility—or the belief that mobility is blocked—leads to demotivation, lower levels of performance, and diminished aspirations for the future. In addition, the work, the working conditions (particularly changing shifts), and the policewomen's personal lives affect their aspirations and commitment. Policing is a "good" job for a single woman because it pays well and entails meeting single men. Patrol work, however, is more difficult to mesh with traditional marriage and motherhood, which most of the policewomen desire and expect; for this reason many female officers were hesitant to make plans or predictions about their futures. Their uncertain personal or family life plans are related to their life situations. Many are not married; others have not completed child-bearing or the early years of child-rearing. Although many of the male officers are in a similar phase of their life cycle, their expectations about domestic demands and responsibilities are different and lead toward rather than away from commitment to a career in policing.

The commitment process often begins before the worker enters a job, although commitment grows through participation in the work and the establishment of a place in the work organization. Policewomen (and other blue-collar women in nontraditional jobs) are likely to have had less anticipatory socialization to their job than their male peers or than women entering nontraditional occupations at the professional level. Thus they are likely to be initially less attached to their chosen occupation. The professional woman's commitment is tested *throughout* a long and costly training process which sensitizes professional women to the barriers they will face on the job and weeds out some of those with wavering commitment. It takes little more than a high school diploma and "good moral character" to become a police officer. For a policewoman commitment develops *after* she becomes an officer. The rookie policewoman is catapulted into a difficult situation on entering the department. New skills and unfamiliar behavior must be learned, the opposition of male coworkers must be taken in stride and the interactional and structural barriers which affect wavering attachment to the job all must be faced at the same time.

Women may be less committed to police work than men because they do not derive a "bonus" in terms of personal identity from their work. While men, too, may enter policing with little dedication to the

organization or occupation, the police role is often sufficient to
motivate them to active law enforcement. In fact, rookie men are often
felt to be too "gung ho" as they seek to prove themselves "real men"
and gain acceptance in the male subcultural world of the police.
Female officers, who have "nothing to prove" as women and who,
instead, may feel their feminine identity is threatened the more they
succeed in being "policelike," often have a different perspective on
their work than men. Although it is obviously too early to determine
whether a similar proportion of policewomen and policemen will
remain in the department until they become eligible for retirement,
from the limited evidence available it appears that women have not
had a higher resignation rate than comparable (new) males, but they
do transfer more frequently from patrol to "inside" assignments than
the men.[3]

IMPLICATIONS FOR THE STUDY
OF WORK AND OCCUPATIONS

Although it has long been understood that a work organization
functions as a complex of occupational and organizational roles that
shape workers' selves, and that sex is a variable which has vast social
consequences extending well beyond the biological differences between males and females, the manner in which gender both affects
institutional arrangements in the workplace and is affected by them is
rarely studied and poorly understood.

Much analysis of occupational behavior has centered on intra- and
inter-role conflicts for workers, yet little attention thus far has been
paid to what Hughes (1945) more than thirty years ago termed
"dilemmas and contradictions of status." Students of work and
occupations instead have produced detailed ethnographic descriptions
of the nature and organization of a myriad of occupations without
explaining or inquiring how sex-segregated occupations reflect and
reinforce gender arrangements for dominants or create conflicts for

---

3. For Bloch's findings with respect to the first group of policewomen, see chapter 5,
footnote 6. With respect to the 55 officers in my interview sample, by December 1977,
18 months after completion of the interviews, five of the men but none of the women
had left the department (four resigned, one retired as a result of injuries). Seven of the
women who had patrol assignments at the time of the interviews had been given "inside"
assignments (in the administrative section, as dispatchers or in youth services) whereas
none of the men were assigned to these duties. About the same number of male and
female officers had transferred to scooter and investigative assignments.

minority workers. What has been missing from the study of work and occupations is the gender variable. Work roles assigned to men were taken as "naturally" assigned to them; those assigned to women were viewed as "appropriate" extensions of women's "natural" more diffuse social role. The differences in male and female access to power and opportunities that shape occupational behavior and, further, the manner in which occupational and organizational arrangements reflect even broader social arrangements between the sexes which they simultaneously reinforce have been largely overlooked.

Goffman (1977) has observed that certain features of social organization function to reflect and magnify gender differences thus confirming gender stereotypes and prevailing arrangements. One such feature is the division of labor; another is selective job placement. We need to better understand the manner in which biological differences of little relevance to the actual work come to be socially elaborated and of great social importance through the phenomenon he termed "institutional reflexivity." Further research is needed on the ways in which gender affects institutional arrangements and simultaneously serves to reflect and confirm prevailing stereotypes and arrangements.

The increasing number of "deviant cases" in which persons of one gender enter occupations normally assigned to the other offer an opportunity to better understand the impact of taken-for-granted gender arrangements on organizational and interactional patterns and vice versa. It is time not only to "bring men back in" (Homans, 1964), but to bring in women as well, and to rethink our understanding of work and occupations in terms of the subtle but pervasive impact of gender.

A GLIMPSE AT THE FUTURE: SEX ROLE, OCCUPATIONAL ROLE, AND SOCIAL CHANGE

In briefly looking toward the future it is necessary to consider not only the impact of social and organizational changes on female officers, but on policemen, the organization, and the occupational role since these tend to have reciprocal and interactive effects. Changes in the occupation have permitted the assignment of women to patrol while, at the same time, patrolwomen foster and intensify the trends that led to their assignment to patrol. While a thorough examination of the implications of sexual integration on policing for the men, the occupational role, and the police organization would require another study, some of these implications will be noted in viewing the future for policewomen.

One growing change in policing is the alteration in the patrol officer's role, and relations with the community, which include an increase in service-related tasks, an official deemphasis on the physical and violent aspects of the work, legal restriction on the use of force by officers, and efforts to "professionalize" the police, which have led to a weakening of "the system" (Wilson, 1963) and tighter bureaucratic control of officers. In addition, changes in recruitment, personnel and training policies have opened the doors of the police station (if only slightly) to a more heterogeneous group of officers (including members of minorities, the college educated, and physically smaller officers) who, in turn, affect the police role. The assignment of women to patrol also was affected by and contributes to on-going changes in societal sex role definitions and norms. The impact of women officers must be viewed in the context of other changes which are likely to affect their future.

For many policemen and citizens alike, one important question is whether the presence of an increasing number of female officers (who are culturally defined as nonviolent) will change the nature of the police role—by definition a forceful and potentially violent one. Will they affect the policemen's pay, prestige, and sense of manhood? If women come to dominate police work or attain representation on the force approaching half the officers, then it is very likely that either the occupational role or the meaning of manhood and womanhood—or, more likely, both—will have to change markedly. It is likely that policing would lose some prestige, the recent acceleration in police salaries would slow down, and the strongly masculine image of police work would disappear. This prospect, however, is very remote due to the strength of our entrenched stereotypes of sex roles, the nature of police work itself, the resistance of departmental leadership to such change, and the slow turnover of police. While some increase in the proportion of women in most departments is predictable, the likelihood is small that women will be represented in more than token numbers in policing during this century.

Yet even women's token presence has led to pressures for acceleration of present trends so that the future of women in policing, despite the barriers detailed in the foregoing chapters, appears to be relatively hopeful. Short term factors that permit a guardedly optimistic appraisal of female officers' situation include: their gradual increase in

Conclusions 217

their assignment to patrol; the birth of an organization of and for
female officers in one major city; signs of increasing acceptance of
their patrol role by citizens; an increasing number of policemen who
regard the presence of policewomen on patrol as a "fact of life" which
they take for granted and even occasionally welcome; the availability
of policewomen as real and media role models for young girls and
women to emulate, facilitating anticipatory socialization.

Longer term signs of a less difficult situation for women in policing
in the future also can be found in changes in sex role norms that are
affecting adults and the socialization of males and females of the next
generation, and changes in patrol work that make it less incompatible
with the newly emerging female role.

In his discussion of the articulation of status sets Merton (1957)
observed that social structures adapt as cultural mandates change.
The more frequent the occurrence of patterned conflict, the more
likely it is that new norms will evolve to govern these situations by
assigning or revising priorities of obligation. The growing number of
women in policing as well as in other nontraditional occupations
make it likely that the trend of change in sex role norms which has
occurred in the past decade will continue and accelerate. This will ease
some of the conflicts currently faced by policewomen and others in
nontraditional occupations as a more "modern" sex role perspective
becomes predominant (Komarovsky, 1946 and 1973). These changes,
plus strong efforts in the past decade to eliminate sexism and sex role
stereotyping in education are likely to result in a generation of women
who have a more positive view of themselves and their occupational
options, and who are more willing to assert themselves to assure that
opportunities materialize. Increased athletic opportunities for girls
and encouragement to develop their physical skills are likely to
diminish the physical differences between men and women. But, as
Goffman (1977) notes, symbolic displays of these physical differences
abound and are likely to persist as subtle reminders of the social
differences that have grown from them.

Finally, the continued modification of the patrol officer's role is
likely to benefit policewomen. For many years, women's police role
was limited to those tasks which were extensions of their traditional
sex role. Change in the patrol officer's role (as well as in sex role
expectations) facilitated women's entry into patrol work. The police
role may be viewed as encompassing a continuum of activities ranging

from control to support. Traditionally the police emphasized the control and law enforcement activities closely associated with "masculine" behavior and disdained the support or service elements of the patrol role as "feminine" activities. Public demand for better service and an end to "police brutality," departmental pressure to "professionalize" the police, and judicial decisions restricting certain police activities have resulted in great pressure on officers to incorporate both control and support. While police work continues to involve the legitimate control of violence, the patrol officer's role has expanded to include social mediation and the provision of services. The result is a wider role repertoire demanded of patrol officers and the need to act both in ways that are stereotypically masculine and stereotypically feminine. Increasingly, police patrol requires a flexible androgynous style of behavior "appropriate" for either male or female officers with a "modern" sex role orientation. The presence of such officers (i.e., the *police*women and men who are modern and moderate in sex role orientation and more service oriented in their occupational role outlook) is thus an encouraging sign that some change has occurred and is likely to continue in the future.

What do these changes mean for the men and the department? They portend the continued weakening of the old officer solidarity based on homogeneity of social class, ethnicity, and shared masculinity and point to the necessity of developing new bases of trust and cooperation (a necessity in police work) founded on a common work experience, as well as a decrease in the separation of the police as a group from the community.

For some policemen whose sense of masculinity is derived from the "manly" nature of their job, the gradual redefinition of masculinity and changes in the role of the police officer incorporating more service elements are threats to their sense of personal and occupational identity. Currently such traditional law enforcement-oriented policemen dominate police organizations and the informal cultural world of police work, thereby limiting the power, opportunities, and numbers of women as well as other "outsiders." Their hegemony, however, is under challenge by a number of groups—blacks, women, service-oriented officers, and the community—and probably will be diminished, particularly if current trends continue. Yet there is a limit: while policing is likely to become somewhat more service oriented, more bureaucratically controlled, and more heterogeneous, the core of the job—exercise of authority and the right to use violence in the face of resistance—will remain, requiring a person who, for some time to come, is more likely to be male than female.

Because the barriers to policewomen are built into the formal and informal structures of the work organization and, more importantly, into the culturally prescribed habits of male-female interaction, only major alteration in both occupational structures and culturally defined patterns of behavior will eliminate them. Such changes appear to be underway at a slow and uncertain pace. The covergence of increased numbers of policewomen (decreasing the effects of tokenism), the effects of time and habit (making the presence of female officers increasingly a taken for granted phenomenon) and changes in both sex and police role norms and behavior all give rise to cautious optimism. Perhaps in the future, cultural and organization changes will permit the emergence of a truly androgynous police force where individual characteristics rather than sex determine the officer's chances of success. Until then, however, as one policewoman wryly observed, female officers will be pressured to "think like men, work like dogs, and act like ladies."

Appendix

Field Research Methods
and Ethical Issues

While I had a longstanding interest in the role of women in the occupational world I had not originally anticipated focusing on policewomen. In the fall of 1973 I began teaching undergraduates, most of whom were police officers, at the Center for the Administration of Justice (CAJ) of The American University. During that semester one such student, who learned of my interest in women's issues, not only spoke with me at great length about the on-going "experiment" with policewomen which was occurring in his district, but made available to me his newspaper clippings and a copy of a term paper he had written on the subject. Previously unaware of their existence, I became curious about women on patrol. Perhaps equally important, he and a number of my other students that semester shattered many of my negative stereotypes about "cops."

During the following year, as I continued to teach for CAJ and develop my research plans, another student suggested that I join the Police Reserve Corps to get an inside view of the police department. The more I considered his suggestion the better it appeared.

Initially I planned to focus this study on the backgrounds and occupational choices of policewomen in comparison with policemen, and a comparison of the male and female officers' role conceptions and role performance, particularly as they related to one specific policing activity—the handling of public inebriates. The focus on police handling of drunks, however, was eliminated quite early in the participant observation phase; the infrequency and low priority of dealing with drunks made gathering observational data difficult and attitudinal statements only weakly related to general occupational role conception.

The choice of the site of the research was easy. Washington, D.C., is my home; its department had the largest percentage of policewomen on patrol in the United States; it had the Police Reserve Corps, which offered the opportunity to do participant observation unlike most other local jurisdictions; I had a number of contacts in that department; and, finally, I hoped to follow-up on the officers studied during their first eighteen months of police service by Bloch and Anderson (1974a and 1974b).

I opted to study only one department in order to control such variables as the nature of the community, and the size, administrative style, and policy of the department, while comparing male and female officers. I realized the limitations of such a case study in terms of generalizing results, but it appeared more feasible for a single researcher and more appropriate for the questions I was seeking to answer.

Initially I had hoped to add longitudinal and qualitative dimensions to the findings reported by Bloch. That study had attempted to determine whether women could effectively function as patrol officers. It assumed that the work tasks, pressures, and informal work environment of the male and female officers were the same. It found, for example, that women made fewer arrests and engaged in less "conduct unbecoming an officer" but made no attempt to determine why this was so. Rather than ask whether women could perform adequately (since that question had been answered in the affirmative) I sought to understand why women became officers, how they defined their job, and how they performed a number of policing tasks in comparison with their male counterparts.

I spent the summer of 1975 reviewing the literature, and sought permission from the Metropolitan Police Department to gain access to departmental records and statistical data, and join the Police Reserve Corps. It proved impossible, however, to obtain either departmental support or data that was necessary for a follow-up on the Bloch study. The department did, however, agree to forward my application to the reserves "without prejudice."

In September I was accepted as a reserve officer, selected a district, and was sworn in. Several weeks later I received my uniform and was permitted to patrol as a reserve. Initially I had viewed the participant observation merely as an exciting and interesting way to become acquainted with departmental organization and policy, the work of police officers, and their informal social world, all of which were unfamiliar to me. The data for the report were to be drawn principally from interviews which I could design on the basis of issues and questions raised by the observation. When other sources of data became unavailable (i.e., official statistics) the importance of participant observation to the study greatly increased. As participant observation progressed it became clear that what was intended to provide background became central to the research endeavor. It both led to a gradual shift in the research questions, and, in a manner similar to that observed by Cain (1973:9): "it served the purpose of establishing *rapport* so that in many cases it would be fair to say that it was the observation work which made the interviews possible . . . and . . . also improved their validity."

On commencing field work I was in a difficult and sometimes uncomfortable position: neither formally accepted by the department to do research nor prohibited from doing so. I had access to the police department from the very bottom and was "on my own" to negotiate the system as a participant. In retrospect I believe my acting like any other new reserve officer assigned to a district, and failing to inform the officials of my district of my research interests, was regrettable both on ethical grounds and because I believe it would have greatly facilitated my entree into the district and opportunities to work with officers of my choice; I was fearful, however, that if I exposed my research the district inspector would not permit me to work as a reserve.

The day I got my uniform, brought it home, and modeled it in front of the mirror, I laughed so hard tears rolled down my cheeks. I could not believe that it was really me with a badge, mace, handcuffs, and nightstick—none of which I knew how to use properly. That night as I drove to the police station the laughter and self-wonder turned to a knot in the pit of my stomach and a panicky "what-am-I-doing-in-a-situation-like-this?" feeling. The sense of strangeness was magnified by my background and lack of familiarity with the police world. I had grown up in a white upper-middle-class suburban community, and until I began teaching at CAJ, had no contact with police except as a participant in civil rights and anti-war demonstrations in the late 1960's and early 1970's.

The first two or three months of work were alternately exhilarating and absorbing and depressing and lonely. I could only rely so far on my reading which included Lofland (1971), Schatzman and Strauss (1973), and Johnson (1975) for "how to do it" instructions supplemented by Hammond (1964), Glaser and Strauss (1967) and Wax (1971); Liebow's (1967) and Whyte's (1955) accounts of successful observation studies; the "police classics" describing the organization and norms of police work; and the discussions by Buckner (1967), Westley (1970), Manning (1972) and Cain (1973) of their experiences as field researchers studying the police. Although they aided in planning the field work, alerted me to some pitfalls, and reminded me that I would feel isolated, I had to find my own way. This was made difficult by several factors: my lowly status as a reserve; my lack of adequate training for street patrol situations; my visibility as a white female; the need to establish trust; and my difficulty in establishing an acceptable identity.

As a reserve I was permitted to attend roll call (which I frequently did) and was permitted to work whenever I wanted. At the station I was assigned to a scout car that had only one officer. I did not have a regular schedule, and worked three or four times per week, usually during the four-to-midnight shift. With no assigned partner I did not receive much systematic instruction or develop close relationships as a "coworker." In retrospect I might have gained greater acceptance and more of an "insider's" view had I worked regularly with only one section for several months; instead I chose to maximize my opportunity to observe and work with a variety of policewomen who were assigned to all three sections. I had hoped to socialize with officers off duty but was not invited to join their informal social activities.

Initially I tried to maintain a low profile. I was frightened of doing anything that would lead to injury, greater ostracism, or my removal from the reserves. My lack of training, coupled with my personal background, was a real handicap. I did not know district geography (and initially was often disoriented), could not use the radio, and was uncomfortable "rapping" with people on the street. I did not know the D.C. Criminal Code and was not well equipped to physically defend myself or my partner. It is hard to describe my terror, and determination to prove myself, in the first months. My field notes for November 8, 1975, indicate some of my feelings:

> I find myself being very edgy about having someone behind me. The problem is that I now expect an attack or am fearful because I don't know how to judge or gauge which situations are dangerous. They all seem potentially dangerous (and are) but I see officers like W— [my partner for that tour of duty] know when to be casual and appear to be

comfortable on the street. I'm jumpy as a cat. Noises, hand movements toward me scare me. I don't know what to do. I startle, back away . . . stay silent, putting myself in a position of being protected. I want to be protected, but don't. I want to establish that I'm O.K. by acting courageously—but how?

Establishing credibility and gaining officers' trust, a key task in fieldwork, was problematic. With each new partner I had to begin the process anew. I discovered that most officers do not like to work with unfamiliar, and therefore unpredictable, partners, and many resent the presence of police reserves. I worked at gaining trust by being uncritical of officers' behavior, playing "dumb" (but occasionally asking too many questions), not repeating any gossip or information about other officers that I had heard, and being helpful (several partners were surprised by my willingness to pump gas, for example). Since I do not smoke and many of the men were clearly bothered by my offer to pay even for a cup of coffee, these normal avenues of simple exchange as a means of building relationships were limited.

Another difficulty was that of establishing an identity. I entered the district as just another reserve officer, although several officers knew me as their current or past instructor at The American University. I tried several identities before finding one that was acceptable both to the officers and me. We finally settled on the professor trying to learn more about police and their work.

Gradually I learned the ways of the stationhouse, mastered radio communication and the geography of the district, and became familiar with the identities and reputations of both officers and officials. As I learned from my partners and from my mistakes, I became more confident and assertive. My presence, while never inconspicuous since there were few white females assigned to the district, slowly normalized; I came to be taken less as a spy for Internal Affairs Division than as an accomplice and personable reserve officer who rode along. While not "of" the police I was taken at least as "for" them. On December 20, 1975, for example, I noted, "I feel like I'm breaking through the veil of propriety and seeing bad policing as well as good." By that time I was occasionally able to work with a partner of my choice, including policewomen.

As the field research progressed, my attention gradually shifted from an emphasis on street incidents and a comparison of male and female officers' role conceptions to concern with the effects of the in-

ternal organization, the men's attitudes and their interpersonal behavior on the policewomen. This resulted both from my observation
in the police station and on the street and from long discussions with
one policewoman who became my informant and good friend during
the project. Introduced by a mutual acquaintance at American University, she proved to be an invaluable source of information about
the department and the problems of women in policing as well as a
source of additional contacts and strong moral support. Her views on
policework are characteristic of *police*women; I have used her words
occasionally in the text. Through her I was able to meet about a dozen
policewomen from other units (representative of both *police*women
and police*women*) at several informal social gatherings and listened
to their discussions which often revolved around their work problems.

Because in police work there are often long periods with little to do,
participant observation served as an excellent form of "conversational
interviewing" (Becker and Geer, 1957). In the scout car, I had a great
deal of opportunity to discuss with my partners a variety of work-
related issues, including women on patrol. Participant observation
overcame some of the problems I could anticipate in interviewing
(Becker and Geer, 1957). I learned the "native language," and
identified topics officers appeared unwilling or unable to talk about
including sexual harassment, which few women admitted experi-
encing, while noting it happened to others, and the threat to their
masculinity posed by women, which men would not discuss. I gained
information on matters people see through distorted lenses including
the "favoritism" given to women and the "discrimination" against
them. The participant observation also permitted me to informally
pre-test many of my interview questions.

During the winter of 1976 I designed the interview schedule and
selected the interview sample, as I continued participant observation.
By March I was ready to begin interviewing.

The initial interview sample included all the women assigned to the
district and an equal number of male officers matched as closely as
possible for length of service and race. Later when it became apparent
that their supervisors' views were important factors in understanding
the problems and coping strategies of the women, I designed a briefer
interview schedule for a small sample of officials.

Interviewing posed a number of logistical problems unique to the
population being interviewed. The first problem, since I did not have
formal access to department personnel records, was getting a list of all

of the officers assigned to the district, their race and length of service, in order to select a sample. A newly compiled district personnel roster noting the officers' race and assignment completed in December 1975 was made available to me by a friendly sergeant with the proviso that I not use the telephone numbers listed to contact the officers. A friend working at the training academy permitted me to use their records to determine when the officers completed their training and were assigned to the district. On the basis of this information (ignoring the fact that some officers had worked undercover before receiving training) I matched a group of male officers to the female population. For the few women with more than three years experience, there were so many potential pairs that the men were chosen largely on the basis of accessibility (i.e., they were still in the section on patrol and I knew them). The sergeants were selected to represent a cross-section of the officials in the district in terms of race (three of the thirteen were black), assignment (eleven patrol sergeants; two with other assignments involving policewomen), experience (ranging from six to more than twenty years of police service), and observed style of supervision (apathetic, military-authoritarian, or relatively democratic and flexible). In addition, one lieutenant and the district inspector were interviewed.

During the period between January 1976, when I determined the sample of officers I would interview, and June 1976, when the interviewing was concluded, some turnover of policewomen occurred. Three of the women on the original interview schedule resigned or were terminated before I could contact them. A number of new women were assigned to the district. I did not seek interviews with the women just out of the training academy; I did interview three additional women who had experience in other assignments before coming to my district. None of the men in the sample left the district during that time.

Five of the 33 women in the sample were not interviewed. Two flatly declined and three others declined after a great deal of excuse-making and several cancelled appointments. Two of the five were white; three were black. Among the males three declined (two were black) and several others failed to keep several appointments and were replaced in the interview sample by others of the same race and length of police experience. Two white sergeants declined to be interviewed. In all 28 female and 27 male officers, 13 sergeants, one lieutenant, and the district inspector were interviewed.

Contacting officers, arranging interviews, and conducting them as scheduled proved difficult. The only way of reaching the officers was at the station, before roll call or after work. This meant that contact was public and often hurried. Although I gave each officer a letter which explained the purpose of the interview and recorded its time and place, many failed to appear. The "selective forgetting" of interview arrangements occurred with such frequency that I concluded this was another way for the officer who did not feel comfortable turning down my request face to face, to refuse to be interviewed. In addition, a variety of work and personal circumstances made scheduling difficult and led to cancelled appointments. It was virtually impossible to plan interviews more than a day or two in advance; many ended up being completed at the spur of the moment when an officer finished a tour of duty and I happened to be around the station.

The final problem was the interview site. Neither I nor the officers had an office. When it was possible and the officer was agreeable, I conducted the interview in her or his home. Others, uncomfortable at this prospect, were interviewed in an empty roll call room or the reserve room at the police station, or at neighborhood bars or restaurants. Use of the station for interviewing inhibited some officers because of the lack of privacy; the local bars, while more private and removed from the police atmosphere, were noisy, making tape recording and even conversation difficult.

While I was conducting the interviews the department initiated a series of seminars for policewomen. All female officers were required to attend one session. I was not permitted to participate or observe any of the seminars, but in a number of interviews conducted after the women attended these meetings, I added questions to the established interview schedule soliciting their impression of the session they had attended and their views of the issues discussed. This proved to be a valuable though unanticipated source of information about their perceptions both of other policewomen and the problems women face as officers.

In addition to interviews in the district in which I was a reserve officer, I arranged interviews with five women who were or had been policewomen, and who had strategic roles in the policewomen on patrol program.

The methods employed in this study raise a number of technical and ethical questions. Although many facets of the data collection were less than ideal, what is lacking in neatness of design was compensated for in familiarity with one district and in the scope of contacts with its patrol officers.

It is impossible to determine to what extent the fact that I was doing research affected the officers' behavior in my presence. I share with Skolnick (1966:36) his assumptions that the more time an observer spends with subjects the more used to his presence they become; participant observation offers less opportunity to the subject to lie than would a questionnaire; and in many situations the police were not free to alter their behavior. The participant observation and interviewing supplemented each other by permitting the corroboration of data. Having familiarity with district operations and some of the personnel enabled me to more accurately detect dishonest or evasive answers and make further probes in the interviews. Having ridden with 19 of the 55 officers either prior to or following the interview, I had the opportunity to compare their statements and behavior.

Research of this sort raises a number of ethical issues, including the effect of my presence on citizens' or defendants' fate; the pretense that I was a police officer in the eyes of citizens; the explanation of my presence to the officers; the use of a citizens' organization to further my research objectives; and the utilization of informal sources of information to draw my sample.

With respect to citizens' fate, the justification for my presence may be found in its consequences. Since it is improbable that police officers would treat suspects more severely or citizens with less respect for their constitutional rights in front of me than if I were not there, my presence probably had a salutary effect. But what effect did my presence have on a citizen's right to privacy when in the company of an officer I entered their homes, in several instances searched suspects, and was confided in by suspects who tried to explain away seemingly culpable actions? The observer must, despite all efforts, in some measure influence the fate of the subjects of study. The ethical line I drew was to minimize all suggestion of active law enforcement on my part. For example, I never suggested taking police action or ticketing a car unless the violation was flagrantly dangerous for other drivers. On several occasions my partners commented on my lack of opinions, which made them uneasy. When a partner solicited my opinion—which was a very infrequent occurrence since I was both a reserve officer and a female—I behaved as any partner would and responded on the basis of my knowledge and the situation. My identity as the "professor" meant that I was consulted on spelling for reports rather than points of law or police actions.

In situations which called for assisting a citizen, I took a more active role without qualm, because in most instances it was consonant with my role as a citizen to offer such help. I searched for a lost dog, assisted my partner in delivering a drunken woman home, assisted and comforted citizens who had been victims of crimes, accidents, or vandalism.

Conducting searches of potential suspects caused me greater discomfort. I was called on, however, only when no other policewoman was available. Had I not conducted the searches on the scene, the arresting officer would have taken the suspect to the station where there was a policewoman on duty. My conducting searches at the site of the suspected crime thus enabled the suspect to avoid longer detainment and the possible embarrassment of being taken to the police station. I attempted to treat the suspects with the dignity and respect I would have wanted given to me.

Arrests were also troublesome but far less frequent than I had imagined. Both of the "disorderly conduct" arrests made in my presence were questionable, but in both situations I acted only as a silent bystander. The other arrests were cases in which the arrestee was apprehended "in the act" and other witnesses were available to testify or the officer consulted with an official who advised on the appropriate action.

I had resolved prior to my entry into the reserves that I would truthfully report about the circumstances of any act or event as I perceived it even if it meant challenging the testimony of another officer. I realized that such behavior would be a violation of "the rule of silence," but was resolved to resign from the reserves rather than perjure myself or sign a false statement should such a situation arise. It never did.

Only once did I consider resigning from the reserves and terminating the research. In that instance, my partner and another officer suggested I remain in the scout car, while they invaded the privacy of a prostitute and john (customer) in their hotel room. I opted to go along and felt upset by the incident. That the man was considered to be "psycho" or dangerous by the initiating officer and several of the streetwalkers, and that he did not have the amount of money promised to the prostitute (a fact ascertained by an illegal search) may explain—but cannot justify—the officers' behavior. Although no legal action was taken, the civil rights of the two were clearly violated.

I attempted to behave as a partner or reserve should ("by the book") and to treat people as I would want to be treated. This standard leaves unanswered the general question of how far a participant observer should aid the police in carrying out their duties. There is no easy answer. I found that the aid I offered as a "peace officer" greatly surpassed that offered in "law enforcement." My personal morality supported my assisting the officers in the apprehension of someone accused of a serious crime in accordance with proper procedures; I was unperturbed by aiding officers who had arrested a woman accused of murder. Because my ability to cope with a physically threatening situation was so seriously doubted (since I was unarmed, untrained, unproven, and female) my partners admitted to "not feeling like working" and being more restrained than usual; they did not want to get into any situation threatening my safety, or where they needed to rely on me for their safety. I had resolved that I would act in self-defense or in defense of my partner, but in several instances where I might have more assertively come to the assistance of my partner, I did not do so. This was less a matter of ethical or moral niceties than hesitation based on ignorance and inexperience.

Perhaps more serious were the ethical questions relating to my responsibility to the police officers with whom I worked and the reserve organization. I had informed the department of my desire to conduct the research and join the reserve corps; the application did not ask why a citizen desired to join that organization. I was not questioned or interviewed, I never deceived anyone in the reserves about my interests or intentions, nor did I have occasion to announce them. My research interests became generally known but were considered irrelevant as long as I performed the duties of a reserve officer in good faith, which I believe I did.

Far more problematic was my presence and presentation of self to the officers with whom I was assigned to work. They had no choice when told by a sergeant that I was to be their partner. At first many were not aware that I was conducting research. Several police acquaintances urged me to hide my real reasons for membership in the reserve corps because they predicted officers would "clam up" or alter their behavior. Because I felt covert observation would have been a violation of the officers' rights, I decided to inform them. Yet there was no one to introduce me and no way to announce my interests.

I had to inform each partner in the course of our working together. Sometimes that was easy, since one of the first questions that partners asked me was, "Why did you join the reserves?" With others it was more difficult either because we immediately were given an assignment or because it did not fit into the flow of conversation. Gradually it became known that I was "writing a book" and officers would ask whether it was done and whether they would be in it. I explained that neither the district nor individuals would be identified and that it would be more than a year before it was written. Once they accepted the fact that I was not a journalist interested in an exposé, some relaxed. Others never did. A few officers sought me out and "sounded off" about their views of the work and department. Some opened up about personal problems, happy to have a sympathetic audience who was "for" but not "of" the police. A few were openly hostile to my presence.

There is no way to ascertain to what extent my unique combination of statuses—white, female, reserve, university instructor, and researcher—affected the officers' reactions to me or altered their behavior in reaction to my presence. I know that as a female I was treated differently from a male. I was excluded from the lockerroom and thus a segment of police life and culture. I could not be "one of the boys" and there was no equivalent "one of the girls." The men readily accepted me as a female and at time I was very uncomfortable about that, particularly when cast into the seductress and pet roles (see chapter 6). Questions about my personal life (such as "Are you sure you're happily married?" and "Do you go out on your husband?") were difficult to handle. Since I wanted to explore the men's views of women, sex roles, and sexual behavior, I did not want to say "mind your own business" or sound too "stuffy," but did not want to encourage sexual relationships.

As a white in an organization in which the number and influence of black officers has rapidly increased, but remains a source of tension and internal political struggle, my race was a barrier to communication and trust. I found interpersonal relations with the white women generally warmer and more open than with the black women. Some of the latter were indeed hospitable and helpful; others were clearly closed and suspicious of me. While we had our sex in common, race, and perhaps differences in life style, remained a barrier. With the men, race was less a perceptible factor. I was treated as "a lady," sex object, or pet by both black and white men.

A final barrier was that of social class. Limitations of my upper middle-class origins, and professional life style and language became painfully clear to me when I discovered many "experience gaps" during the months of participant observation and interviewing. I was often asked where I lived and occasionally questioned about my husband's job and my own work. The responses to their queries set me off as "different" and in some cases may have increased difficulties in understanding and communication.

All research is conducted from a particular perspective. Mine was limited by my ascribed characteristics, my position as a researcher-reserve officer, and by personal biases and shortcomings. I sought to make myself a sensitive human research instrument within the limitations of the research situation. The degree to which I was able to do so is reflected in the findings, and in future research which will more systematically measure the observations presented here.

References

Abrecht, Mary Ellen (with Barbara L. Stern)
  1976 The Making of a Woman Cop. New York: Morrow.
Alex, Nicholas
  1969 Black in Blue: A Study of Negro Policemen. New York: Appleton, Century-Crofts.
  1976 New York Cops Talk Back: A Study of a Beleaguered Minority. New York: Wiley.
Allen, Mary S.
  1925 The Pioneer Policewoman. London: Chatto and Windus.
Angrist, Shirley
  1969 "The Study of Sex Roles." Journal of Social Issues 25:215-32.
Arkin, William and Lynne Dobrofsky
  1978 "Military Socialization and Masculinity." Journal of Social Issues 32: 151-68.
Banton, Michael
  1964 Policemen in the Community. New York: Basic Books.
Bayley, David and Harold Mendelsohn
  1968 Minorities and the Police. New York: Free Press.
Beard, Eugene, Lee P. Brown, and Lawrence E. Gary
  1976 Attitudes and Perceptions of Black Police Officers of the District of Columbia Metropolitan Police Department. Washington: Howard University Institute for Urban Affairs and Research.
Becker, Howard and Blanche Geer
  1957 "Participant Observation and Interviewing: A Comparison." Human Organization 16:28-32.
Berkeley, George
  1969 The Democratic Policeman. Boston: Beacon Press.

235

Bernard, Jessie
1974 "Sex Difference: An Overview." Modular Number 26. New York: MSS Modular Publications, Inc.
1978 Models for the Relationship Between the World of Women and the World of Men. Pp. 219-338 in Louis Kriesberg (ed.), Research in Social Movements, Conflict, and Change. Greenwich, Conn.: JAI Press, Inc.
Biddle, Bruce and E. J. Thomas (eds.)
1966 Role Theory: Concepts and Research. New York: Wiley.
Bittner, Egon
1967 "The Police on Skid Row: A Study in Peacekeeping." American Sociological Review 32:699-715.
1970 The Functions of Police in Modern Society. Chevy Chase, Maryland: National Institute of Mental Health.
Black, Donald
1968 "Police Encounters and Social Organization." Ph.D. dissertation, University of Michigan.
Bloch, Peter B. and Deborah Anderson
1974a Policewomen on Patrol: Final Report: Methodology, Tables, and Instruments. Washington: Urban Institute.
1974b Policewomen on Patrol: Final Report. Washington: Urban Institute.
Bloch, Peter B., Deborah Anderson, and Pam Gervais
1973a D.C. Policewomen Evaluation Vol. III: Instruments. Washington: Urban Institute.
1973b Policewomen on Patrol: Major Findings: First Report. Washington: Urban Institute.
Bordua, David and Albert J. Reiss, Jr.
1966 "Command, Control and Charisma: Reflections on Police Bureaucracy." American Journal of Sociology 72:68-76.
Boyd, Mary
1953 "The Role of the Policewoman." The Police Yearbook. Washington: International Association of Chiefs of Police.
Bradford, David L., Alice Sargent, and Melinda Sprague
1975 "The Executive Man and Woman: The Issue of Sexuality." Pp. 39-58 in Francine E. Gordon and Myra H. Strober (eds.), Bringing Women in Management. New York: McGraw-Hill.
Breece, Constance M. and Gerald R. Garrett
1974 "Women in Policing: Changing Perspectives on the Role." Paper presented at the annual meeting of the American Society of Criminology.
Brown, Roger
1965 Social Psychology. New York: Free Press.
Buckner, H. T.
1967 "The Police: The Culture of a Social Control Agency." Ph.D. dissertation, University of California, Berkeley.

Buwalda, I. W.
1945 "The Policewoman: Yesterday, Today, and Tomorrow." Journal of
Social Hygiene 31:290-93.
Cain, Maureen
1973 Society and the Policeman's Role. London: Routledge, Kegan Paul.
Chappell, Duncan
1975 "Forcible Rape and the Criminal Justice System: Surveying Present
Practices and Projecting Future Trends." Crime and Delinquency
22:125-36.
Chevigny, Paul
1969 Police Power. New York: Vintage.
Coleman, Milton
1978 "'Imbalance' Seen Among D.C. Police Blacks, Women." *Washington
Post*, July 11, B1.
Collins, Randall
1971 "A Conflict Theory of Sexual Stratification." Social Problems 19:
3-21.
Condor, Stella
1960 Woman on the Beat. London: Hale.
Crites, Laura
1973 "Women in Law Enforcement." Management Information Services 5.
Crozier, Michael
1964 The Bureaucratic Phenomenon. Chicago: University of Chicago
Press.
Cumming, Elaine, Ian Cumming, and Laura Edell
1965 "Policeman as Philosopher, Guide and Friend." Social Problems 12:
276-86.
Dalton, Melville
1959 Men Who Manage. New York: Wiley.
David, Deborah and Robert Brannon (eds.)
1976 The Forty-nine Percent Majority: The Male Sex Role. Reading,
Mass.: Addison-Wesley.
Davis, Kenneth C.
1975 Police Discretion. St. Paul: West.
Edmundson, Susan
1975 "Policewomen: How Well are They Doing a Man's Job?" Ladies
Home Journal 93:82-83.
Eisenberg, Terry, Deborah Ann Kent, and Charles Wall
1973 Police Personnel Practices in State and Local Governments. Washington: International Association of Chiefs of Police and Police
Foundation, in Cooperation with the Educational Testing Service.
Epstein, Cynthia F.
1970 Woman's Place: Options and Limits in Professional Careers. Berkeley: University of California Press.

Fagerstrom, Dorothy
1958 "Designed for the Woman in Blue." Law and Order 6:60-61.
1960 "Make the Most of Every Opportunity." Law and Order 8:54-57.
1964 "Practical Handbook for Policewomen." Law and Order 12:37.
Fleming, Alice
1975 New on the Beat: Woman Power in the Police Force. New York: Coward, McCann and Geoghegan.
Fosdick, Raymond
1920 American Police Systems. New York: Century.
Gabower, G.
1945 "Police and Social Workers Cooperate for the Young Delinquent." Washington: The Children's Bureau.
Garmine, Bernard L.
1972 "The Police Role in an Urban Society." Pp. 1-11 in R. Steadman (ed.), The Police and the Community. Baltimore: Johns Hopkins University Press.
Gates, Margaret
1974 "Women in Policing: A Legal Analysis." Pp. 95-132 in Draft Manual: A Symposium About Women in Policing. Washington: Police Foundation.
1976 "Occupational Segregation and the Law." Pp. 61-74 in Martha Blaxall and Barbara Reagan (eds.), Women and the Workplace: The Implications of Occupational Segregation. Chicago: University of Chicago Press.
Gibbons, Thomas J.
1956 "Policewomen Undercover." Law and Order 4:18-19.
Glaser, Barney and Anselm Strauss
1967 The Discovery of Grounded Theory. Chicago: Aldine.
Goffman, Erving
1956 "The Nature of Deference and Demeanor." American Anthropologist 58:473-502.
1961 Encounters. Indianapolis: Bobbs-Merrill.
1976 "Gender Displays." Studies in the Anthropology of Visual Communication 3.
1977 "The Arrangement between the Sexes." Theory and Society 4:301-31.
Gold, Raymond L.
1958 "Roles in Sociological Field Observations." Social Forces 36:217-23.
Goldstein, Joseph
1960 "Police Discretion Not to Invoke the Criminal Process: Low Visibility Decisions in the Administration of Justice." Yale Law Journal 69:551-94.
Goode, William
1960 "A Theory of Role Strain." American Sociological Review 25:483-96.
Gray, Thomas C.
1975 "Selecting for a Police Subculture." Pp. 46-56 in Jerome H. Skolnick

and Thomas C. Gray (eds.), Police in America. Boston: Little Brown.

Gross, Neal, Ward S. Mason, and Alexander W. McEarchen
1958 Explorations in Role Analysis. New York: Wiley.

Hahn, Harlan
1974 "A Profile of Urban Police." Pp. 15-35 in Jack Goldsmith and Sharon Goldsmith (eds.), The Police Community. Pacific Palisades, Calif.: Palisades.

Hamilton, Mary E.
1924 Policewoman: Her Service and Ideals. New York: A. Stokes (reprinted New York Arno Press and New York Times, 1971).

Hammond, Phillip (ed.)
1964 Sociologists at Work. New York: Basic Books.

Harris, Richard
1973 The Police Academy: An Inside View. New York: Wiley.

Henley, Nancy
1970 "The Politics of Touch." Paper presented at American Psychological Association. Reprinted in P. Brown (ed.), Radical Psychology. New York: Harper and Row, 1973.

Henley, Nancy and Jo Freeman
1975 "The Sexual Politics of Interpersonal Behavior." Pp. 391-401 in Jo Freeman (ed.), Women: A Feminist Perspective. Palo Alto, Calif.: Mayfield.

Higgins, Lois L.
1947 "Policewomen's Service in the United States." Master's thesis, Loyola University.
1950 "Women Police Service." Journal of Criminal Law, Criminology and Police Science 41:101-6.
1951 "Historical Background of Policewomen's Services." Journal of Criminal Law, Criminology and Police Science 42.
1956 "Policewomen are Here to Stay." Law Enforcement 10:7-11.
1958a "The Policewomen." Law and Order 6:4.
1958b "The Feminine Force in Crime Prevention." The Police Yearbook: 102-9.
1958c "The Policewoman." Police 3:66-69.
1960 "Golden Anniversary of Women in Police Service." Law and Order 8:4-16.
1961 Policewomen's Manual. Springfield, Ill.: Charles Thomas.
1962a "A Career in Law Enforcement for Women Police." Police 6:46-49.
1962b "Women in Law Enforcement." Law and Order 10:18-22.
1962c "More about Women in Law Enforcement." Law and Order 10: 40-41.
1964 "Bombay and a Lovely Policewoman." Law and Order 12:7.

Hochschild, Arlie R.
1973 "Making It: Marginality and Obstacles to Minority Consciousness." Annals of The New York Academy of Science 208:79-82.

Hodge, Robert W., Paul M. Siegal, and Peter H. Rossi
   1966 "Occupational Prestige in the United States: 1925-1963." Pp. 322-34
       in Reinhard Bendix and Seymour M. Lipset (eds.), Class, Status and
       Power. New York: Free Press.
Homans, George
   1964 "Bringing Men Back In." American Sociological Review 29:809-18.
Horne, Peter
   1972 "Role of Women in Law Enforcement." Master's thesis, California
       State University, Los Angeles.
   1974 Women in Law Enforcement. Springfield, Ill.: Charles Thomas.
Hughes, Everett C.
   1944 "Dilemmas and Contradictions of Status." American Journal of
       Sociology 50:353-59.
   1958 Men and Their Work. Glencoe: Free Press.
   1959 "The Study of Occupations." Pp. 442-58 in Robert Merton, Leonard
       Selznick and Leonard S. Cottrell, Jr. (eds.), Sociology Today. New
       York: Basic Books.
Hurrell, Joseph J., Jr., and William Kroes
   1975 "Stress Awareness." Pp. 234-45 in Kroes, William and Joseph Hur-
       rell, Jr. (eds.), Job Stress and the Police Officer: Identifying Stress
       Reduction Techniques. U.S. Department of HEW, National Institute
       for Occupational Safety and Health.
Hutzel, Eleanor
   1933 The Policewoman's Handbook. New York: Columbia University
       Press.
Jackson, Elton F.
   1962 "Status Inconsistency and Symptoms of Stress." American Socio-
       logical Review 27:469-80.
Johnson, John M.
   1975 Doing Field Research. New York: Free Press.
Jourand, Sidney M.
   1964 The Transparent Self: Self-Disclosure and Well Being. Princeton,
       N.J.: Van Nostrand.
Kahn, Robert, D. M. Wolfe, Robert Quinn, J. D. Snoek, and Robert
   Rosenthal
   1964 Organizational Stress: Studies in Role Conflict and Ambiguity. New
       York: Wiley.
Kanter, Rosabeth Moss
   1974 "Women in Organizations: Change Agent Skills." Paper presented at
       the National Training Laboratory Conference on New Technology in
       Organizational Development. (Printed in Conference Proceedings.)
   1975 "Women and the Structure of Organizations: Explorations in Theory
       and Behavior." Pp. 34-74 in M. Millman and R. M. Kanter (eds.),

Another Voice: Feminist Perspectives on Social Life and Social Science. New York: Doubleday Anchor.

1976a "The Impact of Hierarchical Structures on the Work Behavior of Women and Men." Social Problems 23:415-30.

1976b "Women and Organizations: Sex Roles, Group Dynamics and Change Strategies." In A. Sargent (ed.), Beyond Sex Roles. St. Paul: West.

1977a "Skewed Sex Ratios and Responses to Token Women." American Journal of Sociology 82:965-90.

1977b Men and Women of the Corporation. New York: Basic Books.

Kroes, William
1974 "Psychological Stress and Police Work." Unpublished manuscript presented at 3rd annual Stress Symposium of the American Academy of Stress, St. Charles, Illinois.

Kelly, Rita and Garmon West
1973 "The Racial Transition of a Police Force." Pp. 354-81 in John R. Snibbe and Homa Snibbe (eds.), The Urban Policeman in Transition: A Psychological and Sociological Review. Springfield, Ill.: Charles Thomas.

Kohn, Melvin
1959 "Social Class and Parental Authority." American Sociological Review 24:352-66.

Komarovsky, Mirra
1946 "Cultural Contradictions and Sex Roles." American Journal of Sociology 52:182-89.

1962 Blue Collar Marriage. New York: Random House.

1973 "Cultural Contradictions and Sex Roles: The Masculine Case." Pp. 112-22 in Joan Huber (ed.), Changing Woman in a Changing Society. Chicago: University of Chicago Press.

LaFave, Wayne R.
1965 Arrest. Boston: Little Brown.

Lakoff, Robin
1975 Language and Women's Place. New York: Harper Colophon Books.

Laws, Judith Long
1976 "Work Aspiration of Women: False Leads and New Starts." Pp. 33-50 in Martha Blaxall and Barbara Reagan (eds.), Women and the Workplace: The Implications of Occupational Segregation. Chicago: University of Chicago Press.

Leevy, J. R.
1949 "The Role of the Police Matron." Journal of Criminal Law, Criminology and Police Science 39:538-40.

LeMasters, E. E.
1975 Blue Collar Aristocrats. Madison: University of Wisconsin Press.

Levinson, Daniel
  1959 "Role, Personality and Social Structure." Journal of Abnormal Social Psychology 58:170-80.
Lichtenstein, Grace
  1974 "Rape Squad." New York Times Magazine (March 3). Reprinted pp. 141-50 in Jerome H. Skolnick and Thomas C. Gray (eds.), Police in America. Boston: Little Brown, 1975.
Liebow, Elliot
  1967 Tally's Corner: A Study of Negro Streetcorner Men. Boston: Little Brown.
Lipman-Blumen, Jean
  1976 "Toward a Homosocial Theory of Sex Roles: An Explanation of the Sex Segregation of Social Institutions." Pp. 15-32 in Martha Blaxall and Barbara Reagan (eds.), Women and the Workplace: The Implications of Occupational Segregation. Chicago: University of Chicago Press.
Lipman-Blumen, Jean and Ann Tickamyer
  1975 "Sex Roles in Transition: A Ten-year Perspective." Pp. 297-337 in Alex Inkeles (ed.), Annual Review of Sociology, Volume I. Palo Alto, Calif.: American Reviews, Inc.
Lofland, John
  1971 Analyzing Social Settings: A Guide to Qualitative Observation and Analysis. Belmont, Calif.: Wadsworth.
Maccoby, Eleanor and Carol N. Jacklin
  1974 The Psychology of Sex Differences. Stanford, Calif.: Stanford University Press.
Manning, Peter K.
  1972 "Observing the Police: Deviants, Respectables and the Law." In J. D. Douglas (ed.), Research on Deviance. New York: Random House.
  1977 Police Work: The Social Organization of Policing. Cambridge, Mass.: Massachusetts Institute of Technology Press.
McCombs, Phil
  1976 "Lawmen Adjust to New Era." Washington Post (September 24): 1.
McNamara, John H.
  1967 "Uncertainties in Police Work: Recruits' Background and Training." In David Bordua (ed.), The Police: Six Sociological Essays. New York: Wiley.
Melchionne, Theresa M.
  1960a "Where Policewomen are Better than Men." American City 3:17.
  1960b "Role of the Policewoman in the Investigative Function." The Police Yearbook: 166-70.
  1961 "The Role of the Policewoman Working with Youth: The Bridge Between." Law and Order 9:61-64.
  1964a "Delinquency Control Programs: Part One." Law and Order 12:46.

1964b "Delinquency Control Programs: Part Two." Law and Order 12:26.

1964c "Delinquency Control Programs: Part Three." Law and Order 12:28.

Merton, Robert K.

1957 Social Theory and Social Structure (rev. ed.). Glencoe: Free Press.

Metropolitan Police Department, Washington, D.C.

1975 Annual Report: Fiscal Year 1975.

1976 Annual Report: Fiscal Year 1976.

Miller, Walter

1959 "The Lower Class Gang as a Generating Milieu of Gang Delinquency." Journal of Social Issues 14:5-19.

Miller, Wilbur R.

1973 Cops and Bobbies: Police Authority in New York and London, 1830-1870. Chicago: University of Chicago Press.

Milton, Catherine

1972 Women in Policing. Washington: Police Foundation.

Milton, Catherine, Ava Abamovitz, Laura Crites, Margaret Gates, Ellen Mintz and Georgette Sandler

1974 Women in Policing: A Manual. Washington: Police Foundation.

Muir, William Ker, Jr.

1977 Police: Street Corner Politicians. Chicago: University of Chicago Press.

Niederhoffer, Arthur

1969 Behind the Shield: The Police in Urban Society. Garden City, N.Y.: Anchor Doubleday.

O'Connor, John J.

1955 Opportunities in Law Enforcement. New York: Vocational Guidance Manuals.

Olson, M. G.

1957 "Women in Police Work." The Police Yearbook. Washington: International Association of Chiefs of Police, 99-103.

Owens, J. M.

1958 "Policewomen in the Line." Police 3:21-22.

Owing, Chloe

1968 Women Police. Montclair, N.J.: Patterson Smith.

Parnas, R.

1967 "Police Response to the Domestic Disturbance." Wisconsin Law Review 67:914-60.

The People of the District of Columbia: A Demographic, Social, Economic and Physical Profile of the District of Columbia by Service Areas. Washington: Office of Planning and Management, District of Columbia Government (1973).

President's Commission on Law Enforcement and the Administration of Justice

1967 Task Force Report: The Police. Washington: Government Printing Office.

Psathas, George
    1968 "Toward a Theory of Occupational Choice for Women." Sociology and Social Research 52:253-68.
Purcell, Phillip
    1960 "Use of Policewomen is Valuable Asset to Law Enforcement." FBI Law Enforcement Bulletin 29:3-6.
Radcliffe-Brown, A. R.
    1965 Structure and Function in Primitive Society. New York: Free Press.
Reichley, A. James
    1968 "The Way to Cool the Police Rebellion." Fortune 78: 109ff.
Reiss, Albert J., Jr.
    1971 The Police and the Public. New Haven: Yale University Press.
Richard, Wayne C. and Ronald Fell
    1975 "Health Factors in Police Job Stress." Pp. 73-84 in William Kroes and Joseph Hurrell, Jr. (eds.), Job Stress and the Police Officer: Identifying Stress Reduction Techniques. U.S. Department of HEW, National Institute for Occupational Safety and Health.
Riemer, Jeffrey W.
    1976 "'Deviance' as Fun—A Case of Building Construction Workers at Work." Paper presented at 71st Annual Meeting of American Sociological Association.
Rinck, J. A.
    1963 "Supervising the Juvenile Delinquent." Annals of the American Academy of Political and Social Sciences. Philadelphia: 85.
Rink, S. E.
    1963 "Arresting Females: The Policewomen's Story." Law and Order 1:6-7.
Roberts, Michael
    1975 "Job Stress in Law Enforcement: A Treatment and Prevention Program." Pp. 226-35 in William Kroes and Joseph Hurrell, Jr. (eds.), Job Stress and the Police Officer: Identifying Stress Reduction Techniques. U.S. Department of HEW, National Institute for Occupational Safety and Health.
Roy, Donald
    1953 "Work Satisfaction and Social Reward in Quota Achievement: An Analysis of Piecework Incentive." American Sociological Review 18:507-14.
    1954 "Efficiency and the 'Fix': Informal Intergroup Relations in a Piecework Machine Shop. American Journal of Sociology 60:255-66.
    1974 "Sex in the Factory: Informal Heterosexual Relations between Supervisors and Work Groups." Pp. 44-66 in Clifton Bryant (ed.), Deviant Behavior. Chicago: Rand McNally.
Rubin, Jesse
    1972 "Police Identity and the Police Role." Pp. 12-50 in R. Steadman (ed.), The Police and the Community. Baltimore: Johns Hopkins Press.

Rubinstein, Jonathan
  1974 City Police. New York: Ballantine Books.
Salzbrenner, D.
  1963 "Military Policewomen." Law and Order 11:36.
Sarbin, Theodore
  1954 "Role Theory." Pp. 223-58 in Gardner Lindzey (ed.), Handbook of
       Social Psychology, Vol. 1. Reading, Mass.: Addison-Wesley.
Sarbin, Theodore and Vernon L. Allen
  1968 "Role Theory." Pp. 488-567 in Gardner Lindzey and Elliot Aronson
       (eds.), Handbook of Social Psychology (rev. ed.), Vol. 1. Reading,
       Mass.: Addison-Wesley.
Saunders, Charles B.
  1970 Upgrading the American Police: Education and Training. Washing-
       ton: The Brookings Institution.
Schatzman, Leonard and Anselm L. Strauss
  1973 Field Research: Strategies for a Natural Sociology. Englewood Cliffs,
       N.J.: Prentice Hall.
Sherman, Lewis J.
  1973 "A Psychological View of Women in Policing." Journal of Police
       Science and Administration 21:383-94.
  1975 "An Evaluation of Policewomen on Patrol in a Suburban Police De-
       partment." Journal of Police Science and Administration 3:434-38.
Sherman, M. and L. J. Sherman
  1973 "Bibliography on Policewomen: 1945-1972." Law and Order 21:80-
       83.
Shostak, Arthur
  1969 Blue Collar Life. New York: Random House.
Shpritzer, Felicia
  1959 "A Case for the Promotion of Policewomen in the City of New
       York." Journal of Criminology and Police Science 50:415-19.
Sichel, Joyce L., Lucy N. Friedman, Janet Quint, and Michael E. Smith
  1977 Women on Patrol. A Pilot Study of Police Performance in New York
       City. New York: Vera Institute of Justice (prepublication copy).
Silverman, David
  1971 The Theory of Organizations. New York: Basic Books.
Simon, Rita James
  1975 The Contemporary Women and Crime. Rockville, Md.: National
       Institute of Mental Health.
Skolnick, Jerome H.
  1966 Justice Without Trial. New York: Wiley.
Snow, M.
  1956 "Women's Role in Crime Control." The Police Yearbook. Washing-
       ton: International Association of Chiefs of Police: 71-79.
Spradley, James P. and Brenda J. Mann
  1975 The Cocktail Waitress: Woman's Work in a Man's World. New York:
       Wiley.

Stewart, Phyllis and Muriel Cantor (eds.)
1974 Varieties of Work Experience. Cambridge, Mass.: Schenkman.
Sweeny, F.
1959 "The Policewoman and Crime." Police Chief 26:28.
Sykes, Richard E. and John P. Clark
1975 "A Theory of Deference Exchange in Police-Civilian Encounters." American Journal of Sociology 81:584-600.
Talney, Ronald G.
1969 "Women in Law Enforcement: An Expanded Role." Police 14:49-51.
Tangri, Sandra S.
1972 "Determinants of Occupational Role Innovation Among College Women." Journal of Social Issues 28:177-99.
Tenny, Evabel
1953 "Women's Work in Law Enforcement." Journal of Criminal Law, Criminology and Police Science 44:239-46.
Torres, E. C.
1953 "Policewomen and Crime Prevention." Police Chief 20:8ff.
Turner, Ralph H.
1964 "Some Aspects of Women's Ambition." American Journal of Sociology 70:271-85.
Uhnak, Dorothy
1964 Policewoman. New York: Simon and Schuster.
Ungar, Stanford
1976 "The G-Woman." Potomac supplement to the Washington Post (February 29): 14.
United States Bureau of the Census
1956 U.S. Census of the Population: 1950, Volume 4 Special Reports. Part I, Chapter B—Occupational Characteristics. Washington: Government Printing Office.
1958 Working Paper Number 5. Occupational Trends in the U.S.: 1900-1950. Washington: Government Printing Office.
1963 U.S. Census of the Population: 1960. Subject Reports: Occupational Characteristics—Final Report PC(2)-7A. Washington: Government Printing Office.
1973 U.S. Census of the Population: 1970. Subject Reports: Occupational Characteristics PC(2)-7A. Washington: Government Printing Office.
United States Commission on Civil Rights
1974 The Federal Civil Rights Enforcement Effort—1974. Vol. VI—To Extend Federal Financial Assistance. Washington: Government Printing Office.
United States Department of Justice, National Institute of Law Enforcement
1977 Forcible Rape: A National Survey of the Response by Police (Police Volume 1). Washington: Government Printing Office.

United States Department of Labor, Women's Bureau
  1949 Outlook for Women in Police Work. Washington: Government Printing Office.
  1975 1975 Handbook on Women Workers (Bulletin 297). Washington: Government Printing Office.
United States Equal Employment Opportunity Commission
  1973 Minorities and Women in State and Local Government, 1973: U.S. Summary, Volume I. Washington: Government Printing Office.
United States Federal Bureau of Investigation
  1972 Uniform Crime Report—1971. Washington: Government Printing Office.
  1973 Uniform Crime Report—1972. Washington: Government Printing Office.
  1974 Uniform Crime Report—1973. Washington: Government Printing Office.
  1975 Uniform Crime Report—1974. Washington: Government Printing Office.
  1976 Uniform Crime Report—1975. Washington: Government Printing Office.
  1977 Uniform Crime Report—1976. Washington: Government Printing Office.
Van Maanen, John
  1974 "Working the Street: A Developmental View of Police Behavior." Pp. 83-130 in H. Jacob (ed.), The Potential for Reform of Criminal Justice. Beverly Hills, Calif.: Sage Publications.
  1975 "Police Socialization: A Longitudinal Examination of Job Attitudes in an Urban Police Department." Administrative Science Quarterly 20:207-28.
Van Winkle, Minna
  1924 "The Policewoman," in Proceedings of the 10th Annual Conference of the International Association of Policewomen. Washington.
Vastola, Anthony
  1977 "Women Policing: An Alternative Ideology." Police Chief (January): 62-69.
Washington, Brenda
  1974 The Deployment of Female Police Officers in the United States. Gaithersburg, Md.: International Association of Chiefs of Police.
Wax, Rosalie
  1971 Doing Fieldwork: Warnings and Advice. Chicago: The University of Chicago Press.
Weibel, Kathryn
  1977 Mirror Mirror: Images of Women Reflected in Popular Culture. Garden City, New York: Anchor Books.

Weldy, William O.
  1976 "Women in Policing: A Positive Step Toward Increased Police Enthusiasm." Police Chief (January): 46-47.
Westley, William
  1970 Violence and the Police. Cambridge, Mass.: Massachusetts Institute of Technology Press.
White, Susan O.
  1974 "A Perspective on Police Professionalization." Pp. 39-62 in Jack Goldsmith and Sharon Goldsmith, The Police Community. Pacific Palisades, Calif.: Palisades.
Whyte, William F.
  1955 Street Corner Society. Chicago: University of Chicago Press.
Williams, Carol M.
  1946 The Organization and Practices of Policewomen's Division in the United States. Detroit: National Training School of Public Service.
Willis, F. N., Jr.
  1966 "Initial Speaking Distance as a Function of the Speakers' Relationship." Psychonomic Science 5:221-22.
Wilson, James Q.
  1963 "The Police and Their Problems: A Theory." Public Policy 12:198-216.
  1973 Varieties of Police Behavior. New York: Atheneum.
Wilson, Jerry
  1975 Police Report. Boston: Little Brown.
Wyles, Lilian
  1952 Women at Scotland Yard. London: Faber and Faber.

Index

164-170 *passim*, 176, 181, 182; role distance by citizens, 160; sex status and behavior in, 163-182; and sexual invitations, 170, 173-174; speech patterns and courtesy in, 175; status expectations in, 164

Police departments, 80-88; assignment policies, 56-57, 129-132 (*see also* Assignments); community settings and relations, 36, 50-53, 82, 216; complaints and redress in, 58-59; control of police officers' behavior, 14, 85-86; district organization and units, 53-55; health services of, 134; loyalty to, 189; paramilitary organizational structure of, 13-14, 22, 53, 85; personnel changes in, 52-53, 58-59; policies to accelerate sexual integration in, 210-212; policies differentially affecting male and female officers, 132-135; policies manipulated by white policewomen, 131; political factionalism in, 51; professionalization vs. informal practices in, 58-59; rewards to crime fighters, 82, 83; trial for case of sexual harassment, 135, 135n-136n; uniforms provided by, 111, 132-134, 145, 223. *See also* Washington, D.C., Metropolitan Police Department

Police Foundation, 27; report on employment of policewomen, 37-38

Policemen: altercations among, 96; emotional reserve of, 96-97, 170-171, 177; interaction with female citizens, 168-171; interaction with male citizens, 164-168; motivation and commitment compared to policewomen, 64-75, 212-214; working-class backgrounds of, 60, 87, 90, 91, 96, 153, 156

Policemen, attitudes toward policewomen, xv, xvi, 9, 79, 90-108, 204-205; about assertiveness of policewomen, 95, 104; about authority use, 94-95; about crime-fighting performance, 95-96; moderate views, 106-108; modern views, 104-106; overprotective attitudes, 188; about physical differences and violent confrontations, 91-93, 104; preference for work with incompetent policewomen, 124; reflected in language

use, 141-149; reflected in sex role stereotyping, 151-152; and sexual intimacy, 99-100; and status insecurity of policemen, 100-101; subordinate status of policewomen, 149-151; traditional views, 102-104

Police officers, 59-75; attitudes learned during certification, 121; backgrounds, expectations, and attitudes toward work, 3-11, 60-70; career aspirations and expectations, 70-75; conflict between occupational and family roles, 199-201; education of, 3, 4, 41, 47, 59, 60, 87; effective, 177-178, 181-182; employed as police cadets, 60n-61n; generation gap among, 58-59, 103, 190; interviewed by the researcher, 59-75 (*see also* Interviews); marital and parental statuses of, 59, 73-74; marriages among fellow officers, 200; models of the cowboy and private eye in role of, 90; motivations for police work, 60-70, 212-214; occupational behavior of, 11-16 *passim*; occupations of parents, 60, 61; prior work experience, 60-63, 115; resignation rate among, 214; socioeconomic origins of, 59, 60; stress-related diseases and disorders of, 199; "working personality" of, 14, 84. *See also* Group solidarity among policemen; Police behavior; Social life and off-duty police socializing

Police reform, 36; and the policewomen's movement, 23

Police Reserve Corps, 221; and ethical issues in field research, 231; functions of, ii; participant observation provided by, xiii-xv, 102, 107, 222-223; potential resignation from, 230

Police "riots," 36

Police training academies, 111; academic instruction at, 117, 118; curriculum of, 55; inequality fostered by, 117; and interpersonal skills, 117-118; physical training at, 4-5, 48, 117, 118-121; post-academy training, 8 (*see also* Certification); socialization at, 115-121; unisex programs at, 48

Policewomen: attitudes toward marriage,

Designer: Wendy Calmenson
Compositor: U.C. Press
Printer: Thomson-Shore, Inc.
Binder: Thomson-Shore, Inc.
Text: CompSet 500 Times Roman
Display: Phototypositor Friz Quadrata
Cloth: Holliston Roxite B 53575
Paper: 50 lb P&S offset vellum B-32